healthy eating

This is a Starfire book
First published in 2001

02 04 05 03

3 5 7 9 10 8 6 4 2

Starfire is part of
The Foundry Creative Media Company Limited
Crabtree Hall, Crabtree Lane, Fulham, London, SW6 6TY

Visit the Foundry website: www.foundry.co.uk/recipes

ISBN: 1-903817-09-9

Printed in China

ACKNOWLEDGEMENTS

Authors: Catherine Atkinson, Juliet Barker, Liz Martin, Vickie Smallwood,
Gina Steer, Carol Tennant, Mari Mererid Williams, Elizabeth Wolf-Cohen, and Simone Wright
Photography: Colin Bowling, Paul Forrester, and Stephen Brayne
Home Economists and Stylists: Jacqueline Bellefontaine,
Mandy Phipps, Vicki Smallwood, and Penny Stephens

All props supplied by Barbara Stewart at Surfaces

NOTE
Recipes using uncooked eggs should be avoided by infants,
the elderly, pregnant women, and anyone suffering from an illness.

LET'S COOK

healthy eating

STAR FIRE

CONTENTS

SOUPS & STARTERS

FISH & SHELLFISH

MEAT

POULTRY

POULTRY

VEGETARIAN

VEGETABLES AND SALADS

ENTERTAINING

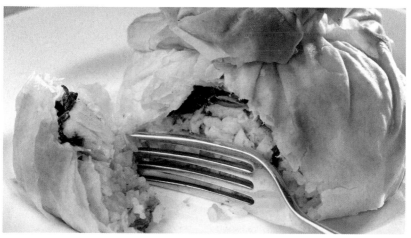

CLEANLINESS IN THE KITCHEN

I t is well worth remembering that many foods can carry some form of bacteria. In most cases, the worst it will lead to is a bout of food poisoning or gastroenteritis, although for certain groups this can be more serious—the risk can be reduced or eliminated by good food hygiene and proper cooking.

Do not buy food that is past its sell-by date and do not consume any food that is past its use-by date. When buying food, use the eyes and nose. If the food has a bad color or a rank, acrid, or simply bad smell, do not buy or eat it under any circumstances.

Take special care when preparing raw meat and fish. A separate chopping board should be used for each; wash the knife, board, and the hands thoroughly before handling or preparing any other food.

Regularly clean, defrost, and clear out the refrigerator or freezer—it is worth checking the packaging to see exactly how long each product is safe to freeze.

Avoid handling food if suffering from an upset stomach, as bacteria can be passed through food preparation.

Dish towels must be washed and changed regularly. Ideally, use disposable paper towels that can be discarded after use. More durable cloths should be left to soak in bleach, then washed in the washing machine in hot water.

Keep your hands, cooking utensils, and food preparation surfaces clean, and do not allow pets to climb onto any work surfaces.

BUYING

A void bulk buying where possible, especially of meat, poultry, fish, fruit, and vegetables, unless buying to store in the freezer. Fresh foods lose their nutritional value rapidly so buying a little at a time minimizes loss of nutrients. It also eliminates a packed refrigerator, which can reduce the effectiveness of the refrigeration process.

When buying prepackaged goods, such as cream and yogurt, check that the packaging is intact and not damaged or pierced at all. Cans should not be dented, pierced or rusty. Check the sell-by dates for cans and packages of dry ingredients, such as flour and rice, as well. Store fresh foods in the refrigerator as soon as possible –don't leave them in your car.

When buying frozen foods, ensure that they are not heavily iced on the outside and the contents feel completely frozen. Ensure that the frozen foods have been stored at the correct storage level and that the temperature is below -0°F. Bring home and place in the freezer as soon as possible after purchase.

PREPARATION

M ake sure that all work surfaces and utensils are clean and dry. Hygiene should be given priority at all times.

Separate chopping boards should be used for raw and cooked meats, fish, and vegetables. Currently, a variety of good-quality plastic boards come in various designs and colors. This makes differentiating easier, and the plastic has the added hygienic advantage of being washable at high temperatures in the dishwasher. NB: If using the board for fish, first wash in cold water, then in hot to prevent odor. Also, remember that knives and utensils should always be thoroughly cleaned after use.

When cooking, be particularly careful to keep cooked and raw food separate to avoid any contamination. It is worthwhile to wash all fruits and vegetables, regardless of whether they are going to be eaten raw or lightly cooked. This rule should apply even to prewashed herbs and salads.

Do not reheat food more than once. If using a microwave, always check that the food is piping hot all the way through. In theory, the food should reach 168 °F and needs to be cooked at that temperature for at least three minutes to ensure that all bacteria are killed.

All frozen poultry must be thoroughly thawed before using, including chicken and game hen. Remove the food to be thawed from the freezer and place in a shallow dish to contain the juices. Leave the food in the refrigerator until it is completely thawed. A 3 lb. whole chicken will take about 26 to 30 hours to thaw. To speed up the process, immerse the chicken in cold water. However, make sure that the water is changed regularly. When the joints can move freely and no ice crystals remain in the cavity, the bird is completely thawed.

Once thawed, remove the wrapper and pat the chicken dry. Place the chicken in a shallow dish, cover lightly, and store as close to the bottom of the refrigerator as possible. The chicken should be cooked as soon as possible.

Some foods can be cooked from frozen, including many prepackaged foods such as soups, sauces, casseroles, and breads. Where applicable follow the manufacturer's instructions.

Vegetables and fruits can also be cooked from frozen, but meats and fish should be thawed first. The only time food can be refrozen is when the food has been thoroughly thawed, then cooked. Once the food has cooled, it can be frozen again. On such occasions the food can only be stored for one month.

All poultry and game (except for duck) must be cooked thoroughly. When cooked, the juices will run clear from the thickest part of the bird—the best area to try is usually the thigh. Other meats, like ground meat and pork, should be cooked all the way through. Fish should turn opaque, be firm in texture, and break easily into large flakes.

When cooking leftovers, make sure they are reheated until piping hot and that any sauce or soup reaches boiling point first.

STORING
REFRIGERATING AND FREEZING

Meat, poultry, fish, seafood, and dairy products should all be refrigerated. The temperature of the refrigerator should be between 34–41° F while the freezer should not rise above 0° F.

To ensure the optimum refrigerator and freezer temperature, avoid leaving the door open for a long time. Try not to overstock the refrigerator as this reduces the airflow inside and reduces the effectiveness of the cooling system.

When refrigerating cooked food, let it cool completely before refrigerating. Hot food will raise the temperature of the refrigerator and possibly affect, or spoil, other food that is stored inside.

Food within the refrigerator and freezer should always be covered. Raw and cooked food should be stored in separate parts of the refrigerator. Cooked food should be kept on the top shelves of the refrigerator, while raw meat, poultry, and fish should be placed on bottom shelves to avoid drips and cross-contamination. It is recommended that eggs should be refrigerated in order to maintain their freshness and shelf life.

Take care that frozen foods are not stored in the freezer for too long. Blanched vegetables can be stored for one month; beef, lamb, poultry, and pork for six months; and unblanched vegetables and fruits in syrup for a year. Oily fish and sausages can be stored for three months. Dairy products can last four to six months, while cakes and pastries can be kept in the freezer for three to six months.

HIGH-RISK FOODS

C ertain foods may carry risks to people who are considered vulnerable, such as the elderly, the ill, pregnant women, babies, young infants, and those suffering from a reccuring illness.

It is advisable to avoid those foods listed below which belong to a higher-risk category.

There is a slight chance that some eggs carry the bacteria salmonella. Cook the eggs until both the yolk and the white are firm to eliminate this risk. Pay particular attention to dishes and products incorporating lightly cooked or raw eggs, which should be eliminated from the diet. Sauces such as hollandaise and mayonnaise, mousses, soufflés, and meringues all use raw or lightly cooked eggs, as do custard-based dishes, ice creams, and sorbets. These are all considered high-risk foods to the vulnerable groups mentioned above.

Certain meats and poultry also carry the potential risk of salmonella and so should be cooked thoroughly until the juices run clear and there is no pinkness left. Unpasteurized products such as milk, cheese (especially soft cheese), pâté, and meat (both raw and cooked) all have the potential risk of listeria and should be avoided.

When buying seafood, buy from a reputable source that has a high turnover to ensure freshness. Fish should have bright, clear eyes, shiny skin, and bright pink or red gills. The fish should feel stiff to the touch, with a slight smell of sea air and iodine. The flesh of fish steaks and fillets should be translucent with no signs of discoloration. Mollusks, such as scallops, clams and mussels, are sold fresh and are still alive. Avoid any that are open or do not close when tapped lightly. In the same way, univalves should withdraw back into their shells when prodded lightly. When choosing cephalopods, such as squid and octopus, they should have a firm flesh and pleasant sea smell.

As with all fish, whether it is shellfish or seafish, care is required when freezing it. It is imperative to check whether the fish has been frozen before. If it has been frozen, then it should not be frozen again under any circumstances.

NUTRITION
The Role of Essential Nutrients

A healthy and well-balanced diet is the body's primary energy source. In children, it constitutes the building blocks for future health as well as providing lots of energy. In adults, it encourages self-healing and regeneration within the body. A well-balanced diet will provide the body with all the essential nutrients it needs. This can be achieved by eating a variety of foods, demonstrated in the pyramid below:

FATS

milk, yogurt,
and cheese

PROTEINS

meat, fish, poultry, eggs,
nuts, and beans

FRUITS AND
VEGETABLES

STARCHY CARBOHYDRATES
cereals, potatoes, bread, rice, and pasta

FATS

F ats fall into two categories: saturated and unsaturated fats. It is very important that a healthy balance is achieved within the diet. Fats are an essential part of the diet and a source of energy, and provide essential fatty acids and fat soluble vitamins. The right balance of fats should boost the body's immunity to infection and keep muscles, nerves, and arteries in good condition. Saturated fats are of animal origin and are hard when stored at room temperature. They can be found in dairy produce, meat, eggs, margarines, and hard white cooking fat (lard) as well as in manufactured products such as pies, cookies and cakes. A high intake of saturated fat over many years has been proven to increase heart disease and high blood cholesterol levels, and often leads to weight gain. The aim of a healthy diet is to keep the fat content low in the foods that we eat. Lowering the amount of saturated fat that we consume is very important, but this does not mean that it is good to consume lots of other types of fat.

There are two kinds of unsaturated fats: poly-unsaturated fats and monounsaturated fats. Poly-unsaturated fats include the following oils: safflower oil, soybean oil, corn oil, and sesame oil. Within the polyunsaturated group are Omega oils. The Omega-3 oils are of significant interest because they have been found to be particularly beneficial to coronary health and can encourage brain growth, and development. Omega-3 oils are derived from oily fish such as salmon, mackerel, herring, and sardines. It is recommended that we should eat these types of fish at least once a week. However, for those who do not eat fish or are vegetarian, liver oil supplements are available in most supermarkets and health stores. It is suggested that these supplements should be taken on a daily basis. The most popular oil that is high in monounsaturates is olive oil. The Mediterranean diet, which is based on a diet high in mono-unsaturated fats, is recommended for heart health. Also, monounsaturated fats are known to help reduce the levels of LDL (the bad) cholesterol.

PROTEINS

C omposed of amino acids (proteins' building bricks), proteins perform a wide variety of essential functions for the body, including sup-plying energy and building, and repairing tissues. Good sources of proteins are eggs, milk, yogurt, cheese, meat, fish, poultry, eggs, nuts, and beans. (See the second level of the pyramid.) Some of these foods, however, contain saturated fats. To strike a nutritional balance eat generous amounts of vegetable protein foods such as soy beans, lentils, peas, and nuts.

FRUITS AND VEGETABLES

N ot only are fruits and vegetables the most visually appealing foods, but they are extremely good for us, providing essential vitamins and minerals essential for growth, repair, and protection in the human body. Fruits and vegetables are low in calories and are responsible for regulating the body's metabolic processes, and controlling the composition of its fluids and cells.

MINERALS

CALCIUM Important for healthy bones and teeth, nerve transmission, muscle contraction, blood clotting, and hormone function. Calcium promotes a healthy heart, improves skin, relieves aching muscles and bones, main-tains the correct acid-alkaline balance, and reduces menstrual cramps. Good sources are dairy products, small bones of small fish, nuts, beans, fortified white flours, breads, and green leafy vegetables.

CHROMIUM Part of the glucose tolerance factor, chromium balances blood sugar levels, helps to normalize hunger and reduce cravings, improves lifespan, helps protect DNA, and is essential for heart function. Good sources are brewer's yeast, wholewheat bread, rye bread, oysters, potatoes, green bell peppers, butter, and parsnips.

IODINE Important for the manufacture of thyroid hormones and for normal development. Good sources of iodine are seafood, seaweed, milk and other dairy products.

IRON As a component of hemoglobin, iron carries oxygen around the body. It is vital for normal growth and development. Good sources are liver, red meat, fortified breakfast cereals, beans, green leafy vegetables, egg yolk, and cocoa and its products.

MAGNESIUM Important for efficient functioning of metabolic enzymes and development of the skeleton. Magnesium promotes healthy muscles by helping them to relax and is therefore good for PMS. It is also important for heart muscles and the nervous system. Good sources are nuts, green vegetables, meat, cereals, milk, and yogurt.

PHOSPHORUS Forms and maintains bones and teeth, builds muscle tissue, helps maintain pH of the body, aids metabolism and energy production. Phosphorus is present in almost all foods.

POTASSIUM Enables nutrients to move into cells, while waste products move out. It promotes healthy nerves and muscles, maintains fluid balance in the body, helps secretion of insulin for blood sugar control to produce constant energy, relaxes muscles, maintains heart functioning, and stimulates gut movement to encourage proper elimination. Good sources are fruit, vegetables, milk, and bread.

SELENIUM Antioxidant properties help to protect against free radicals and carcinogens. Selenium reduces inflammation, stimulates the immune system to fight infections, promotes a healthy heart, and helps vitamin E's action. It is also required for the male reproductive

system and is needed for metabolism. Good sources are tuna, liver, kidney, meat, eggs, cereals, nuts, and dairy products.

SODIUM Important in helping to control body fluid and balance, preventing dehydration. Sodium is involved in muscle and nerve function and helps move nutrients into cells. All foods are good sources, however, processed, pickled, and salted foods are richest in sodium.

ZINC Important for metabolism and the healing of wounds. It also aids ability to cope with stress, promotes a healthy nervous system and brain, especially in the growing fetus, aids bones and teeth formation, and is essential for constant energy. Good sources are liver, meat, beans, whole-grain cereals, nuts, and oysters.

VITAMINS

VITAMIN A Important for cell growth and development, and for the formation of visual pigments in the eye. Vitamin A comes in two forms: retinol and beta-carotenes. Retinol is found in liver, meat and meat products, and whole milk and its products. Beta-carotene is a powerul antioxidant and is found in red and yellow fruits and vegetables such as carrots, mangoes, and apricots.

VITAMIN B1 Important in releasing energy from carboydrate-containing foods. Good sources are yeast and its products, bread, fortified breakfast cereals, and potatoes.

VITAMIN B2 Important for metabolism of proteins, fats, and carbohydrates to produce energy. Good sources are meat, yeast extracts, fortified breakfast cereals, and milk and its products.

VITAMIN B3 Required for the metabolism of food into energy production. Good sources are milk and its products, fortified breakfast cereals, beans, meat, poultry, and eggs.

VITAMIN B5 Important for the metabolism of food and energy production. All foods are good sources, but especially fortified breakfast cereals, whole-grain bread, and dairy products.

VITAMIN B6 Important for metabolism of protein and fat. Vitamin B6 may also be involved with the regulation of sex hormones. Good sources are liver, fish, pork, soybeans, and peanuts.

VITAMIN B12 Important for the production of red blood cells and DNA. It is vital for growth and the nervous system. Good sources are meat, fish, eggs, poultry, and milk.

BIOTIN Important for metabolism of fatty acids. Good sources of biotin are liver, kidney, eggs, and nuts. Microorganisms also manufacture this vitamin in the gut.

VITAMIN C Important for healing wounds and the formation of collagen, which keeps skin and bones strong. It is an important antioxidant. Good sources are fruit, soft summer fruit and vegetables.

VITAMIN D Important for absorption and handling of calcium to help build bone strength. Good sources are oily fish, eggs, whole milk and its products, margarine, and of course, sufficient exposure to sunlight, as vitamin D is made in the skin.

VITAMIN E Important as an antioxidant vitamin helping to protect cell membranes from damage. Good sources are vegetable oils, margarines, seeds, nuts, and green vegetables.

FOLIC ACID Critical during pregnancy for the development of the brain and nerves. It is always essential for brain and nerve function, and is needed for utilizing protein and red blood cell formation. Good sources are whole-grain cereals, fortified breakfast cereals, green leafy vegetables, oranges, and liver.

VITAMIN K Important for controlling blood clotting. Good sources are cauliflower, Brussels sprouts, lettuce, cabbage, beans, broccoli, peas, asparagus, potatoes, corn oil, tomatoes, and milk.

CARBOHYDRATES

C arbohydrates are an energy source and come in two forms: starch and sugar carbohydrates. Starch carbohydrates are also known as complex carbohydrates and they include all cereals, potatoes, breads, rice, and pasta. (See the fourth level of the pyramid). Eating whole-grain varieties of these foods also provides fiber. Diets high in fiber are believed to be beneficial in helping to prevent bowel cancer, and can also keep cholesterol down. High-fiber diets are also good for those concerned about weight gain. Fiber is bulky so fills the stomach, therefore reducing hunger pangs. Sugar carbohydrates, which are also known as fast-release carbohydrates (because of the quick fix of energy they give to the body) include sugar and sugar-sweetened products, such as jellies and syrups. Milk provides lactose, which is a milk sugar and fruit provide fructose, which is a fruit sugar.

VARIETIES OF POTATOES AND STORAGE

The humble potato is generally taken for granted and the versatility and huge number of varieties of this delicious vegetable are often forgotten. Worldwide, there are thousands of different types of potatoes and for about two-thirds of the world, they are the staple food. In this country, almost three-quarters of main crop potatoes are made up of just five varieties. Consumers, however, have gradually become more demanding, so a wider range of potatoes suitable for different uses is now available. Although you will still find bags simply labeled "red" and "white" in super-markets, alongside them is also a selection of named varieties. Many of the old varieties of potato are currently being revived, as well as new ones being created.

Potatoes are classified according to how early in the season they are ready for harvesting, and are named as follows: first early, second early, and main crop. The first earlies are the first new potatoes on the market; they are very fresh and young, and the skins can be simply rubbed off. The second earlies are still new potatoes, but their skins will have begun to set. These potatoes will be difficult to scrape and are better cooked in their skins. Main crop potatoes are available all year round and may have been stored for several months. Individual potato varieties have their own characteristics. Some main crop varieties are better for boiling than baking and vice versa, so choose the most appropriate type of potato for the dish being prepared. Check the label, ask your retailer or refer to the list below for guidance.

AILSA (MAIN CROP) These medium-sized potatoes are round or oval with white skins and creamy-colored, floury flesh. Ailsa potatoes are excellent for boiling and for french fries.

ANYA (SECOND EARLY) These speciality, knobbly, oval-shaped potatoes have a pinkish skin and white flesh. They have a nutty flavor and waxy texture, and are at their best when boiled or used in salads.

ARRAN COMET (FIRST EARLY) These round, and sometimes oval, new potatoes have a white skin and creamy flesh. Large ones are good for fries.

ARRAN PILOT (FIRST EARLY) The firm flesh of these potatoes makes them an ideal choice for salads. They have white flesh and skins.

ARRAN VICTORY (MAIN CROP) These oval-shaped potatoes have a deep purple skin and a bright white flesh. They are the oldest variety of Arran potatoes still available. Arran Victory potatoes have a very floury texture and flavor, and are excellent for baking and boiling. Currently they are undergoing a revival—it is worthwhile seeking this variety out.

ASPERGE (SECOND EARLY) Also known as la ratte and cornichon, these potatoes have a yellow skin and a creamy, very waxy flesh. They are good steamed or boiled and are perfect for salads.

BELLE DE FONTENAY (EARLY MAIN CROP) These long potatoes often have a curved shape. Their skins are pale yellow and their flesh is firm, waxy, and yellow. They have a wonderful buttery flavor and are particularly good boiled, in salads or mashed.

BINTJE (MAIN CROP) With a pale yellow skin and flesh, these potatoes are suitable for all cooking methods and make particularly good french fries.

CARA (LATE MAIN CROP) These potatoes may be white or red, round or oval. The flesh is creamy-colored with a mild flavor and waxy texture. Cara are good all-around potatoes.

CATRIONA (SECOND EARLY) Kidney-shaped potatoes with purple markings around the eyes on the skin and a pale yellow flesh. They have a delicious flavor and are ideal for baking, boiling, and mashing.

CHARLOTTE (MAIN CROP) Oval or pear-shaped potatoes with pale yellow skin and flesh, a firm, waxy texture, and a flavor not unlike chestnuts. They are particulary good boiled, steamed, and in salads, but can also be baked.

CLEOPATRA (FIRST EARLY) These oval, new potatoes are suitable for boiling, have pink or red skin and a light-yellow, dense flesh.

COLMO (FIRST EARLY) Medium round or oval, these potatoes have a white skin and golden, firm flesh. Their texture and color make them particularly good for mashing.

DESIREE (MAIN CROP) Probably the world's most popular red-skinned potatoes with pale yellow flesh, a firm texture, and good flavor. These potatoes are good all-arounders and are great for both mashing, and roasting. They also hold their shape well enough for boiling.

DIAMONT (MAIN CROP) These potatoes were a common and popular variety in the 1930s, and are still available now. They are long and oval shaped with a rough, white skin, and a firm, waxy yellow interior. Their flavor is slightly sharp and nutty.

DUKE OF YORK (FIRST EARLY) These long, oval, new potatoes have a sweet flavor, firm texture, pale creamy skins and light yellow flesh. A red-skinned variety is also available.

EPICURE (FIRST EARLY) Round potatoes with white or sometimes pink-tinged skin, creamy, firm flesh, and a distinctive flavor. Suitable for both boiling and baking.

ESTIMA (SECOND EARLY) Oval-shaped potatoes with a light yellow skin and flesh. Their firm, moist texture, and subtle flavor make them

good baking potatoes. These potatoes were the first yellow-fleshed potatoes to become popular.

GOLDEN WONDER (LATE MAIN CROP)
These large, oval potatoes have a dark, russet-colored skin, and light yellow flesh. They are excellent for baking and their floury texture makes them especially good for potato chips.

HOME GUARD (FIRST EARLY) Round or slightly oval, with white skins and creamy-colored flesh, these potatoes have a dry, floury texture, and a good flavor with slightly bitter overtones. These potatoes are ideal for boiling, roasting, and French fries. They were a favorite during the Second World War and are one of the first varieties of new potatoes available.

JERSEY ROYALS (SECOND EARLY) The best and most popular new potatoes, Jersey Royals have a creamy-colored skin and flesh, and can be served both hot or cold. When cooked (boiled or steamed), they are tender rather than firm,

and are best served whole, with or without the skins.

KERR'S PINK (LATE MAIN CROP) Round, pink-skinned potatoes with creamy-white flesh and a floury texture, these potatoes are suitable for boiling, baking, mashing, roasting, and for fries.

KING EDWARD (MAIN CROP) These large, white-skinned potatoes are among the best known and most popular. They have creamy-colored, very floury flesh, and are good all-arounders. They are particularly suited to roasting and baking, but are not so good for salads.

MARFONA (SECOND EARLY) These are good baking potatoes, also suitable for boiling, but not for roasting.

MARIS BARD (FIRST EARLY) These white-skinned potatoes have firm, waxy flesh with a slightly earthy taste. They are good for boiling and suitable for most other methods. They should be

avoided, however, late in the season when they lose their flavor and are in danger of disintegrating during cooking.

MARIS PEER (SECOND EARLY) These potatoes have white flesh and skins with an excellent flavor. They are good for salads as well as boiling and steaming.

MORAG (MAIN CROP) These potatoes have a pale skin and a white, waxy flesh. Serve them boiled, steamed, or baked.

NADINE (SECOND EARLY) These potatoes are available in two sizes. There are the small new potatoes and the slightly larger-sized potatoes, which are suitable for baking. Nadine potatoes have creamy-yellow skins and white, waxy flesh, but their flavor is somewhat bland.

PENTLAND JAVELIN (FIRST EARLY) These new potatoes have very white, smooth skins, and milky-white flesh. These potatoes are ideal for salads, but are also good boiled or steamed.

PENTLAND SQUIRE (MAIN CROP) Usually white skinned, but occasionally russet, the flesh of these potatoes is very white. Their floury texture makes them perfect for baking. They are also good for boiling and mashing, but are poor in salads.

PINK FIR APPLE (MAIN CROP) These knobbly, misshapen potatoes have white skins with a pinkish blush and a pale yellow flesh. They are firm and waxy with a delicious nutty flavor and have many of the characteristics of new potatoes. They are best cooked in their skins as their shape makes them extremely difficult to peel and are good steamed, boiled, and served cold in salads.

SHELAGH (MAIN CROP) This Scottish variety has a creamy flesh and pinkish patches all over the skin. The waxy texture of these potatoes makes them good for boiling, steaming, or for fries.

WILJA (SECOND EARLY) These potatoes have pale yellow skins and flesh. They are good, flavorsome all-arounders, and hold their shape when cooked, so are particularly suitable for salads, boiling, and steaming. They can also be used for baking and roasting.

SWEET POTATOES These potatoes are imported from tropical areas of the Americas and from many other hot countries around the world. Their skins are red and the flesh inside is either white or orange. Orange-fleshed sweet potatoes have a denser, waxier texture, and tend to hold their shape better, whereas white-fleshed ones are starchier and not quite as sugary. It is impossible to tell from the outside what color the flesh will be within, so unless labeled you may need to scrape off a small patch of skin. Treat in much the same way as ordinary potatoes—bake, mash or cook.

BUYING AND STORAGE

W hen buying potatoes, always choose ones with smooth, firm skins. When purchasing new potatoes, check that they are really young and fresh by scraping the skin—it should peel away very easily. Only buy the quantity you need and use within a couple of days. Check main crop potatoes to make sure they are firm and not sprouting or showing any signs of mold. Avoid buying and discard any potatoes with greenish patches or carefully cut them out. These parts of the potato are toxic and a sign that they have been stored in light.

Potatoes should be stored in a cool, dark place but not in the refrigerator as the dampness will make them sweat, causing mold to grow. If the potatoes come in plastic bags, take them out and store in a paper bag or on a vegetable rack. If you prefer to buy in bulk, keep the potatoes in a cold, dark, dry place, such as a pantry or garage, making sure they do not freeze in cold weather.

Sweet potatoes should be stored in a cool, dry place, but unlike ordinary potatoes, do not need to be kept in the dark.

VARIETIES OF RICE AND STORAGE

R ice is the staple food of many countries throughout the world. Every country and culture has its own repertoire of rice recipes, for example, India has the aromatic biryani, Spain has the saffron-scented paella, and Italy has the creamy risotto. Rice is grown on marshy, flooded land where other cereals cannot thrive, and because it is grown in so many different areas, there is a huge range of rice types.

LONG-GRAIN WHITE RICE This is probably the most widely used type of rice. Long-grain white rice has been milled so that the husk, bran, and germ is removed. If you buy it loose, it is sometimes whitened with chalk or other substances, so thorough rinsing under cold running water is essential. Easy-cook long-grain white rice has been steamed under pressure before milling. This makes it difficult to overcook, therefore separate dry and fluffy grains are virtually guaranteed. Precooked rice, also known as parboiled or converted rice, is polished white rice, which is half cooked after milling, then dried again. It is quick and simple to cook, but has a rather bland flavor. Java rice is one of the slightly shorter long-grain rices and because it is particularly absorbent it is often used in baked rice dishes.

Rice is sometimes referred to by the country or region in which it was originally grown. Patna rice is a term used to describe a type of long-grain rice, which originated from Patna in north-east India. Long-grain rice is rarely labeled by country of origin, as it now mostly comes from the United States. Carolina is simply another name for long-grain rice and refers to the region in the united states where rice was first planted.

LONG-GRAIN BROWN RICE Here the outer husk is removed, leaving the bran and germ behind, so retaining a lot more of the fiber, vitamins, and minerals. It has a nutty, slightly chewy texture and because it is less refined takes longer to cook than long-grain white rice.

BASMATI RICE This slender long-grain rice, which may be white or brown, is grown in the foothills of the Himalaya Mountains. After harvesting, it matures for a year, giving it a unique aromatic flavor, hence its name, which means fragrant. Its perfect, separate, white, and fluffy grains frequently feature in Indian cooking.

RISOTTO RICE Grown in the north of Italy, this is the only rice that is suitable for making Italian risotto. The grains are plump and stubby, and have the ability to absorb large quantities of liquid without becoming too soft, cooking to a creamy texture with a slight bite. The starchiness of risotto rice makes it a good addition to soups where it acts as thickener. It can also be made into molded rice dishes, such as timbales, as the grains hold together without being too sticky. There are two grades of risotto rice: superfino and fino. Arborio rice is the most widely sold variety of the former, but you can also find carnaroli, Roma, and baldo in Italian food stores and delicatessens. Fino rice, such as vialone nano, has a slightly shorter grain, but the flavor is still excellent.

VALENCIA RICE Traditionally used for Spanish paella, Valencia rice is soft and tender when ready. The medium-sized grains break down easily, so

RICE PRODUCTS

N umerous Japanese ingredients are made from rice. Japan's national drink, sake, is a spirit distilled from rice, and is often used in cooking. Mirin is a sweet rice wine used as a marinade in dishes such as teriyaki. Rice vinegar is made from soured and fermented wine. Japanese rice vinegar has a soft, mellow flavor, whereas Chinese rice vinegar has a very sharp taste.

Sometimes Japanese rice vinegars are made into flavored vinegars by mixing the vinegar with soy sauce, for example, to make dashi. Most rice vinegars are a clear, pale golden color, but brown rice vinegar, made from whole-grain rice, is deep brown.

Amasake is a rice drink, often sold in healthfood stores and is made by adding enzymes to whole-grain dessert rice. It can be used in desserts and baking as an alternative to milk.

Rice paper is made from a mixture of rice flour, salt, and water. Machines roll the mixture out until it is extremely thin and transparent, then it is dried out. Rice paper comes in hard circles and triangles and

is easily softened by placing between two dampened dish towels. When soft, the rice paper can be wrapped around a filling, then steamed or cooked, to make dishes such as dim sum.

should be left unstirred during cooking to absorb the flavor of the stock and other ingredients.

JASMINE RICE Also known as Thai fragrant rice, this long-grain rice has a delicate, almost perfumed aroma and flavor, and has a soft, sticky texture.

GLUTINOUS RICE White or black (unpolished), these short grains are high in starch and feature in Chinese and Japanese cooking, as the grains stick together when cooked, making them easy to eat with chopsticks. This rice has a slightly sweet taste and is used for making dim sum as well as sweet, sticky desserts.

JAPANESE SUSHI RICE This is similar to glutinous rice in that it has a sticky texture. When mixed with rice vinegar it is easy to roll up with a filling inside to make sushi. Much of the sushi rice eaten in the West is now grown in California.

DESSERT RICE This rounded, short-grain rice is ideal for rice desserts. The grains swell and absorb large quantities of milk during cooking, giving desserts a rich and soft creamy consistency. Brown dessert rice is also available.

RED RICE This is grown in small amounts in the Camargue, a marshy region in Provence in France. It is similar to brown rice in taste and texture, but when cooked its red color develops, making it an attractive addition to salads and other rice dishes.

WILD RICE Strictly speaking this is an aquatic grass, which is grown in North America rather than a true variety of rice. Some wild rice is now grown commercially, which has reduced the price slightly, but much of it is still found growing wild in North America's vast lakes, where only native Americans have the right to gather it. The black grains are long and slender, and after harvesting and cleaning are toasted to remove the chaff, and intensify the nutty flavor and slight chewiness. Although wild rice is much more expensive than other rices, a small quantity goes a long way—it is often sold as a mixture with either long-grain white or basmati rice.

FLAKED RICE White or brown rice grains are steamed and rolled to paper thinness to make flaked rice. It is extremely quick to cook and is mainly used to make creamy desserts, but may also be used for baking. It is sometimes found in commercially made muesli mixtures.

GROUND RICE This type of rice is made by grounding white rice to the size of fine sand. Like flaked rice, it can be used to make fast rice desserts and is also frequently used in baking, especially for making cookies such as shortbread.

RICE FLOUR Raw rice can be ground finely to make rice flour, which may be used to thicken sauces (you need about 1 tablespoon to thicken 1¼ cups of liquid) or as a vital ingredient in sticky Asian cakes and desserts. It is also used to make fresh and dried rice noodles. When rice flour is ground even more finely, it becomes rice powder and has a fine consistency like cornstarch. It can be found in Asian grocery stores.

BUYING AND STORING RICE

R ice will keep for several years if kept in sealed packages, however, it is at its best when fresh. To ensure freshness, always buy rice from reputable stores with a good turnover and buy in small quantities. Once opened, store the rice in an airtight container in a cool, dry place to keep out moisture. Most rice (but not risotto) benefit from washing before cooking—tip into a strainer and rinse under cold running water for a minute or so, until the water runs clear.

Cooked rice will keep well for up to two days if cooled rapidly and stored in a bowl covered with plastic wrap in the refrigerator. If eating rice cold, serve within 24 hours–after this time it should be reheated thoroughly. To reheat rice, place it in a heavy—bottomed saucepan with 2–3 tablespoons of water, cover, and heat until piping hot, shaking the pan occasionally. Alternatively, reheat the bowl of cooled rice in the microwave, piercing the plastic wrap first.

COOKING TECHNIQUES FOR POTATOES

G enerally, new potato varieties have a firm and waxy texture which do not break up during cooking, so are ideal for boiling, steaming, and salads. Main crop potatoes, on the other hand, have a more floury texture and lend themselves to mashing and roasting–both types are suitable for french fries. When cooking potatoes, it is important to make sure the potatoes that you are using are the correct type for the dish being prepared. Whichever way you choose to serve potatoes, allow 1-1½ per person.

BOILING POTATOES
NEW POTATOES

Most of the new potatoes available nowadays are fairly clean—especially those sold in supermarkets — and simply need a light scrub before cooking in their skins. If the potatoes are very dirty, use a small scrubbing brush or scourer to remove both the skins and dirt. Add them to a saucepan of cold, salted water, and bring to a boil. Cover the pan with a lid and let simmer for 12–15 minutes, or until tender. Add a couple of sprigs of fresh herbs to the pan, if you like—fresh mint is traditionally used to flavor potatoes. Drain the potatoes thoroughly and serve hot, tossed in a little melted butter, or for a change, 1 tablespoon of pesto. The skins of first early new potatoes will peel away easily, but second earlies should be served in their skins or peeled when cooked (hold the hot potatoes with a fork to make this easier). Very firm new potatoes can be added to boiling water, simmered for 8 minutes, then left to stand in the hot water for an additional 10 minutes until cooked through.

OLD POTATOES

Choose a main crop potato suitable for boiling, then thinly peel and cut into even-size pieces. Add to a saucepan of cold, salted water and bring to a boil. Cover the saucepan with a lid and let simmer for 20 minutes, or until tender.

Alternatively, you can cook the potatoes in their skins and peel them after cooking. (It is particularly important to cook floury potatoes gently, or the outsides may start to fall apart before they are tender in the center. Drain the potatoes in a strainer, then return to the saucepan to dry out over a very low heat for 1–2 minutes.) If you are planning to serve the potatoes mashed, coarsely mash them then add a pat of butter and 2 tablespoons of milk per person. Mash until smooth, either with a hand masher, mouli grater, or a potato ricer. Season to taste with salt, freshly ground black pepper, and a little freshly grated nutmeg, if liked, then beat for a few seconds with a wooden spoon until fluffy. As an alternative to butter, use a good-quality olive oil or sour cream. Finely chopped red and green chilies, crispy-cooked crumbled bacon, fresh herbs, or grated Parmesan cheese can also be stirred in for additional flavor.

STEAMING POTATOES

All potatoes are suitable for steaming. Floury potatoes, however, are ideal for this method of cooking as they fall apart easily.

New and small potatoes can be steamed whole, but larger ones should be cut into even-sized pieces. Place the potatoes in a steamer, colander, or sieve over a pan of boiling water and cover. Steam for 10 minutes if the potatoes are very small, or if they are large, cut into chunks and cook for 20–25 minutes.

FRYING POTATOES
POTATOES FOR FRENCH FRIES

To make french fries wash, peel, and cut the potatoes into ⅜ inch slices. Cut the slices into long strips about ⅜ inches wide. Place the strips in a bowl of cold water and leave for 20 minutes, then drain and dry well on paper towels—moisture will make the fat spit. Pour some oil into a deep, heavy-

bottomed saucepan or deep-fat fryer, making sure that the oil does not go any further than halfway up the sides of the pan. Heat the oil to 375° F, or until a fry dropped into the fat rises to the surface straight away and is surrounded by bubbles. Put the fries into a wire basket, lower into the oil and cook for 7–8 minutes or until golden. Remove and increase the heat of the oil to 400° F. Lower the fries into the oil again and cook for 2–3 minutes, or until they are crisp and golden brown. Drain on paper towels before serving.

Slightly finer french fries are known as *pommes frites*, even finer ones as *pommes allumettes* and the finest of all as *pommes pailles* (straw fries). Paper-thin slices of peeled potatoes, cut with a sharp knife or using a mandoline or food processor, can be deep-fried a few at a time to make potato chips.

HEALTHY FRENCH FRIES

To make reduced-fat french fries, preheat the oven to 400° F/Gas Mark 6 and place a non-stick baking tray in the oven to heat up. Cut the potatoes into french fries or into chunky wedges, if preferred. Put the fries or wedges in a saucepan of cold water and quickly bring to a boil. Let simmer for 2 minutes, then drain in a strainer. Leave for a few minutes to dry, then drizzle over 1½–2 tablespoons of olive or corn oil, and toss to coat. Tip onto the heated baking sheet and cook in the preheated oven for 20–25 minutes, turning occasionally, until golden brown and crisp.

SAUTÉED POTATOES

Cut peeled potatoes into rounds about ¼ inch thick and pat dry. Heat ¼ stick unsalted butter and 2 tablespoons of oil in a large, heavy-bottomed skillet until hot. Add the potatoes in a single layer and cook for 4–5 minutes or until the undersides are golden. Turn with a large spatula and cook the other side until golden and tender. Drain on paper towels and sprinkle with a little salt before serving.

BAKING POTATOES

Allow 1 medium potato per person and choose a variety such as Maris Piper, Cara, or King Edward. Wash and dry the potatoes, prick the skins lightly, then rub each one with a little oil and sprinkle with salt. Bake in a preheated oven at 400° F for 1–1½ hours or until the skins are crisp and the centers are very soft. To speed up the cooking time, thread onto metal skewers as this conducts heat to the center of the potatoes.

ROASTING POTATOES

For crisp and brown outsides and fluffy centers choose potatoes suitable for baking. Thinly peel the potatoes and cut into even-sized pieces. Drop them into a saucepan of boiling, salted water and let simmer for 5 minutes. Turn off the heat and let stand for 3–4 minutes. Drain well and return the potatoes to the pan over a low heat for a minute to dry them and to roughen the edges. Carefully transfer them to a roasting pan containing hot oil. Baste well then bake in a preheated oven at 425° F for 20 minutes. Turn them and cook for an additional 20–30 minutes, turning and basting at least one more time. Serve as soon as the potatoes are ready.

POTATO CROQUETTES

Mash dry, boiled potatoes with just a little butter or olive oil, then stir in 1 egg yolk mixed with 1–2 tablespoons of milk or sour cream to make a firm mixture. Shape the mashed potatoes into small cylinders about 2 inches long, rolling them in flour. Dip in beaten egg then in fresh, white bread crumbs. Chill the croquettes in the refrigerator for 30 minutes. Place a little unsalted butter and oil in a heavy-bottomed skillet and slowly heat until the butter has melted. Pan fry the croquettes, turning occasionally, until they are golden brown and crisp.

ROSTI

Parboil peeled, waxy potatoes in boiling, salted water for 8 minutes, drain, and let cool before coarsely grating into a bowl. Season well with salt and freshly ground black pepper, and freshly chopped herbs, if liked. Heat a mixture of unsalted butter and oil in a heavy-bottomed skillet until bubbling. Add tablespoonfuls of the grated potato into the pan and flatten with the back of a spatula. Cook over a medium heat for about 7 minutes, or until crisp and golden. Turn and cook the other side.

COOKING POTATOES IN A CLAY POT

Terracotta potato pots can cook up to 3 medium or 1 lb of whole potatoes at a time. Soak the clay pot for at least 20 minutes before use, then add even-sized, preferably smallish potatoes. Drizzle over a little olive oil and season generously with salt and freshly ground black pepper. Cover the pot with the lid and put in a cold oven, setting the temperature to 400° F. The potatoes will take about 45 minutes to cook.

MICROWAVED POTATOES

This method of cooking is suitable for boiling and baking potatoes, providing you do not want the skins to be crispy. To cook new potatoes, prick the skins with a skewer to prevent them from bursting, then place in a bowl with 3 tablespoons of boiling water. Cover with plastic wrap, which has been pierced two or three times and cook on High for 12–15 minutes, or until tender. Peeled chunks of potato can be cooked in the same way. To bake potatoes, place each potato on a circle of paper towels. Make several cuts in each to ensure that the skins do not burst. Transfer to the microwave plate and cook on High for 4–6 minutes per potato, allowing an extra 3–4 minutes for every additional potato. Turn the potatoes at least once during cooking. Let stand for 5 minutes before serving.

HEALTH AND NUTRITION

Potatoes are high in complex carbohydrates, providing sustained energy. They are also an excellent source of vitamins B and C, and minerals such as iron and potassium. They contain almost no fat and are high in dietary fiber.

MUSHROOM & SHERRY SOUP

INGREDIENTS   Serves 4

4 slices day-old white bread
1 tsp. lemon zest
1 tbsp. lemon juice
salt and freshly ground
  black pepper
1¾ cups assorted wild
  mushrooms, lightly rinsed
1¾ cups baby button
  mushrooms, wiped

2 tsp. olive oil
1 garlic clove, peeled
  and crushed
6 scallions, trimmed
  and diagonally sliced
2½ cups chicken stock
4 tbsp. dry sherry
1 tbsp. freshly cut chives, to
  garnish

1 Preheat the oven to 350° F. Remove the crusts from the bread and cut the bread into small cubes.

2 In a large bowl, toss the cubes of bread with the lemon zest and juice, 2 tablespoons of water, and plenty of freshly ground black pepper.

3 Spread the bread cubes onto a lightly greased baking sheet and cook in the preheated oven for 20 minutes until golden and crisp.

4 If the wild mushrooms are small, leave some whole. Otherwise, thinly slice all the mushrooms and set aside.

5 Heat the oil in a saucepan. Add the garlic and scallions, and cook for 1–2 minutes.

6 Add the mushrooms and cook for 3–4 minutes until they start to soften. Add the chicken stock and stir to mix.

7 Bring to a boil, then reduce the heat to a gentle simmer. Cover the pan with a lid and cook for 10 minutes.

8 Stir in the sherry, and season to taste with a little salt and pepper. Pour into warmed bowls, sprinkle the chives on top, and serve the soup immediately with the lemon croutons.

HELPFUL HINT

To achieve very fine shreds, use a zester, available from all kitchen stores. Or, thinly peel the fruit with a vegetable peeler, then shred with a small, sharp knife. When grating fruit, use a clean, dry pastry brush to remove the rind from the grater.

CHINESE CHICKEN SOUP

INGREDIENTS

Serves 4

8 oz. cooked chicken
1 tsp. oil
6 scallions, trimmed
  and diagonally sliced
1 red chili, seeded and
  finely chopped
1 garlic clove, peeled
  and crushed
1-in. piece fresh ginger, peeled
  and finely grated
4 cups chicken stock

1½ cups medium
  egg noodles
1 carrot, peeled and cut
  into matchsticks
¾ cup bean sprouts
2 tbsp. soy sauce
1 tbsp. fish sauce
fresh cilantro leaves,
  to garnish

1 Remove any skin from the chicken. Place on a chopping board and use 2 forks to tear the chicken into fine shreds.

2 Heat the oil in a large saucepan and fry the scallions and chili for 1 minute.

3 Add the garlic and ginger, and cook for another minute.

4 Stir in the chicken stock and gradually bring the mixture to a boil.

5 Break up the noodles a little and add to the boiling stock, along with the carrot.

6 Stir to mix, then reduce the heat to a simmer and cook for 3–4 minutes.

7 Add the shredded chicken, bean sprouts, soy sauce, and fish sauce, and stir.

8 Cook for an additional 2–3 minutes until piping hot. Spoon the soup into bowls and sprinkle with a few fresh cilantro leaves. Serve immediately.

TASTY TIP

If possible, buy corn-fed chicken for this recipe. Since this soup is chicken stock-based, the use of corn-fed chicken will make the soup much more flavorful.
For added nutritional value, substitute the egg noodles with the whole-wheat variety and use sesame oil in step 2. Increase the vegetable content by adding ¾ cups each of water chestnuts and bamboo shoots, and ½ cup of snow peas and baby corn in step 7.

CARROT & GINGER SOUP

INGREDIENTS

Serves 4

4 slices of bread,
  crusts removed
1 tsp. yeast extract
2 tsp. olive oil
1 onion, peeled and chopped
1 garlic clove, peeled
  and crushed
½ tsp. ground ginger
2½ cups carrots, peeled
  and chopped
4 cups vegetable stock

1-in. piece of ginger, peeled
  and finely grated
salt and freshly ground
  black pepper
1 tbsp. lemon juice

TO GARNISH:
chives
lemon zest

1 Preheat the oven to 350° F. Coarsely chop the bread. Dissolve the yeast extract in 2 tablespoons of warm water, and mix with the bread.

2 Spread the bread cubes over a lightly greased baking sheet and cook for 20 minutes, turning halfway through. Remove from the oven and set aside.

3 Heat the oil in a large saucepan. Gently cook the onion and garlic for 3–4 minutes.

4 Stir in the ground ginger and cook for 1 minute to release the flavor.

5 Add the chopped carrots, then stir in the stock and the fresh ginger. Simmer gently for 15 minutes.

6 Remove from the heat and allow to cool slightly. Blend until smooth, then season to taste with salt and pepper. Stir in the lemon juice. Garnish with the chives and lemon zest, and serve immediately.

TASTY TIP

This soup would be delicious for special occasions if served with a spoonful of lightly whipped cream or low-fat sour cream. Serve with slices of bruschetta, which can be easily made by lightly broiling thick slices of ciabatta bread on both sides. While still warm, rub the top of the bruschetta with a whole, peeled clove of garlic, and drizzle with a little good-quality extra-virgin olive oil.

ITALIAN BEAN SOUP

INGREDIENTS

Serves 4

2 tsp. olive oil
1 leek, washed and chopped
1 garlic clove, peeled
  and crushed
2 tsp. dried oregano
¾ cup green beans, trimmed
  and cut into bite-size pieces

14-oz. can lima beans, drained
  and rinsed
¾ cup small pasta shapes
4 cups vegetable stock
8 cherry tomatoes
salt and freshly ground
  black pepper
3 tbsp. freshly torn basil

1 Heat the oil in a large saucepan. Add the leek, garlic, and oregano, and cook for 5 minutes, stirring occasionally.

2 Stir in the green beans and the lima beans. Sprinkle in the pasta and pour in the stock.

3 Bring the stock mixture to a boil, then reduce the heat to a simmer.

4 Cook for 12–15 minutes or until the vegetables are tender and the pasta is cooked to al dente. Stir occasionally.

5 In a heavy skillet, fry the tomatoes over a high heat until they soften and the skins begin to blacken.

6 Gently crush the tomatoes in the skillet with the back of a spoon, and add to the soup.

7 Season to taste with salt and pepper. Stir in the shredded basil and serve immediately.

TASTY TIP

This soup will taste even better the day after it has been made. Make the soup the day before you intend to serve it, and add a little extra stock when reheating.

FOOD FACT

The majority of Italian cooking takes advantage of the abundance of freshly grown herbs, especially when used in tomato-based dishes. With a few exceptions, it is worth trying to use fresh herbs to draw out the other flavors of the dish. However, if you decide to use dried herbs, remember that they are much more pungent. 1 teaspoon of dried herbs equals roughly 1 tablespoon of fresh herbs.

TOMATO & BASIL SOUP

INGREDIENTS

Serves 4

7 medium, ripe tomatoes,
  cut in half
2 garlic cloves
1 tsp. olive oil
1 tbsp. balsamic vinegar
1 tbsp. dark brown sugar
1 tbsp. tomato paste

1¼ cups vegetable stock
6 tbsp. low-fat plain yogurt
2 tbsp. freshly chopped basil
salt and freshly ground
  black pepper
small basil leaves,
  to garnish

1 Preheat the oven to 400° F. Evenly spread the tomato halves and unpeeled garlic in a single layer in a large roasting pan.

2 Mix the oil and vinegar together. Drizzle over the tomatoes and sprinkle with the dark brown sugar.

3 Roast the tomatoes in the preheated oven for 20 minutes until tender and lightly charred in places.

4 Remove from the oven and allow to cool slightly. When cool enough to handle, squeeze the softened flesh of the garlic from the papery skin. Place with the charred tomatoes in a strainer over a saucepan.

5 Press the garlic and tomato through the strainer with the back of a wooden spoon.

6 When all the flesh has been strained, add the tomato paste and the vegetable stock to the pan. Heat gently, stirring occasionally.

7 In a small bowl beat the yogurt and basil together, and season to taste with salt and pepper. Stir the basil yogurt into the soup. Garnish with basil leaves and serve immediately.

TASTY TIP

Use the sweetest type of tomatoes available, as it makes a big difference to the flavor of the soup. Many supermarkets now stock special tomatoes, grown slowly and matured for longer on the vine to give them an intense flavor. If these are unavailable, add a little extra sugar to bring out the flavor.

SHRIMP & CHILI SOUP

INGREDIENTS

Serves 4

2 scallions, trimmed
8 oz. whole, raw jumbo
  shrimp
3 cups fish stock
2 tsp. finely grated lime rind
1 tbsp. lime juice
1 tbsp. fish sauce

1 red chili, seeded
  and chopped
1 tbsp. soy sauce
1 lemongrass stalk
2 tbsp. rice vinegar
4 tbsp. freshly chopped
  cilantro

1 To make the scallion curls, finely shred the scallions lengthwise. Place in a bowl of ice-cold water and set aside.

2 Remove the heads and shells from the shrimp, leaving the tails intact.

3 Split the shrimp almost in two to form a butterfly shape, and individually remove the black vein that runs down the back of each.

4 In a large saucepan, heat the stock with the lime rind and juice, fish sauce, chili, and soy sauce.

5 Bruise the lemongrass by crushing it along its length with a rolling pin, then add to the stock mixture.

6 When the stock mixture is boiling, add the shrimp and cook until they are pink.

7 Remove the lemongrass and add the rice vinegar and cilantro.

8 Spoon into bowls and garnish with the scallion curls. Serve immediately.

TASTY TIP

For a more substantial dish, cook ¼ cup Thai fragrant rice for 12–15 minutes or until just cooked. Drain, then place a little in the soup bowl and spoon the prepared soup on top.

CURRIED PARSNIP SOUP

INGREDIENTS

Serves 4

1 tsp. cumin seeds
2 tsp. coriander seeds
1 tsp. oil
1 onion, peeled and chopped
1 garlic clove, peeled
  and crushed
½ tsp. turmeric
¼ tsp. chili powder
1 cinnamon stick

2 cups parsnips, peeled and
  chopped
4 cups vegetable stock
salt and freshly ground
  black pepper
2–3 tbsp. low-fat plain yogurt,
  to serve
fresh cilantro leaves,
  to garnish

1 In a small skillet, fry the cumin and coriander seeds over a moderately high heat for 1–2 minutes. Shake the skillet during cooking until the seeds are lightly toasted.

2 Set aside until cooled. Grind the toasted seeds with a mortar and pestle.

3 Heat the oil in a saucepan. Cook the onion until softened and starting to turn golden.

4 Add the garlic, turmeric, chili powder, and cinnamon stick to the pan. Continue to cook for an additional minute.

5 Add the parsnips and stir well. Pour in the stock and bring to a boil. Cover and simmer for 15 minutes or until the parsnips are cooked.

6 Allow the soup to cool. Once cooled, remove the cinnamon stick and discard.

7 Blend the soup in a food processor until very smooth.

8 Transfer to a saucepan and reheat gently. Season to taste with salt and pepper. Garnish with fresh cilantro leaves, and serve immediately with yogurt.

FOOD FACT

Parsnips vary in color from pale yellow to a creamy white. They are at their best when they are the size of a large carrot. If larger, remove the central core, which can be woody.

MUSHROOM & RED WINE PÂTÉ

INGREDIENTS

Serves 4

3 large slices of white bread, crusts removed
2 tsp. oil
1 small onion, peeled and finely chopped
1 garlic clove, peeled and crushed
3¾ cup button mushrooms, wiped and finely chopped
⅔ cup red wine
½ tsp. dried mixed herbs

1 tbsp. freshly chopped parsley
salt and freshly ground black pepper
2 tbsp. low-fat cream cheese

TO SERVE:
finely chopped cucumber
finely chopped tomato

1 Preheat the oven to 350° F. Cut the bread in half diagonally. Place the bread triangles on a baking sheet and cook for 10 minutes.

2 Remove from the oven and split each bread triangle in half to make 12 triangles, and return to the oven until golden and crisp. Allow to cool on a wire rack.

3 Heat the oil in a saucepan and gently cook the onion and garlic until transparent.

4 Add the mushrooms and cook, stirring for 3–4 minutes or until the mushroom juices start to run.

5 Stir the wine and herbs into the mushroom mixture and bring to a boil. Reduce the heat and simmer uncovered until all the liquid is absorbed.

6 Remove from the heat and season to taste with salt and pepper. Allow to cool.

7 When cold, beat in the cream cheese and season lightly. Place in a small, clean bowl and chill in the refrigerator until needed. Serve the toast triangles with the cucumber and tomato.

TASTY TIP

This pâté is also delicious served as a bruschetta topping. Toast slices of ciabatta, generously spread the pâté on top, and garnish with a little arugula.

THAI FISH CAKES

INGREDIENTS

Serves 4

1 red chili, seeded
  and coarsely chopped
4 tbsp. coarsely chopped
  fresh cilantro
1 garlic clove, peeled
  and crushed
2 scallions, trimmed
  and coarsely chopped
1 lemongrass, outer
  leaves discarded and
  coarsely chopped

3 oz. shrimp, defrosted if
  frozen
10 oz. cod fillet, skinned, pin
  bones removed, and cubed
salt and freshly ground
  black pepper
sweet chili dipping sauce,
  to serve

1 Preheat the oven to 375° F. Place the chili, cilantro, garlic, scallions, and lemongrass in a food processor, and blend together.

2 Pat the shrimp and cod dry with paper towels.

3 Add to the food processor and blend until the mixture is coarsely chopped.

4 Season to taste with salt and pepper, and blend to mix.

5 Dampen your hands, then shape heaping tablespoons of the mixture into 12 little patties.

6 Place the patties on a lightly greased baking sheet, and cook in the preheated oven for 12–15 minutes or until piping hot and cooked through. Turn the patties over halfway through the cooking time.

7 Serve the fish cakes immediately with the sweet chili sauce for dipping.

TASTY TIP

A horseradish dip could be used in place of the sweet chili sauce, if a creamier dip is preferred. Mix together 2 tablespoons of grated horseradish (from a jar) with 3 tablespoons each of plain yogurt and low-calorie mayonnaise. Add 3 finely chopped scallions, a squeeze of lime, and salt and pepper to taste.

HOISIN CHICKEN PANCAKES

INGREDIENTS   Serves 4

3 tbsp. hoisin sauce
1 garlic clove, peeled
   and crushed
1-in. piece ginger, peeled and
   finely grated
1 tbsp. soy sauce
1 tsp. sesame oil
salt and freshly ground
   black pepper

4 skinless chicken thighs
½ cucumber, peeled (optional)
12 store-bought Chinese
   pancakes
6 scallions, trimmed
   and cut lengthwise
sweet chili dipping sauce,
   to serve

1 Preheat the oven to 375°F. In a nonmetallic bowl, mix the hoisin sauce with the garlic, ginger, soy sauce, sesame oil, and seasoning.

2 Add the chicken thighs and coat in the mixture. Cover loosely with plastic wrap, and leave in the refrigerator to marinate for 3–4 hours, turning the chicken occasionally.

3 Remove the chicken from the marinade and place in a roasting pan. Set the marinade aside. Cook in the preheated oven for 30 minutes, basting occasionally with the marinade.

4 Cut the cucumber in half lengthwise, and remove the seeds by running a teaspoon down the center to scoop them out. Cut into thin pieces.

5 Place the pancakes in a steamer to warm, according to package instructions. Thinly slice

the hot chicken, and arrange on a plate with the shredded scallions, cucumber, and pancakes.

6 Place a spoonful of the chicken in the center of each warmed pancake, and top with pieces of cucumber, scallion, and some of the dipping sauce. Roll up and serve immediately.

TASTY TIP

For those with wheat allergies or who want to make this tasty dish more substantial, stir-fry the scallions and cucumber pieces in a little peanut oil. Add a carrot cut into batons and mix in the thinly sliced chicken and extra marinade (as prepared in step 3). Serve with steamed rice—Thai fragrant rice is particularly good.

ROASTED RED BELL PEPPER, TOMATO, & RED ONION SOUP

INGREDIENTS

Serves 4

fine spray of oil
2 large red bell peppers,
  seeded and coarsely
  chopped
1 red onion, peeled and
  coarsely chopped
2 medium tomatoes, halved

1 small, crusty French loaf
1 garlic clove, peeled
2½ cups vegetable stock
salt and freshly ground
  black pepper
1 tsp. Worcestershire sauce
4 tbsp. low-fat sour cream

1 Preheat the oven to 375° F. Spray a large roasting pan with the oil, and place the bell peppers and the onion in the base. Cook in the preheated oven for 10 minutes. Add the tomatoes, and cook for an additional 20 minutes or until the bell peppers are soft.

2 Cut the bread into ½ inch slices. Cut the garlic clove in half and rub the cut edge of the garlic over the bread.

3 Place all the bread slices on a large baking sheet, and cook in the oven for 10 minutes, turning halfway through, until golden and crisp.

4 Remove the vegetables from the oven and allow to cool slightly, then blend in a food processor until smooth. Strain the vegetable mixture through a large strainer into a saucepan to remove the seeds and skin. Add the stock, season to taste with salt and pepper, and stir to mix. Heat the soup gently until piping hot.

5 In a small bowl, beat together the Worcestershire sauce with the sour cream.

6 Pour the soup into warmed bowls and swirl a spoonful of the sour cream mixture into each bowl. Serve immediately with the garlic toast.

HELPFUL HINT

A quick way to remove the skin from bell peppers once they have been roasted or broiled is to place them in a plastic bag. Leave for 10 minutes or until cool enough to handle, then peel the skin away from the flesh.

HOT HERBED MUSHROOMS

INGREDIENTS

Serves 4

4 thin slices of white bread,
 crusts removed
1¾ cups chestnut mushrooms,
 wiped and sliced
1¾ cups oyster mushrooms,
 wiped
1 garlic clove, peeled
 and crushed
1 tsp. mustard

1¼ cups chicken stock
salt and freshly ground
 black pepper
1 tbsp. freshly chopped
 parsley
1 tbsp. freshly cut chives, plus
 extra to garnish
mixed lettuce leaves, to serve

1 Preheat the oven to 350° F. With a rolling pin, roll each piece of bread out as thinly as possible.

2 Press each piece of bread into a 4-inch tartlet pan. Push each piece firmly down, then bake in the preheated oven for 20 minutes.

3 Place the mushrooms in a skillet with the garlic, mustard, and chicken stock, and stir-fry over a moderate heat until the mushrooms are tender and the liquid is reduced by half.

4 Using a slotted spoon, carefully remove the mushrooms from the skillet, and transfer to a heat-resistant dish. Cover with foil and place in the bottom of the oven to keep the mushrooms warm.

5 Boil the remaining juices until reduced to a thick sauce. Season with salt and pepper.

6 Stir the parsley and chives into the mushroom mixture.

7 Place one bread tartlet shell on each plate, and divide the mushroom mixture among them.

8 Spoon over the juices, garnish with the chives, and serve immediately with mixed lettuce leaves.

FOOD FACT

Mushrooms are an extremely nutritious food, rich in vitamins and minerals, which help to boost our immune system.
 This recipe could be adapted to include shiitake mushrooms, which studies have shown can significantly boost and protect the body's immune system, and can also strengthen the body's protection against cancer.

CILANTRO CHICKEN & SOY SAUCE CAKES

INGREDIENTS

Serves 4

- ¼ cucumber, peeled
- 1 shallot, peeled and thinly sliced
- 6 radishes, trimmed and sliced
- 12 oz. skinless, boneless chicken thigh
- 4 tbsp. coarsely chopped fresh cilantro
- 2 scallions, trimmed and coarsely chopped
- 1 red chili, seeded and chopped
- 2 tsp. finely grated lime rind
- 2 tbsp. soy sauce
- 1 tbsp. sugar
- 2 tbsp. rice vinegar
- 1 red chili, seeded and finely sliced
- freshly chopped cilantro, to garnish

1 Preheat the oven to 375° F. Halve the peeled cucumber lengthwise, remove the seeds, and dice.

2 In a bowl, mix the shallot and radishes together. Chill until ready to serve.

3 Place the chicken thighs in a food processor, and blend until coarsely chopped.

4 Add the cilantro and scallions to the chicken with the chili, lime zest, and soy sauce. Blend again until mixed.

5 Using slightly damp hands, shape the chicken mixture into 12 small rounds.

6 Place the rounds on a lightly greased baking sheet and cook in the preheated oven for 15 minutes or until golden.

7 In a small saucepan, heat the sugar with 2 tablespoons of water until dissolved. Simmer until syrupy.

8 Remove from the heat and allow to cool a little, then stir in the vinegar and chili slices. Pour over the cucumber, radish, and shallot salad. Garnish with the freshly chopped cilantro, and serve the chicken cakes with the salad immediately.

FOOD FACT

In this recipe, the chicken cakes can be altered so that half chicken and half lean pork is used. This alters the flavor of the dish and works really well if a small 1-inch piece of fresh ginger is grated and added in Step 4.

ROASTED EGGPLANT DIP WITH PITA STRIPS

INGREDIENTS   Serves 4

4 pita breads
2 large eggplants
1 garlic clove, peeled
¼ tsp. sesame oil
1 tbsp. lemon juice

½ tsp. cumin
salt and freshly ground
  black pepper
2 tbsp. freshly chopped parsley
fresh lettuce leaves, to serve

1 Preheat the oven to 350° F. On a chopping board, cut the pita breads into strips, and spread in a single layer onto a large baking sheet.

2 Cook in the preheated oven for 15 minutes or until golden brown and crisp. Allow to cool on a wire rack.

3 Trim the eggplants, rinse lightly, and set aside. Heat a griddle pan until almost smoking. Cook the eggplants and garlic for about 15 minutes.

4 Turn the eggplants frequently until very tender, with wrinkled and charred skins. Remove from the heat. Let cool.

5 When the eggplants are cool enough to handle, cut in half, and scoop out the cooked flesh and place in a food processor.

6 Squeeze the softened garlic flesh from the papery skin, and add to the eggplant in the food processor.

7 Blend the eggplant and garlic until smooth, then add the sesame oil, lemon juice, and cumin, and blend again to mix.

8 Season to taste with salt and pepper, stir in the parsley, and serve with the pita strips and mixed lettuce leaves.

FOOD FACT

This dish is a variation on the traditional Arabic dish known as *baba ghanouj*, which translates to "spoiled old man." As well as being great with pita strips or grissini, this dish is fantastic as a side dish when served hot.

GRILLED GARLIC & LEMON SQUID

INGREDIENTS   Serves 4

½ cup long-grain rice
1¼ cups fish stock
8 oz. squid, cleaned
1 tbsp. grated lemon rind
1 garlic clove, peeled
  and crushed
1 shallot, peeled and
  finely chopped

2 tbsp. freshly chopped
  cilantro
2 tbsp. lemon juice
salt and freshly ground
  black pepper

1 Rinse the rice until the water runs clear, then place in a saucepan with the stock.

2 Bring to a boil, then reduce the heat. Cover and simmer gently for 10 minutes.

3 Turn off the heat and leave the saucepan covered so the rice can steam while you cook the squid.

4 Remove the tentacles from the squid, and set aside.

5 Cut the body cavity in half. Using the tip of a small, sharp knife, score the inside flesh of the body cavity in a diamond pattern. Do not cut all the way through.

6 Mix the lemon rind, crushed garlic, and chopped shallot together.

7 Place the squid in a shallow bowl, sprinkle the lemon mixture on top, and stir.

8 Heat a griddle pan until almost smoking. Cook the squid for 3–4 minutes until cooked through, then slice.

9 Sprinkle with the cilantro and lemon juice. Season to taste with salt and pepper. Drain the rice and serve immediately with the squid.

HELPFUL HINT

To prepare squid, peel the tentacles from the squid's pouch, and cut away the head just below the eye. Discard the head. Remove the quill and the soft innards from the squid, and discard. Peel off any dark skin that covers the squid, and discard. Rinse the tentacles and pouch thoroughly. The squid is now ready to use.

CREAMY SALMON WITH DILL IN PHYLLO BASKETS

INGREDIENTS   Serves 4

1 bay leaf	2½ cups baby spinach leaves
6 black peppercorns	8 tbsp. low-fat sour cream
1 large sprig of fresh parsley	2 tsp. mustard
6 oz. salmon fillet	2 tbsp. freshly chopped dill
4 large sheets phyllo pastry	salt and freshly ground
fine spray of oil	black pepper

1 Preheat the oven to 400° F. Place the bay leaf, peppercorns, parsley, and salmon in a large skillet, and add enough water to barely cover the fish.

2 Bring to a boil, reduce the heat, and cook the fish for 5 minutes until it flakes easily. Remove from the skillet. Set aside.

3 Spray each sheet of phyllo pastry lightly with the oil. Scrunch up the pastry to make a nest shape approximately 5 inches in diameter.

4 Place on a lightly greased baking sheet, and cook in the preheated oven for 10 minutes until golden and crisp.

5 Blanch the baby spinach leaves in a saucepan of lightly salted boiling water for 2 minutes. Drain thoroughly and keep warm.

6 Mix the sour cream, mustard, and dill together, then warm gently. Season to taste with salt and pepper. Divide the spinach among the phyllo pastry nests, and flake the salmon onto the spinach.

7 Spoon the mustard and dill sauce over the phyllo pastry baskets, and serve immediately.

FOOD FACT

This is a highly nutritious dish, combining calcium-rich salmon with vitamin- and mineral-rich spinach. The low-fat sour cream in this recipe can be replaced with low-fat yogurt if you want to aid digestion and give your immune system a real boost!

SMOKED SALMON SUSHI

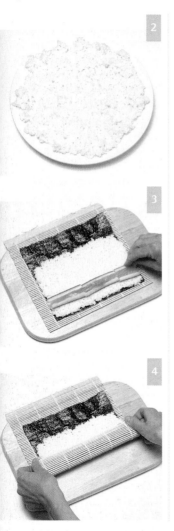

INGREDIENTS
Serves 4

¾ cup sushi rice
2 tbsp. rice vinegar
4 tsp. sugar
½ tsp salt
2 sheets sushi nori
2½ oz. smoked salmon
¼ cucumber, cut into fine strips

TO SERVE:
wasabi
soy sauce
pickled ginger

1 Rinse the rice thoroughly in cold water until the water runs clear, then place in a large saucepan with 1¼ cups of water. Bring to a boil and cover with a tight-fitting lid. Reduce to a simmer and cook gently for 10 minutes. Turn the heat off, but keep the saucepan covered to allow the rice to steam for an additional 10 minutes.

2 In a small saucepan, gently heat the rice vinegar, sugar, and salt until the sugar has dissolved. When the rice has finished steaming, pour over the vinegar mixture and stir well to mix. Empty the rice out onto a large, flat surface (a chopping board or large plate is ideal). Fan the rice to cool and to produce a shinier rice.

3 Lay one sheet of sushi nori on a sushi mat (if you do not have a sushi mat, improvise with a stiff piece of fabric that is a little larger than the sushi nori), and spread with half the cooled rice. Dampen your hands while doing this, to prevent the rice from sticking to your hands. On the nearest edge, place half the salmon and half the cucumber strips.

4 Roll up the rice and smoked salmon tightly. Dampen the blade of a sharp knife and cut the sushi into slices about ¾ inch thick. Repeat with the remaining sushi nori, rice, smoked salmon, and cucumber. Serve with wasabi, soy sauce, and pickled ginger.

TASTY TIP

If wasabi is unavailable, use a little horseradish. If you cannot find sushi nori (seaweed sheets), shape the rice into small bite-size oblongs, then drape a piece of smoked salmon over each one, and garnish with chives.

HONEY & GINGER SHRIMP

INGREDIENTS   Serves 4

1 carrot
¾ cup bamboo shoots
4 scallions
1 tbsp. honey
1 tbsp. ketchup
1 tsp. soy sauce
1-in. piece fresh ginger, peeled
    and finely grated
1 garlic clove, peeled
    and crushed
1 tbsp. lime juice

6 oz. peeled shrimp, defrosted
    if frozen
2 heads romaine lettuce
2 tbsp. freshly chopped
    cilantro
salt and freshly ground
    black pepper

TO GARNISH:
sprigs of fresh cilantro
lime slices

1 Cut the carrot into matchstick-size pieces, coarsely chop the bamboo shoots, and finely slice the scallions.

2 Combine the bamboo shoots with the carrot matchsticks and scallions.

3 In a wok or large skillet, gently heat the honey, ketchup, soy sauce, ginger, garlic, and lime juice with 3 tablespoons of water. Bring to a boil.

4 Add the carrot mixture and stir-fry for 2–3 minutes until the vegetables are hot.

5 Add the shrimp and continue to stir-fry for 2 minutes.

6 Remove the wok or skillet from the heat, and set aside until cooled slightly.

7 Divide the romaine lettuce into leaves, and rinse lightly under cold running water.

8 Stir the chopped cilantro into the shrimp mixture, and season to taste with salt and pepper. Spoon into the lettuce leaves, and serve immediately, garnished with sprigs of fresh cilantro and lime slices.

HELPFUL HINT

This highly versatile dish can be adapted to suit any diet by increasing and varying the vegetable content. If desired, raw jumbo shrimp can be used for this recipe—make sure that, if using raw shrimp, the black vein that runs along the back is removed.

TUNA CHOWDER

INGREDIENTS   Serves 4

2 tsp. oil
1 onion, peeled and
  finely chopped
2 sticks of celery, trimmed
  and finely sliced
1 tbsp. all-purpose flour
2⅓ cups nonfat milk
7-oz. can tuna in water

11-oz. can of corn, drained
2 tsp. freshly chopped thyme
salt and freshly ground
  black pepper
pinch of cayenne pepper
2 tbsp. freshly chopped
  parsley

1 Heat the oil in a large, heavy saucepan. Add the onion and celery, and gently cook for about 5 minutes, stirring from time to time until the onion is softened.

2 Stir in the flour and cook for about 1 minute to thicken.

3 Take the saucepan off the heat and gradually pour in the milk, stirring throughout.

4 Add the tuna and its liquid, the drained corn, and the freshly chopped thyme.

5 Mix gently, then bring to a boil. Cover with a lid and simmer for 5 minutes.

6 Remove the saucepan from the heat and season to taste with salt and pepper.

7 Sprinkle the chowder with the cayenne pepper and chopped parsley. Divide among soup bowls and serve immediately.

TASTY TIP

To make this soup even more colorful, use a can of corn with bell peppers. For those who particularly like fish and seafood, add 4 oz. of shelled shrimp for an extra-special flavor.

TASTY TIP

This creamy soup also works well using equivalent amounts of canned crabmeat instead of the tuna. For a contrasting taste and to enhance the delicate creaminess of this soup, add a spoonful of low-fat sour cream to the top of the soup. Sprinkle with cayenne pepper, and then garnish with a few chopped chives.

ASIAN GROUND CHICKEN ON ARUGULA & TOMATO

INGREDIENTS   Serves 4

2 shallots, peeled
1 garlic clove, peeled
1 carrot, peeled
½ cup water chestnuts
1 tsp. oil
12 oz. fresh ground chicken

1 tsp. Chinese five spice
  powder
pinch of chili powder
1 tsp. soy sauce
1 tbsp. fish sauce
8 cherry tomatoes
1¼ cups arugula

1 Finely chop the shallots and garlic. Cut the carrot into matchsticks, thinly slice the water chestnuts, and set aside. Heat the oil in a large wok or heavy skillet, and add the chicken. Stir-fry for 3–4 minutes over a moderately high heat, breaking up any large pieces of chicken.

2 Add the garlic and shallots and cook for 2–3 minutes until softened. Sprinkle with the Chinese five spice powder and chili powder, and continue to cook for about 1 minute.

3 Add the carrot, water chestnuts, soy and fish sauce, and 2 tablespoons of water. Stir-fry for an additional 2 minutes. Remove from the heat and set aside to cool slightly.

4 Seed the tomatoes and cut into thin wedges. Toss with the arugula and divide among 4 serving plates. Spoon the warm chicken mixture over the arugula and tomato wedges, and serve immediately to keep the arugula from wilting.

TASTY TIP

This is a very versatile dish. In place of the chicken, you could use any lean cut of meat, or even shrimp. To make this dish a main meal, replace the arugula and tomatoes with stir-fried vegetables and rice. Another alternative that works very well is to serve the chicken mixture in Step 3 in lettuce leaves. Place a spoonful of the mixture into a lettuce leaf and roll up into a small pocket.

RUTABAGA, TURNIP, PARSNIP, & POTATO SOUP

INGREDIENTS

Serves 4

2 large onions, peeled
2 tbsp. butter
2 medium carrots, peeled and
  roughly chopped
1 cup peeled and roughly
  chopped rutabaga
¾ cup peeled and roughly
  chopped turnip
¾ cup peeled and roughly
  chopped parsnips

1 cup peeled and roughly
  chopped potatoes
4¼ cups vegetable stock
½ tsp. freshly grated nutmeg
salt and freshly ground black
  pepper
4 tbsp. vegetable oil, for frying
½ cup heavy cream
warm crusty bread, to serve

1 Finely chop 1 onion. Melt the butter in a large saucepan and add the onion, carrots, rutabaga, turnip, parsnip, and potatoes. Cover and cook gently for about 10 minutes, without browning, stirring occasionally.

2 Add the stock, and season to taste with the nutmeg, salt, and pepper. Cover and bring to a boil, then reduce the heat and simmer gently for 15–20 minutes or until the vegetables are tender. Remove from the heat and let cool for 30 minutes.

3 Heat the oil in a large heavy-based skillet. Add the onions and cook over a medium heat for about 2–3 minutes, stirring frequently, until golden brown. Remove the onions with a slotted spoon and drain well on paper towels. As they cool, they will turn crispy.

4 Pour the cooled soup into a food processor or blender, and process to form a smooth purée. Return to the cleaned pan, adjust the seasoning, then stir in the cream. Gently reheat, and top with the crispy onions. Serve immediately with chunks of bread.

HELPFUL HINT

For a lower-fat version of this delicious soup, add milk (skim milk if desired) rather than cream when reheating.

POTATO & FENNEL SOUP

INGREDIENTS

Serves 4

2 tbsp. butter
2 large onions, peeled and
  thinly sliced
2–3 garlic cloves, peeled and
  crushed
1 tsp. salt
2 medium potatoes, about
  1 lb. in weight, peeled and
  diced

1 fennel bulb, trimmed and
  finely chopped
½ tsp. caraway seeds
4¼ cups vegetable stock
freshly ground black pepper
2 tbsp. freshly chopped parsley
4 tbsp. crème fraîche
roughly torn pieces of French
  bread, to serve

1 Melt the butter in a large heavy-based saucepan. Add the onions with the garlic and half the salt, and cook over a medium heat, stirring occasionally for 7–10 minutes or until the onions are very soft and beginning to turn brown.

2 Add the potatoes, fennel bulb, caraway seeds, and the remaining salt. Cook for about 5 minutes, then pour in the vegetable stock. Bring to a boil, partially cover, and simmer for 15–20 minutes or until the potatoes are tender. Stir in the chopped parsley and adjust the seasoning to taste.

3 For a smooth-textured soup, allow to cool slightly, then pour into a food processor or blender and blend until smooth. Reheat the soup gently, then ladle into individual soup bowls. For a chunky soup, omit this blending stage and ladle straight from the saucepan into soup bowls.

4 Swirl a spoonful of crème fraîche into each bowl and serve immediately with roughly torn pieces of French bread.

FOOD FACT

A fennel bulb is, in fact, the swollen stem of a plant known as "Florence fennel." Originating in Italy, Florence fennel has a distinct aniseed flavor, which mellows and sweetens when cooked. Look for well-rounded bulbs with bright green fronds. Fennel is at its best when fresh, so use as soon as possible after buying. It may be stored in the refrigerator for a few days.

CAWL

INGREDIENTS

Serves 4–6

1½ lbs. neck slices or rib chops of lamb
pinch of salt
2 large onions, peeled and thinly sliced
3 large potatoes, peeled and cut into chunks
2 parsnips, peeled and cut into chunks

1 rutabaga, peeled and cut into chunks
3 large carrots, peeled and cut into chunks
2 leeks, trimmed and sliced
freshly ground black pepper
4 tbsp. freshly chopped parsley
warm, crusty bread, to serve

1 Put the lamb in a large saucepan, cover with cold water, and bring to a boil. Add a generous pinch of salt. Simmer gently for 1½ hours, then set aside to cool completely, preferably overnight.

2 The next day, skim the fat off the surface of the lamb liquid and discard. Return the saucepan to the heat and bring back to a boil. Simmer for 5 minutes. Add the onions, potatoes, parsnips, rutabaga, and carrots, and return to a boil. Reduce the heat, cover, and cook for about 20 minutes, stirring occasionally.

3 Add the leeks and season to taste with salt and pepper. Cook for an additional 10 minutes or until all the vegetables are tender.

4 Using a slotted spoon, remove the meat from the saucepan, and take it off the bone. Discard the bones and any gristle, then return the meat to the pan. Adjust the seasoning to taste, stir in the parsley, then serve immediately with plenty of warm, crusty bread.

FOOD FACT

Many traditional Welsh recipes, such as cawl, feature lamb. This soup was once a staple dish, originally made with scraps of mutton or lamb and vegetables cooked together in a broth. Use Welsh lamb if possible for this modern version. The meat is lean and tender, and may have the delicate flavor of herbs if the sheep have been grazing on the wild thyme and rosemary that grow in the mountains.

POTATO, LEEK, & ROSEMARY SOUP

INGREDIENTS

Serves 4

¼ cup butter
1 lb. leeks, trimmed and finely sliced
4 cups peeled and roughly chopped potatoes
3¾ cups vegetable stock
4 sprigs of fresh rosemary
2 cups whole milk

2 tbsp. freshly chopped parsley
2 tbsp. crème fraîche
salt and freshly ground black pepper
whole-wheat rolls, to serve

1 Melt the butter in a large saucepan, add the leeks, and cook gently for 5 minutes, stirring frequently. Remove 1 tablespoon of the cooked leeks and set aside for garnishing.

2 Add the potatoes, vegetable stock, rosemary sprigs, and milk. Bring to a boil, then reduce the heat, cover, and simmer gently for 20–25 minutes or until the vegetables are tender.

3 Cool for 10 minutes. Discard the rosemary, then pour into a food processor or blender, and blend well to form a smooth-textured soup.

4 Return the soup to the cleaned saucepan and stir in the chopped parsley and crème fraîche. Season to taste with salt and pepper. If the soup is too thick, stir in a little more milk or water. Reheat gently, without boiling, then ladle into warm soup bowls. Garnish the soup with the set-aside leeks and serve immediately with whole-wheat rolls.

TASTY TIP

This rosemary-scented version of vichyssoise is equally delicious served cold. Allow the soup to cool before covering, then chill in the refrigerator for at least 2 hours. The soup will thicken as it chills, so you may need to thin it to the desired consistency with more milk or stock, and season before serving. It is important to use fresh rosemary rather than dried for this recipe. If unavailable, use 2 bay leaves, or add a bruised, fresh lemongrass stalk.

CREAM OF SPINACH SOUP

INGREDIENTS

Serves 6–8

1 large onion, peeled and chopped
5 large garlic cloves, peeled and chopped
2 medium potatoes, peeled and chopped
3¼ cups cold water
1 tsp. salt
1 lb. spinach, washed and large stems removed

¼ cup butter
3 tbsp. flour
3¾ cups milk
½ tsp. freshly grated nutmeg
freshly ground black pepper
6–8 tbsp. crème fraîche or sour cream
warm foccacia bread, to serve

1 Place the onion, garlic, and potatoes in a large saucepan and cover with the cold water. Add half the salt and bring to a boil. Cover and simmer for 15–20 minutes or until the potatoes are tender. Remove from the heat and add the spinach. Cover and set aside for 10 minutes.

2 Slowly melt the butter in another saucepan, add the flour, and cook over a low heat for about 2 minutes. Remove the saucepan from the heat and add the milk a little at a time, stirring continuously. Return to the heat and cook, stirring continuously for 5–8 minutes or until the sauce is smooth and slightly thickened. Add the freshly grated nutmeg or pepper to taste.

3 Blend the cooled potato and spinach mixture in a food processor or blender to a smooth purée, then return to the saucepan and gradually stir in the white sauce. Season to taste with salt and pepper, and gently reheat, taking care not to allow the soup to boil. Ladle into soup bowls and top with spoonfuls of crème fraîche or sour cream. Serve immediately with warm foccacia bread.

HELPFUL HINT

When choosing spinach, always look for fresh, crisp, dark-green leaves. Store in a cool place until needed and use within 1–2 days of buying. To prepare, wash several times to remove any dirt or grit, and shake off as much excess water as possible or use a salad spinner. Remove the central stems only if they are large and tough—this is not necessary if you buy baby spinach leaves.

RICE & TOMATO SOUP

INGREDIENTS

Serves 4

heaping ¾ cup easy-cook basmati rice
1¾ cups chopped tomatoes
2 garlic cloves, peeled and crushed
grated zest of ½ lime
2 tbsp. extra-virgin olive oil
1 tsp. sugar
salt and freshly ground pepper

1¼ cups vegetable stock or water

FOR THE CROUTONS:
2 tbsp. prepared pesto sauce
2 tbsp. olive oil
6 thin slices ciabatta bread, cut into ½-in. cubes

1 Preheat the oven to 425° F. Rinse and drain the rice. Place the tomatoes with their juice in a large heavy-based saucepan with the garlic, lime zest, oil, and sugar. Season to taste with salt and pepper. Bring to a boil, then reduce the heat, cover, and simmer for 10 minutes.

2 Add the boiling vegetable stock or water and the rice, then cook uncovered for an additional 15–20 minutes or until the rice is tender. If the soup is too thick, add a little more water. Set aside and keep warm if the croutons are not ready.

3 Meanwhile, to make the croutons, mix the pesto and olive oil in a large bowl. Add the bread cubes and toss until they are coated completely with the mixture. Spread on a cookie sheet, and bake in the preheated oven for 10–15 minutes until

golden and crisp, turning them over halfway through cooking. Serve the soup immediately, sprinkled with the warm croutons.

HELPFUL HINT

Pesto is a vivid green sauce made from basil leaves and olive oil. Store-bought pesto is fine for this quick soup, but try making your own during the summer when fresh basil is plentiful. To make ⅔ cup of pesto, put 1 cup fresh basil leaves, 1 peeled garlic clove, 1 tbsp. pine nuts, 4 tbsp. olive oil, salt, and black pepper in a blender or food processor and blend together at high speed until very creamy. Stir in ¼ cup freshly grated Parmesan cheese. Store in the refrigerator for up to 2 weeks in an airtight jar.

COCONUT CHICKEN SOUP

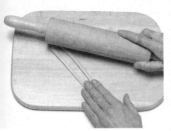

INGREDIENTS

Serves 4

2 lemongrass stalks
3 tbsp. vegetable oil
3 medium onions, peeled and finely sliced
3 garlic cloves, peeled and crushed
2 tbsp. fresh ginger, finely grated
2–3 kaffir lime leaves
1½ tsp. turmeric
1 red bell pepper, deseeded and diced
1¾ cups coconut milk

5 cups vegetable or chicken stock
1½ cups easy-cook long-grain rice
1½ cups roughly diced cooked chicken meat
1½ cups corn
3 tbsp. freshly chopped cilantro
1 tbsp. Thai fish sauce
freshly chopped pickled chilies, to serve

1 Discard the outer leaves of the lemongrass stalks, then place on a chopping board and, using a mallet or rolling pin, pound gently to bruise; set aside.

2 Heat the vegetable oil in a large saucepan and cook the onions over a medium heat for about 10–15 minutes until soft and beginning to change color.

3 Lower the heat, stir in the garlic, ginger, lime leaves, and turmeric, and cook for 1 minute. Add the red bell pepper, coconut milk, stock, lemongrass, and rice. Bring to a boil, cover, and simmer gently over a low heat for about 10 minutes.

4 Add the chicken and then stir it into the soup with the corn and the freshly chopped cilantro. Add a few dashes of

Thai fish sauce to taste, then reheat gently, stirring frequently. Serve immediately with a few chopped pickled chilies to sprinkle on top.

FOOD FACT

Small, dark, glossy kaffir lime leaves come from a wild citrus tree and are usually imported from southeast Asia. They impart a strong and sharp, spicy, citrus flavor and are frequently featured in Thai and Indonesian soups. If you have difficulty finding them, substitute a large strip of lime or lemon zest instead, remembering to remove before serving.

HOT & SOUR MUSHROOM SOUP

INGREDIENTS

Serves 4

4 tbsp. sunflower oil
3 garlic cloves, peeled and
  finely chopped
3 shallots, peeled and finely
  chopped
2 large red chilies, deseeded
  and finely chopped
1 tbsp. brown sugar
large pinch of salt
4¼ cups vegetable stock
1½ cups Thai fragrant rice
5 kaffir lime leaves, torn
2 tbsp. soy sauce

grated zest and juice of 1
  lemon
½ lb. oyster mushrooms,
  wiped and cut into pieces
2 tbsp. freshly chopped
  cilantro

TO GARNISH:
2 green chilies, deseeded and
  finely chopped
3 scallions, trimmed and finely
  chopped

1 Heat the oil in a skillet, add the garlic and shallots, and cook until golden brown and starting to crisp. Remove from the pan and set aside. Add the chilies to the pan and cook until they start to change color.

2 Place the garlic, shallots, and chilies in a food processor or blender. Blend to a smooth purée with ⅔ cup water. Pour the purée back into the pan, add the sugar with a large pinch of salt, then cook gently, stirring, until dark in color. Take care not to burn the mixture.

3 Pour the stock into a large saucepan, add the garlic purée, rice, lime leaves, soy sauce, and the lemon zest and juice. Bring to a boil, then reduce the heat, cover, and simmer gently for about 10 minutes.

4 Add the mushrooms and simmer for an additional 10 minutes or until the mushrooms and rice are tender. Remove the lime leaves, stir in the chopped cilantro, and ladle into bowls. Place the chopped green chilies and scallions in small bowls and serve separately to sprinkle on top of the soup.

HELPFUL HINT

There are many kinds of chilies, varying in both size and color, and many have a hot, spicy flavor. They contain volatile oils which can irritate your skin, so during preparation take great care not to touch your eyes, and wash your hands immediately after handling.

BACON & SPLIT PEA SOUP

INGREDIENTS

Serves 4

⅓ cup dried split peas
2 tbsp. butter
1 garlic clove, peeled and finely chopped
1 medium onion, peeled and thinly sliced
1 cup long-grain rice
2 tbsp. tomato paste
5 cups vegetable or chicken stock

1 cup peeled and finely diced carrots
4 slices bacon, finely chopped
salt and freshly ground black pepper
2 tbsp. freshly chopped parsley
4 tbsp. light cream
warm, crusty garlic bread, to serve

1 Cover the dried split peas with plenty of cold water, cover loosely, and leave to soak for a minimum of 12 hours, preferably overnight.

2 Melt the butter in a heavy-based saucepan, add the garlic and onion, and cook for 2–3 minutes, without browning. Add the rice, drained split peas, and tomato paste, and cook for 2–3 minutes, stirring constantly to prevent sticking. Add the stock, bring to a boil, then reduce the heat and simmer for 20–25 minutes or until the rice and peas are tender. Remove from the heat and let cool.

3 Blend about three quarters of the soup in a food processor, or blender, to form a smooth purée. Pour this into the remaining soup in the saucepan. Add the carrots and cook for an additional 10–12 minutes or until the carrots are tender.

4 Meanwhile, place the bacon in a nonstick skillet, and cook over a gentle heat until the bacon is crisp. Remove and drain on paper towels.

5 Season the soup with salt and pepper to taste, then stir in the parsley and cream. Reheat for 2–3 minutes, then ladle into soup bowls. Sprinkle with the bacon, and serve immediately with warm garlic bread.

HELPFUL HINT

You can use either green or yellow split peas for this satisfying soup—there is no difference in flavor. For a quicker alternative, use red split lentils, as they are quick to cook and do not need presoaking.

SQUASH & SMOKED HADDOCK SOUP

INGREDIENTS

Serves 4–6

2 tbsp. olive oil
1 medium onion, peeled and chopped
2 garlic cloves, peeled and chopped
3 celery stalks, trimmed and chopped
1½ lbs. squash, peeled, deseeded and cut into chunks

2⅔ cups peeled and coarsely diced potatoes
3¼ cups chicken stock, heated
½ cup dry sherry
½ lb. smoked haddock fillet
⅔ cup milk
freshly ground black pepper
2 tbsp. freshly chopped parsley

1 Heat the oil in a large heavy-based saucepan and gently cook the onion, garlic, and celery for about 10 minutes. This will release the sweetness but not brown the vegetables. Add the squash and potatoes to the saucepan and stir to coat the vegetables with the oil.

2 Gradually add the stock and bring to a boil. Cover, then reduce the heat and simmer for 25 minutes, stirring occasionally. Stir in the dry sherry, then remove the saucepan from the heat and let cool for 5–10 minutes.

3 Blend the mixture in a food processor, or blender, to form a chunky purée, and return to the cleaned saucepan.

4 Meanwhile, place the fish in a skillet. Pour in the milk with 3 tablespoons of water and bring

almost to the boiling point. Reduce the heat, cover, and simmer for 6 minutes or until the fish is cooked and flakes easily. Remove from the heat and, using a slotted spoon, remove the fish from the liquid, setting aside both liquid and fish.

5 Discard the skin and any bones from the fish and flake into pieces. Stir the fish liquid into the soup, together with the flaked fish. Season with freshly ground black pepper, stir in the parsley, and serve immediately.

TASTY TIP

Use smoked salmon if haddock is unavailable. Butternut squash works nicely in this recipe.

ZUCCHINI & TARRAGON TORTILLA

INGREDIENTS   Serves 6

1½ lbs. potatoes
3 tbsp. olive oil
1 onion, peeled and thinly
  sliced
salt and freshly ground black
  pepper

1 zucchini, trimmed and thinly
  sliced
6 medium eggs
2 tbsp. freshly chopped
  tarragon
tomato wedges, to serve

1 Peel the potatoes and slice thinly. Dry the slices in a clean dishtowel to get them as dry as possible. Heat the oil in a large heavy-based skillet, add the onion, and cook for 3 minutes. Add the potatoes along with a little salt and pepper, then stir the potatoes and onion lightly to coat in the oil.

2 Reduce the heat to the lowest possible setting, cover, and cook gently for 5 minutes. Turn the potatoes and onion over and continue to cook for an additional 5 minutes. Give the pan a shake every now and again to ensure that the potatoes do not stick to the base or burn. Add the zucchini, then cover and cook for 10 more minutes.

3 Beat the eggs and tarragon together, and season to taste with salt and pepper. Pour the egg mixture over the vegetables and return to the heat. Cook on a low heat for up to 20–25 minutes or until there is no liquid egg left on the surface of the tortilla.

4 Turn the tortilla over by inverting the pan onto the lid or a large flat plate. Slide the tortilla back into the pan. Return the pan to the heat and cook for a final 3–5 minutes or until the underside is golden brown. If preferred, place the tortilla under a preheated broiler for 4 minutes or until set and golden brown on top. Cut into small squares, and serve hot or cold with tomato wedges.

FOOD FACT

Almost regarded as the national dish of Spain, the tortilla is a substantial omelette traditionally made from eggs, potatoes, and onions. Here, zucchini and tarragon are added for extra flavor and color. Use even-sized, waxy potatoes, which do not break up during cooking.

SMOKED SALMON SUSHI

INGREDIENTS

Serves 4

¾ cup sushi rice or round long-
   grain pudding rice
2 tbsp. cider vinegar
1 tbsp. granulated sugar
1 tsp. salt
2 green leeks, trimmed

½ lb. smoked salmon
1 tsp. Japanese soy sauce

TO GARNISH:
fresh chives
lemon or lime wedges

1 Wash the rice in plenty of cold water, then drain. Put the rice and ¾ cup cold water in a saucepan, and leave to soak for 30 minutes. Place the saucepan over a medium heat and bring to a boil, stirring frequently. Lower the heat, cover, and cook the rice for about 15 minutes or until the grains are tender and the water has been absorbed. Remove from the heat and set aside, still covered, for an additional 10–15 minutes.

2 Place the vinegar, sugar, and salt in a small saucepan. Heat gently, stirring to dissolve the sugar. Turn the rice into a large bowl, sprinkle over the vinegar mixture, and mix together.

3 Cut the trimmed leeks in half lengthwise, then blanch in boiling water for 3–4 minutes. Drain, place in ice-cold water for 5 minutes, then drain again.

4 Separate the leek leaves. Cut both the leek leaves and the smoked salmon slices lengthwise into 1 x 3 in. strips, setting aside 2

wide leek leaves. Lay a leek slice neatly on top of each slice of smoked salmon.

5 Spoon the rice onto the salmon and leek slices, then roll. Using the tip of a sharp knife, slice the additional leek leaves lengthwise into long strips. Tie the strips around the smoked salmon rolls. Sprinkle the rolls with a few drops of the soy sauce, garnish with the chives and lemon wedges, and serve.

FOOD FACT

It takes many years of training to qualify as a sushi chef, but these smoked salmon and leek canapés are simple to make, although a little time consuming. Rolled sushi like these are known as *hosomaki* in Japan. Use the rice right after cooking—it cannot be stored in the refrigerator or it will harden and be difficult to work with.

POTATO PANCAKES

INGREDIENTS

Serves 6

FOR THE SAUCE:
4 tbsp. crème fraîche
1 tbsp. horseradish sauce
grated zest and juice of 1 lime
1 tbsp. freshly cut chives

1⅓ cups floury potatoes,
  peeled and coarsely diced
1 small egg white
2 tbsp. milk
2 tsp. self-rising flour

1 tbsp. freshly chopped thyme
large pinch of salt
a little vegetable oil, for frying
½ lb. smoked mackerel fillets,
  skinned and roughly
  chopped
fresh herbs, to garnish

1 To make the sauce, mix together the crème fraîche, horseradish, lime zest and juice, and chives. Cover and set aside.

2 Place the potatoes in a large saucepan, and cover with lightly salted, boiling water. Bring back to a boil, cover, and simmer for 15 minutes or until the potatoes are tender. Drain and mash until smooth. Cool for 5 minutes, then beat in the egg white, milk, flour, thyme, and salt to form a thick, smooth batter. Let stand for 30 minutes, then stir before using.

3 Heat a little oil in a heavy-based skillet. Add 2–3 large spoonfuls of batter to make a small pancake and cook for 1–2 minutes until golden. Turn the pancake over and cook for an additional minute or until golden. Repeat with the rest of the batter to make 8 pancakes.

4 Arrange the pancakes on a plate and top with the smoked mackerel. Garnish with herbs and serve immediately with spoonfuls of the horseradish sauce.

HELPFUL HINT

Keep the pancakes warm as you make them by stacking on a warmed plate. Place wax paper between each pancake to keep them separate, and fold a clean dishtowel loosely over the top. If desired, they can be made in advance and frozen, interleaved with nonstick baking parchment. To serve, thaw, then reheat the stack of pancakes, covered in aluminum foil, in a warm oven.

SWEET POTATO CHIPS WITH MANGO SALSA

INGREDIENTS

Serves 6

FOR THE SALSA:
1 large mango, peeled, pitted, and cut into small cubes
8 cherry tomatoes, quartered
½ cucumber, peeled and finely diced
1 red onion, peeled and finely chopped
pinch of sugar
1 red chili, deseeded and finely chopped
2 tbsp. rice vinegar
2 tbsp. olive oil
grated zest and juice of 1 lime
2⅔ cups peeled and thinly sliced sweet potatoes, vegetable oil, for deep frying
sea salt
2 tbsp. freshly chopped mint

1 To make the salsa, mix the mango with the tomatoes, cucumber, and onion. Add the sugar, chili, vinegar, oil, and the lime zest and juice. Mix together thoroughly, cover, and leave for 45–50 minutes.

2 Soak the potatoes in cold water for 40 minutes to remove as much of the excess starch as possible. Drain and dry thoroughly on a clean dishtowel or paper towel.

3 Heat the oil to 375° F in a deep fryer. When at the correct temperature, place half the potatoes in the frying basket, then carefully lower the potatoes into the hot oil and cook for 4–5 minutes or until they are golden brown. Shake the basket often so that the potatoes do not stick together.

4 Drain the potato chips on paper towels, sprinkle with sea salt, and place under a preheated broiler for a few seconds to dry out. Repeat with the remaining potatoes. Stir the mint into the salsa and serve with the potato chips.

HELPFUL HINT

Take care when deep-fat frying. Use a deep heavy-based saucepan or special deep-fat fryer, and fill the pan by no more than one third with oil. If you do not have a food thermometer, check the temperature by dropping a cube of bread into the oil. At the correct heat, it will turn golden brown in 40 seconds.

STUFFED GRAPE LEAVES

INGREDIENTS

Serves 6–8

heaping ¾ cup long-grain rice
½ lb. fresh or preserved grape
  leaves
1 red onion, peeled and finely
  chopped
3 baby leeks, trimmed and
  finely sliced
1 cup freshly chopped parsley
1 cup freshly chopped mint
1 cup freshly chopped dill
⅔ cup extra-virgin olive oil
salt and freshly ground black
  pepper

¼ cup currants
½ cup finely chopped dried
  apricots
2½ tbsp. pine nuts
juice of 1 lemon
2½–3¼ cups boiling stock
lemon wedges or slices, to
  garnish
4 tbsp. plain yogurt, to serve

1 Soak the rice in cold water for 30 minutes. If using fresh vine leaves, blanch them, 5–6 leaves at a time, in salted, boiling water for a minute. Rinse and drain. If using preserved vine leaves, soak in tepid water for at least 20 minutes, drain, rinse, and pat dry with a paper towel.

2 Mix the onion and leeks with the herbs and half the oil. Add the drained rice, mix, and season with salt and pepper. Stir in the currants, apricots, pine nuts, and lemon juice. Spoon 1 teaspoon of the filling at the stalk end of each leaf. Roll, tucking the side flaps into the center to create a neat pocket. Continue until all the filling is used.

3 Layer half the remaining vine leaves over the base of a large

skillet. Put the little pockets in the skillet, and cover with the remaining leaves.

4 Pour in enough stock just to cover the vine leaves, add a pinch of salt, and bring to a boil. Reduce the heat, cover, and simmer for 45–55 minutes or until the rice is sticky and tender. Let stand for 10 minutes. Drain off any remaining stock. Garnish with lemon wedges, and serve hot with the yogurt.

FOOD FACT

The use of grape leaves in cooking goes back as far as the early cultivation of vines. Particularly popular in Middle Eastern cooking, they give a delicious, tart flavor to dishes.

POTATO SKINS

INGREDIENTS

Serves 4

4 large baking potatoes
2 tbsp. olive oil
2 tsp. paprika
¾ cup roughly chopped
  pancetta or bacon
6 tbsp. heavy cream
⅓ cup diced blue cheese, such
  as Gorgonzola

1 tbsp. freshly chopped
  parsley

TO SERVE:
mayonnaise
sweet chili dipping sauce
tossed green salad

1 Preheat the oven to 400° F. Scrub the potatoes, then prick a few times with a fork or skewer and place directly on the top shelf of the oven. Bake in the preheated oven for at least 1 hour or until tender. The potatoes are cooked when they yield gently to the pressure of your hand.

2 Set the potatoes aside until cool enough to handle, then cut in half and scoop the flesh into a bowl and set aside. Preheat the broiler, and line the pan with aluminum foil.

3 Mix together the oil and paprika, and use half to brush the outside of the potato skins. Place on the foil-lined pan under the preheated broiler, and cook for 5 minutes or until crisp, turning as necessary.

4 Heat the remaining paprika-flavored oil and gently fry the pancetta until crisp. Add to the potato flesh along with the cream, blue cheese, and parsley.

Halve the potato skins, and fill with the blue-cheese filling. Return to the oven for an additional 15 minutes to heat through. Sprinkle with a little more paprika, and serve immediately with mayonnaise, sweet chili sauce, and a green salad.

FOOD FACT

A popular Italian cheese, Gorgonzola was first made over 1100 years ago, in the village of the same name, near Milan. Now mostly produced in Lombardy, it is made from pasteurized cow's milk and allowed to ripen for at least 3 months, giving it a rich, but not overpowering, flavor. Unlike most blue cheeses, it should have a greater concentration of veining toward the center of the cheese.

RED BEET RISOTTO

INGREDIENTS

Serves 6

6 tbsp. extra-virgin olive oil
1 onion, peeled and finely
chopped
2 garlic cloves, peeled and
finely chopped
2 tsp. freshly chopped thyme
1 tsp. grated lemon zest
2 cups Arborio rice
⅔ cup dry white wine
3¾ cups vegetable stock,
heated

2 tbsp. heavy cream
1½ cups peeled and finely
chopped cooked beet
2 tbsp. freshly chopped
parsley
¾ cup freshly grated Parmesan
cheese
salt and freshly ground black
pepper
sprigs of fresh thyme, to
garnish

1 Heat half the oil in a large heavy-based skillet. Add the onion, garlic, thyme, and lemon zest. Cook for 5 minutes, stirring frequently, until the onion is soft and transparent, but not browned. Add the rice and stir until it is well coated in the oil.

2 Add the wine, then bring to a boil and boil rapidly until the wine has almost evaporated. Reduce the heat.

3 Keeping the pan over a low heat, add a ladleful of the hot stock to the rice, and cook, stirring constantly, until the stock is absorbed. Continue gradually adding the stock in this way until the rice is tender; this should take about 20 minutes. You may not need all the stock.

4 Stir in the cream, chopped beet, parsley, and half the grated Parmesan cheese. Season to taste with salt and pepper. Garnish with sprigs of fresh thyme, and serve immediately, with the remaining grated Parmesan cheese.

TASTY TIP

If you buy ready-cooked beets, choose small ones, which are sweeter. Make sure that they are not packed in vinegar (i.e., pickled), as this would spoil the flavor of the dish. If cooking your own, try baking them instead of boiling. Leave the stems intact and gently scrub to remove any dirt. Put them in a baking dish, cover loosely, and cook in a preheated oven at 325° F for 2 hours. Once cool enough to handle, the skins should slip right off.

GINGER & GARLIC POTATOES

INGREDIENTS   Serves 4

1½ lbs. potatoes
1-in. piece of ginger, peeled
   and coarsely chopped
3 garlic cloves, peeled and
   chopped
½ tsp. turmeric
1 tsp. salt
½ tsp. cayenne pepper
5 tbsp. vegetable oil
1 tsp. whole fennel seeds
1 large apple, cored and diced

6 scallions, trimmed and sliced
   diagonally
1 tbsp. freshly chopped
   cilantro

TO SERVE:
dark-green lettuce
mayonnaise, seasoned with
   curry to taste

1 Scrub the potatoes, then place, unpeeled, in a large saucepan and cover with boiling, salted water. Bring to a boil and cook for 15 minutes, then drain and leave the potatoes to cool completely. Peel and cut into 1-in. cubes.

2 Place the ginger, garlic, turmeric, salt, and cayenne pepper in a food processor and blend for 1 minute. With the motor still running, slowly add 3 tablespoons of water and blend into a paste. Alternatively, pound the ingredients to a paste with a mortar and pestle.

3 Heat the oil in a large heavy-based skillet and when hot, but not smoking, add the fennel seeds, and fry for a few minutes. Stir in the ginger paste, and cook for 2 minutes, stirring frequently. Take care not to burn the mixture.

4 Reduce the heat, then add the potatoes and cook for 5–7 minutes, stirring frequently, until the potatoes have a golden-brown crust. Add the diced apple and scallions, then sprinkle with the freshly chopped cilantro. Heat for 2 minutes, then serve on lettuce with curry-flavored mayonnaise.

FOOD FACT

Turmeric is a rhizome that comes from the same family as ginger. When the root is dried, it has a dull yellow appearance and can be ground to a powder. Turmeric powder can be used in a wide range of savory dishes. It has a warm, spicy flavor and gives food a wonderful golden color.

THAI CRAB CAKES

INGREDIENTS

Serves 4

heaping 1 cup easy-cook
basmati rice
2 cups chicken stock, heated
½ lb. cooked crabmeat
¼ lb. white fish fillet, skinned
and ground or finely
chopped
5 scallions, trimmed and finely
chopped
1 lemon grass stalk, outer
leaves discarded and finely
chopped
1 green chili, deseeded and
finely chopped

1 tbsp. freshly grated ginger
1 tbsp. freshly chopped
cilantro
1 tbsp. all-purpose flour
1 medium egg
salt and freshly ground black
pepper
2 tbsp. vegetable oil, for frying

TO SERVE:
sweet chili dipping sauce
fresh lettuce

1 Put the rice in a large saucepan and add the hot stock. Bring to a boil, cover, and simmer over a low heat, without stirring, for 18 minutes or until the grains are tender and all the liquid is absorbed.

2 To make the cakes, place the crabmeat, fish, scallions, lemongrass, chili, ginger, cilantro, flour, and egg in a food processor. Blend until all the ingredients are mixed thoroughly, then season to taste with salt and pepper. Add the rice to the processor and blend once more, but do not overmix.

3 Remove the mixture from the processor, and place on a clean work surface. With damp hands, divide into 12 even-sized patties. Transfer to a plate, cover,

and chill in the refrigerator for about 30 minutes.

4 Heat the oil in a heavy-based skillet and cook the crab cakes, four at a time, for 3–5 minutes on each side until crisp and golden. Drain on paper towels and serve immediately with a chili dipping sauce.

HELPFUL HINT

For the best flavor and texture, use freshly cooked crab for this dish, choosing the white rather than brown meat. Canned crabmeat will still give good results. Simply drain in a sieve and rinse very briefly under cold water to remove the excess brine before using.

RICE & PAPAYA SALAD

INGREDIENTS

Serves 4

1 cup easy-cook basmati rice
1 cinnamon stick, bruised
1 bird's eye chili, deseeded
   and finely chopped
zest and juice of 2 limes
zest and juice of 2 lemons
2 tbsp. Thai fish sauce
1 tbsp. light brown sugar
1 papaya, peeled and seeded
1 mango, peeled and stone
   removed

1 green chili, deseeded and
   finely chopped
2 tbsp. freshly chopped
   cilantro
1 tbsp. freshly chopped mint
1¼ cups finely shredded
   cooked chicken meat
½ cup chopped roasted
   peanuts
strips of pita bread, to serve

1 Rinse and drain the rice, and pour into a saucepan. Add 2 cups salted, boiling water and the cinnamon stick. Bring to a boil, reduce the heat to a very low setting, cover, and cook, without stirring, for 15–18 minutes or until all the liquid is absorbed. The rice should be light and fluffy, and have steam holes on the surface. Remove the cinnamon stick and stir in the zest from 1 lime.

2 To make the dressing, place the bird's eye chili, remaining zest and lime and lemon juice, fish sauce, and sugar in a food processor, and mix for a few minutes until blended. Alternatively, place all these ingredients in an airtight jar and shake vigorously until well blended. Pour half the dressing over the hot rice and toss until the grains glisten.

3 Slice the papaya and mango into thin slices, then place in a bowl. Add the chopped green chili, cilantro, and mint. Add the cooked chicken to the bowl with the chopped peanuts.

4 Add the remaining dressing to the chicken mixture and stir until all the ingredients are lightly coated. Spoon the rice onto a platter, pile the chicken mixture on top, and serve with strips of warm pita bread.

HELPFUL HINT

The papaya's skin turns from green, when unripe, to yellow and orange. To prepare, cut in half lengthwise, scoop out the black seeds with a spoon, and discard. Cut away the thin skin before slicing.

GINGERED COD STEAKS

INGREDIENTS   Serves 4

1-in. piece fresh ginger, peeled
4 scallions
2 tsp. freshly chopped parsley
1 tbsp. brown sugar
4 6-oz. cod steaks

salt and freshly ground
   black pepper
¼ stick reduced-fat butter
freshly cooked vegetables,
   to serve

1 Preheat the broiler and line the broiler rack with a layer of foil. Coarsely grate the piece of fresh ginger. Trim the scallions and cut into thin strips.

2 Mix the scallions, ginger, chopped parsley, and sugar together. Add 1 tablespoon of water.

3 Wipe the fish steaks. Season to taste with salt and pepper. Place onto 4 separate 8 x 8 inch foil squares.

4 Carefully spoon the scallions and ginger mixture evenly over the fish.

5 Cut the butter into small cubes and place over the fish.

6 Loosely fold the foil over the steaks to enclose the fish and to make a pocket.

7 Place under the preheated broiler and cook for 10–12 minutes or until cooked and the flesh has turned opaque.

8 Place the fish pockets on individual serving plates. Serve immediately with the freshly cooked vegetables.

HELPFUL HINT

This recipe will also work well with other fish steaks. Try salmon, fresh haddock, or monkfish fillets. The monkfish fillets may take a little longer to cook.

TASTY TIP

Why not serve this dish with roasted new potatoes *en papillote*? Place the new potatoes into double-thickness baking parchment with a few cloves of peeled garlic. Drizzle with a little olive oil and season well with salt and black pepper. Fold all the edges of the waxed paper together, and roast in the preheated oven at 350° F for 40–50 minutes before serving in the paper casing.

SEARED PANCETTA-WRAPPED COD

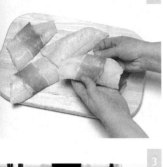

INGREDIENTS   Serves 4

4 6-oz. cod fillets
4 very thin slices of pancetta
3 tbsp. capers, in vinegar
1 tbsp. vegetable or corn oil
2 tbsp. lemon juice
1 tbsp. olive oil
freshly ground black pepper

1 tbsp. freshly chopped
  parsley, to garnish

TO SERVE:
freshly cooked vegetables
new potatoes

1 Wipe the cod fillets and wrap each one with the pancetta. Secure each fillet with a toothpick and set aside.

2 Drain the capers and soak in cold water for 10 minutes to remove any excess salt, then drain and set aside.

3 Heat the oil in a large skillet and sear the wrapped pieces of cod fillet for about 3 minutes on each side, turning carefully with a spatula so as not to break up the fish.

4 Lower the heat, then continue to cook for 2–3 minutes or until the fish is cooked thoroughly.

5 Meanwhile, place the remaining capers, lemon juice, and olive oil in a small saucepan. Add the black pepper.

6 Place the saucepan over a low heat and bring to a gentle simmer, stirring continuously for 2–3 minutes.

7 Once the fish is cooked, garnish with the parsley and serve with the warm caper dressing, freshly cooked vegetables, and new potatoes.

FOOD FACT

Pancetta is Italian-cured belly pork, which is often delicately smoked and sold either finely sliced or chopped coarsely into small cubes. The slices of pancetta can be used to encase poultry and fish, whereas chopped pancetta is often used in sauces. To cook chopped pancetta, fry for 2–3 minutes and set aside. Use the oil to seal meat or to fry onions, then return the pancetta to the pan.

MUSSELS LINGUINE

INGREDIENTS   Serves 4

4½ lbs. fresh mussels, washed
   and scrubbed
pat of butter
1 onion, peeled and
   finely chopped
1¼ cups medium-dry
   white wine

FOR THE SAUCE:
1 tbsp. corn oil
4 baby onions, peeled
   and quartered

2 garlic cloves, peeled
   and crushed
14-oz. can chopped tomatoes
large pinch of salt
3 cups dried linguine
   or tagliatelle
2 tbsp. freshly chopped
   parsley

1 Soak the mussels in plenty of cold water. Leave in the refrigerator until needed. When ready to use, scrub the shells, removing any barnacles or beards. Discard any open mussels.

2 Melt the butter in a large saucepan. Add the mussels, onion, and wine. Cover and steam for 5–6 minutes, shaking the pan gently to ensure even cooking. Discard any mussels that have not opened, then strain and set the liquid aside.

3 To make the sauce, heat the oil in a medium saucepan, and gently cook the quartered onion and garlic for 3–4 minutes until soft and transparent. Stir in the tomatoes and half the set-aside liquid. Bring to a boil, and simmer for 7–10 minutes or until the sauce begins to thicken.

4 Cook the pasta in boiling, salted water for 7 minutes or or until al dente. Drain the pasta, saving 2 tablespoons of the cooking liquid, then return the pasta and liquid to the pan.

5 Remove the meat from half the mussel shells. Stir into the sauce, along with the remaining mussels. Pour the hot sauce over the cooked pasta and toss gently. Garnish with the parsley and serve immediately.

TASTY TIP

Serving mussels in their shells is a fantastic way to eat them. Every mussel is surrounded with the delicious sauce, adding flavor to every mouthful. Clams, which often have a sweeter flavor, could also be used in this recipe.

BARBECUED FISH KABOBS

INGREDIENTS   Serves 4

1 lb. herring or mackerel fillets,
   cut into chunks
2 small red onions, peeled and
   quartered
16 cherry tomatoes
salt and freshly ground
   black pepper
couscous, to serve

FOR THE SAUCE:
⅔ cup fish stock
5 tbsp. ketchup
2 tbsp. Worcestershire sauce
2 tbsp. wine vinegar
2 tbsp. brown sugar
2 drops hot chili sauce
2 tbsp. tomato paste

1 Line a broiler rack with a single layer of foil, and preheat the broiler.

2 If using wooden skewers, soak in cold water for 30 minutes to keep them from burning during cooking.

3 Meanwhile, prepare the sauce. Add the fish stock, ketchup, Worcestershire sauce, vinegar, sugar, hot chili sauce, and tomato paste to a small saucepan. Stir well and leave to simmer for 5 minutes.

4 When ready to cook, drain the skewers, if necessary, then thread the fish chunks, the quartered red onions, and the cherry tomatoes alternately onto the skewers.

5 Season the kabobs to taste with salt and pepper, and brush with the sauce. Broil under the preheated broiler for 8–10 minutes, basting with the sauce occasionally during cooking. Turn

the kabobs often to ensure that they are cooked thoroughly and evenly on all sides. Serve immediately with couscous.

TASTY TIP

This dish would be ideal for a light summertime evening meal. Instead of cooking indoors, cook these kabobs on the barbecue for a delicious charcoal flavor. Light the barbecue at least 20 minutes before use in order to allow the coals to heat up. (The coals will have a gray-white ash when ready.) Barbecue some bell peppers and red onions, and serve with a mixed salad as an accompaniment to the fish kabobs.

RATATOUILLE MACKEREL

INGREDIENTS

Serves 4

1 red bell pepper
1 tbsp. olive oil
1 red onion, peeled
1 garlic clove, peeled and
   thinly sliced
2 zucchini, trimmed and sliced
14-oz. can chopped tomatoes
sea salt and freshly ground
   black pepper

4 10-oz. small mackerel,
   cleaned and heads removed
spray of olive oil
lemon juice, for drizzling
12 fresh basil leaves
couscous or rice mixed with
   chopped parsley, to serve

1 Preheat the oven to 375° F. Cut the top off the red bell pepper, remove the seeds and membrane, then cut into chunks. Cut the red onion into thick wedges.

2 Heat the oil in a large saucepan, and cook the onion and garlic for 5 minutes or until beginning to soften.

3 Add the bell pepper chunks and zucchini slices, and cook for an additional 5 minutes.

4 Pour in the chopped tomatoes with their juice, and cook for an additional 5 minutes. Season to taste with salt and pepper, and pour into an ovenproof dish.

5 Season the fish with salt and pepper and arrange on top of the vegetables. Spray with a little olive oil and lemon juice. Cover and cook in the preheated oven for 20 minutes.

6 Remove the cover, add the basil leaves, and return to the oven for an additional 5 minutes. Serve immediately with couscous or rice mixed with parsley.

FOOD FACT

Ratatouille is a traditional French dish using onions, tomatoes, zucchini, and often eggplant. It is a very versatile dish to which many other vegetables can be added. For that extra kick, why not add a little chopped chili?

COD WITH FENNEL & CARDAMOM

INGREDIENTS
Serves 4

1 garlic clove, peeled
  and crushed
1 tbsp. grated lemon rind
1 tsp. lemon juice
1 tbsp. olive oil

1 fennel bulb
1 tbsp. cardamom pods
salt and freshly ground
  black pepper
4 6-oz. cod fillets

1 Preheat the oven to 375° F. Place the garlic in a small bowl with the lemon zest, juice, and olive oil, and stir well.

2 Cover with plastic wrap and leave to infuse for at least 30 minutes. Stir well before using.

3 Trim the fennel bulb, thinly slice, and place in a bowl.

4 Place the cardamom pods in a mortar and pestle, and lightly pound to crack the pods.

5 Alternatively, wrap in a piece of plastic wrap and pound gently with a rolling pin. Add the crushed cardamom to the fennel slices.

6 Season the fish with salt and pepper, and place onto 4 separate 8-inch squares of baking parchment.

7 Spoon the fennel mixture over the fish and drizzle with the infused oil, then fold the baking parchment over to enclose the fish and form a pocket.

8 Place the pockets on a baking sheet and cook in the preheated oven for 8–10 minutes or until cooked. Serve immediately in the paper pockets.

FOOD FACT

When buying fresh fish, look for fish that does not smell. Any fish smelling of ammonia should be avoided.
The flesh should be plump and firm-looking. The eyes should be bright, not sunken. If in doubt, choose frozen fish. This is cleaned and packed almost as soon as it is caught. It is often fresher and contains more nutrients than its fresh counterparts.

SEARED TUNA WITH PERNOD & THYME

INGREDIENTS

Serves 4

4 tuna or swordfish steaks
salt and freshly ground
 black pepper
3 tbsp. Pernod
1 tbsp. olive oil
3 tsp. each lime zest and juice

2 tsp. fresh thyme leaves
4 sun-dried tomatoes

TO SERVE:
freshly cooked mixed rice
tossed green salad

1 Wipe the fish steaks with a damp cloth or dampened paper towels.

2 Season both sides of the fish to taste with salt and pepper, then place in a shallow bowl and set aside.

3 Mix together the Pernod, olive oil, lime zest, and juice with the fresh thyme leaves.

4 Finely chop the sun-dried tomatoes, and add to the Pernod mixture.

5 Pour the Pernod mixture over the fish and chill in the refrigerator for about 2 hours, occasionally spooning the marinade over the fish.

6 Heat a griddle or heavy skillet. Drain the fish, setting aside the marinade. Cook the fish for 3–4 minutes on each side for a steak that is still slightly pink in the center. Alternatively, cook the fish for 1–2 minutes longer on each side if you prefer your fish cooked through.

7 Place the remaining marinade in a small saucepan, and bring to a boil. Pour the marinade over the fish, and serve immediately with the mixed rice and salad.

HELPFUL HINT

Tuna is now widely available all year round in supermarkets. Tuna is an oily fish that is rich in omega-3 fatty acids and helps in the prevention of heart disease by lowering blood cholesterol levels. Tuna is usually sold in steaks, and the flesh should be dark red in color.

HADDOCK WITH AN OLIVE CRUST

INGREDIENTS

Serves 4

12 pitted ripe olives,
  finely chopped
¾ cup fresh white
  bread crumbs
1 tbsp. freshly chopped
  tarragon
1 garlic clove, peeled
  and crushed
3 scallions, trimmed and
  finely chopped

1 tbsp. olive oil
4 thick, skinless haddock
  fillets, 6 oz. each

TO SERVE:
freshly cooked carrots
freshly cooked beans

1 Preheat the oven to 375° F. Place the olives in a small bowl with the bread crumbs, and add the chopped tarragon.

2 Add the crushed garlic to the olives with the chopped scallions and the olive oil. Mix together lightly.

3 Wipe the fillets with either a clean, damp cloth or damp paper towels, then place on a lightly greased baking sheet.

4 Place spoonfuls of the olive and bread crumb mixture on top of each fillet, and press the mixture down lightly and evenly over the top of the fish.

5 Bake the fish in the preheated oven for 20–25 minutes or until the fish is cooked thoroughly, and the topping is golden brown. Serve immediately with the freshly cooked carrots and beans.

HELPFUL HINT

Any firm-fleshed fish will be suitable for this delicious and tasty dish. Try substituting cod, monkfish, or even salmon.

TASTY TIP

Why not try experimenting by adding other ingredients to the crust? Adding 2 cloves of roasted garlic gives the crust a delicious flavor. Simply mash the garlic and add to the crumbs. Also, a combination of white and whole-wheat bread crumbs can be used for a nuttier, malty taste.

CITRUS MONKFISH KABOBS

INGREDIENTS

Serves 4

FOR THE MARINADE:
1 tbsp. corn oil
2 tsp. finely grated lime rind
1 tbsp. lime juice
1 tbsp. lemon juice
1 sprig of freshly chopped
  rosemary
1 tbsp. mustard
1 garlic clove, peeled and
  crushed
salt and freshly ground
  black pepper

FOR THE KABOBS:
1 lb. monkfish tail
8 raw jumbo shrimp
1 small green zucchini,
  trimmed and sliced
4 tbsp. low-fat sour cream

1 Preheat the broiler and line the broiler rack with foil. Mix all the marinade ingredients together in a bowl, and set aside.

2 Using a sharp knife, cut down both sides of the fish tail. Remove the bone and discard. Cut away and discard any skin, then cut the fish into bite-size cubes.

3 Shell the shrimp, leaving the tails intact, and remove the black vein that runs down the back of each. Place the fish and shrimp in a shallow dish.

4 Pour the marinade over the fish and shrimp. Cover lightly and leave to marinate in the refrigerator for 30 minutes. Spoon the marinade over the fish and shrimp occasionally during this time. Soak the skewers in cold water for 30 minutes, then drain.

5 Thread the cubes of fish, shrimp, and zucchini onto the drained skewers.

6 Arrange on the broiler rack, then place under the preheated broiler and cook for 5–7 minutes or until cooked thoroughly and the shrimp have turned pink. Occasionally brush with the remaining marinade, and turn the kabobs during cooking.

7 Mix 2 tablespoons of the marinade with the sour cream and serve as a dip with the kabobs.

FOOD FACT

Monkfish is so versatile—it can be roasted in the oven, poached, baked, or broiled. Its firm flesh is ideal for kabobs.

SARDINES WITH RED CURRANTS

INGREDIENTS
Serves 4

2 tbsp. red currant jelly
2 tsp. finely grated lime rind
2 tbsp. medium-dry sherry
1 lb. fresh sardines, cleaned
  and heads removed
sea salt and freshly ground
  black pepper
lime wedges, to garnish

TO SERVE:
fresh red currants
fresh green salad

1 Preheat the broiler and line the broiler rack with foil 2–3 minutes before cooking.

2 Warm the red currant jelly in a bowl standing over a pan of gently simmering water and stir until smooth. Add the lime rind and sherry to the bowl, and stir until blended.

3 Lightly rinse the sardines and pat dry with absorbent paper towels.

4 Place on a chopping board and with a sharp knife, make several diagonal cuts across the flesh of each fish. Season the sardines inside the cavities with salt and pepper.

5 Gently brush the warm marinade over the skin and inside the cavities of the sardines.

6 Place on the broiler rack and cook under the preheated broiler for 8–10 minutes or until the fish are cooked.

7 Carefully turn the sardines over at least once during broiling. Baste occasionally with the remaining red currant and lime marinade. Garnish with the red currants. Serve immediately with the salad and lime wedges.

COOK'S TIP

Most fish are sold cleaned, but it is easy to do yourself. Using the back of a knife, scrape off the scales from the tail toward the head. Using a sharp knife, make a small slit along the belly. Carefully scrape out the entrails and rinse thoroughly under cold running water. Pat dry with absorbent paper towels.

HOT SALSA-FILLED SOLE

INGREDIENTS
Serves 4

8 6-oz. sole fillets, skinned
⅔ cup orange juice
2 tbsp. lemon juice

FOR THE SALSA:
1 small mango
8 cherry tomatoes, quartered
1 small red onion, peeled
  and finely chopped
pinch of sugar
1 red chili
2 tbsp. rice vinegar

2 tsp. lime zest
1 tbsp. lime juice
1 tbsp. olive oil
sea salt and freshly ground
  black pepper
2 tbsp. freshly chopped mint
lime wedges, to garnish
lettuce leaves, to serve

1 First, make the salsa. Peel the mango and cut the flesh away from the pit. Chop finely and place in a small bowl. Add the cherry tomatoes to the mango, along with the onion and sugar.

2 Cut the top of the chili. Slit down the side, and discard the seeds and membrane (the skin to which the seeds are attached). Finely chop the chili and add to the mango mixture with the vinegar, lime zest, juice, and oil. Season to taste with salt and pepper. Mix thoroughly and let stand for 30 minutes to allow the flavors to develop.

3 Lay the fish fillets on a chopping board, skinned-side up, and pile the salsa on the tail end of the fillets. Fold in half, season, and place in a large, shallow skillet. Pour over the orange and lemon juice.

4 Bring to a gentle boil, then reduce the heat to a simmer. Cover and cook on a low heat for 7–10 minutes, adding a little water if the liquid is evaporating. Remove the cover, add the mint, and cook uncovered for an additional 3 minutes. Garnish with lime wedges and serve immediately with the salad.

HELPFUL HINT

Your skin may burn after handling chilies. Take care not to touch your eyes, and wash your hands immediately.

TASTY TIP

To temper the hotness of the salsa, add 1–2 teaspoons of warm honey.

SMOKED HADDOCK RÖSTI

INGREDIENTS   Serves 4

1 lb. potatoes, peeled and
   coarsely grated
1 large onion, peeled and
   coarsely grated
2–3 garlic cloves, peeled
   and crushed
1 lb. smoked haddock
1 tbsp. olive oil

salt and freshly ground
   black pepper
2 tsp. finely grated lemon rind
1 tbsp. freshly chopped
   parsley
2 tbsp. low-fat sour cream
lettuce leaves, to garnish
lemon wedges, to serve

1 Dry the grated potatoes in a clean dishtowel. Rinse the grated onion thoroughly in cold water, dry in a clean dishtowel, and add to the potatoes.

2 Stir the garlic into the potato mixture. Skin the smoked haddock and remove as many of the tiny pin bones as possible. Cut into thin slices and set aside.

3 Heat the oil in a large nonstick skillet. Add half the potatoes and press down in the skillet. Season to taste with salt and pepper.

4 Add a layer of fish and a sprinkling of lemon rind, parsley, and a little black pepper.

5 Top with the remaining potatoes and press down firmly. Cover with a sheet of foil, and cook on the lowest heat for 25–30 minutes.

6 Preheat the broiler 2–3 minutes before the end of the cooking time. Remove the foil and place the rösti under the broiler to brown. Turn out onto a warmed serving dish, and serve immediately with spoonfuls of sour cream, lemon wedges, and mixed lettuce leaves.

HELPFUL HINT

These delicious fish rosti are best if they are prepared, cooked, and then eaten right away.

SWEET-&-SOUR SHRIMP WITH NOODLES

INGREDIENTS   Serves 4

15-oz. can pineapple chunks in
   natural juice
1 green bell pepper, seeded
   and cut into quarters
1 tbsp. peanut oil
1 onion, cut into thin wedges
3 tbsp. brown sugar
⅔ cup chicken stock
4 tbsp. wine vinegar

1 tbsp. tomato paste
1 tbsp. light soy sauce
1 tbsp. cornstarch
12 oz. raw jumbo shrimp,
   shelled
5 cups bok choy, shredded
4¾ cups medium egg noodles
fresh cilantro leaves,
   to garnish

1 Make the sauce by draining the pineapple and setting aside 2 tablespoons of the juice.

2 Remove the membrane from the quartered bell pepper and cut into thin strips.

3 Heat the oil in a saucepan. Add the onion and pepper, and cook for about 4 minutes or until the onion has softened.

4 Add the pineapple, the sugar, stock, vinegar, tomato paste, and the soy sauce.

5 Bring the sauce to a boil and simmer for about 4 minutes. Blend the cornstarch with the pineapple juice and stir into the saucepan, stirring until the sauce has thickened.

6 Clean the shrimp if necessary. Wash the bok choy thoroughly, then shred.

7 Add the shrimp and bok choy to the sauce. Simmer for 3 minutes or until the shrimp are cooked and have turned pink.

8 Cook the noodles in boiling water for 4–5 minutes until just tender.

9 Drain and arrange the noodles on a warmed serving plate and pour over the shrimp. Garnish with a few cilantro leaves and serve immediately.

HELPFUL HINT

This dish works well with Thai jasmine steamed rice and also whole-wheat noodles, which have more nutritional value. When using raw jumbo shrimp, make sure that the black vein that runs along their backs has been completely removed.

SALMON FISH CAKES

INGREDIENTS

Serves 4

8 oz. potatoes, peeled
1 lb. salmon fillet, skinned
1 medium carrot, trimmed
  and peeled
2 tbsp. grated lemon rind
2–3 tbsp. freshly chopped
  cilantro
1 medium egg yolk
salt and freshly ground
  black pepper

2 tbsp. all-purpose flour
few fine sprays of oil

TO SERVE:
prepared tomato sauce
tossed green salad
crusty bread

1 Cube the potatoes and cook in lightly salted, boiling water for 15 minutes. Drain and mash the potatoes. Place in a large bowl and set aside.

2 Place the salmon in a food processor and blend to form a chunky purée. Add the purée to the potatoes and mix together.

3 Coarsely grate the carrot and add to the fish, along with the lemon rind and the cilantro.

4 Add the egg yolk, season to taste with salt and pepper, then gently mix the ingredients together. With damp hands, form the mixture into 4 large fish cakes.

5 Coat with flour, then place on a plate. Cover loosely and chill for at least 30 minutes.

6 When ready to cook, spray a griddle pan with a few fine sprays of oil and heat the pan. When hot, add the fish cakes and cook on both sides for 3–4 minutes or until the fish is cooked. Add an extra spray of oil if needed during the cooking.

7 When the fish cakes are cooked, serve immediately with the tomato sauce, green salad, and crusty bread.

FOOD FACT

Salmon is now easily affordable due to salmon farming. It is readily available year-round, and is often cheaper to buy than cod. It is an excellent source of omega-3 fatty acids, which help lower blood cholesterol levels.

CITRUS-BROILED FLOUNDER

INGREDIENTS

Serves 4

1 tsp. corn oil
1 onion, peeled and chopped
1 orange bell pepper, seeded
   and chopped
¾ cup long-grain rice
⅔ cup orange juice
2 tbsp. lemon juice
1 cup vegetable stock
spray of oil
4 6-oz. flounder fillets, skinned
1 orange
1 lemon

¼ stick reduced-fat butter
   or 2 tbsp. low-fat spread
2 tbsp. freshly chopped
   tarragon
salt and freshly ground
   black pepper
lemon wedges, to garnish

1 Heat the oil in a large skillet, then cook the onion, bell pepper, and rice for 2 minutes.

2 Add the orange and lemon juice, and bring to a boil. Reduce the heat, add half the stock, and simmer for 15–20 minutes or until the rice is tender, adding the remaining stock as necessary.

3 Preheat the broiler. Finely spray the base of the broiler pan with oil. Place the flounder fillets in the base and set aside.

4 Finely grate the orange and lemon rind. Squeeze the juice from half of each fruit.

5 Melt the butter or low-fat spread in a small saucepan. Add the grated rind, juice, and half of the tarragon, and use to baste the flounder fillets.

6 Cook one side only of the fish under the preheated broiler at a medium heat for 4–6 minutes, basting continuously.

7 Once the rice is cooked, stir in the remaining tarragon, and season to taste with salt and pepper. Garnish the fish with the lemon wedges, and serve immediately with the rice.

TASTY TIP

Flounder is caught mainly in cold Atlantic waters. It can be bought fresh or frozen, whole or in fillets, and can be fried, poached, or broiled. Sole or halibut can be used in place of flounder, but they are more expensive.

FISH LASAGNA

INGREDIENTS

Serves 4

¾ cup mushrooms
1 tsp. vegetable oil
1 onion, peeled and chopped
1 tbsp. freshly chopped
  oregano
14-oz. can chopped tomatoes
1 tbsp. tomato paste
salt and freshly ground
  black pepper
1 lb. cod or haddock fillets,
  skinned
9–12 sheets precooked lasagna
  verde

FOR THE TOPPING:
1 medium egg, beaten
½ cup cottage cheese
½ cup low-fat plain yogurt
½ cup reduced-fat cheddar
  cheese, shredded

TO SERVE:
mixed lettuce leaves
cherry tomatoes

1 Preheat the oven to 375° F. Wipe the mushrooms, trim the stalks, and chop. Heat the oil in a large, heavy saucepan, add the onion, and gently cook the onion for 3–5 minutes or until soft.

2 Stir in the mushrooms, the oregano, and the chopped tomatoes with their juice.

3 Blend the tomato paste with 1 tablespoon of water. Stir into the pan, and season to taste with salt and pepper.

4 Bring the sauce to a boil, then simmer uncovered for 5–10 minutes.

5 Remove as many of the tiny pin bones as possible from the fish, and cut the fish into cubes and add to the tomato sauce mixture. Stir gently and remove from the heat.

6 Cover the base of an ovenproof dish with 2–3 sheets of the lasagna verde. Top with half of the fish mixture. Repeat the layers, finishing with the lasagna sheets.

7 To make the topping, mix together the beaten egg, cottage cheese, and yogurt. Pour over the lasagna and sprinkle with the cheese.

8 Cook the lasagna in the preheated oven for 40–45 minutes or until the topping is golden brown and bubbling. Serve the lasagna immediately with the mixed lettuce leaves and cherry tomatoes.

FRUITS DE MER STIR-FRY

INGREDIENTS

Serves 4

1 lb. mixed fresh shellfish,
  such as jumbo shrimp,
  squid, scallops,
  and mussels
1-in. piece fresh ginger
2 garlic cloves, peeled and
  crushed
2 green chilies, seeded and
  finely chopped
3 tbsp. light soy sauce
2 tbsp. olive oil

2 cups baby corn, rinsed
1¾ cups asparagus tips,
  trimmed and cut in half
1 cup snow peas, trimmed
2 tbsp. plum sauce
4 scallions, trimmed and
  shredded, to garnish
freshly cooked rice, to serve

1 Prepare the shellfish. Shell the shrimp, and if necessary, remove the thin black veins from the back of each. Lightly rinse the squid rings and clean the scallops if needed.

2 Remove and discard any mussels that are open. Scrub and debeard the remaining mussels, removing any barnacles from the shells. Cover the mussels with cold water until needed.

3 Peel the fresh ginger and either coarsely grate or shred finely with a sharp knife, and place into a small bowl.

4 Add the garlic and chilies to the small bowl, pour in the soy sauce, and mix well.

5 Place the mixed shellfish, except the mussels, in a bowl and pour over the marinade. Stir, cover, and leave for 15 minutes.

6 Heat a wok until hot, then add the oil and heat until almost smoking. Add the prepared vegetables, stir-fry for 3 minutes, then stir in the plum sauce.

7 Add the shellfish and the mussels with the marinade, and stir-fry for an additional 3–4 minutes or until the fish is cooked. Discard any mussels that have not opened. Garnish with the scallions, and serve immediately with the freshly cooked rice.

HELPFUL HINT

When stir-frying, it is important that the wok is heated before the oil is added. This ensures that the food does not stick to the wok.

ZESTY WHOLE-BAKED FISH

INGREDIENTS

Serves 8

4 lbs. whole salmon, cleaned
sea salt and freshly ground
  black pepper
¼ cup low-fat spread
1 garlic clove, peeled and
  sliced
1 tbsp. lemon zest
1 tbsp. lemon juice
1 tbsp. orange zest
1 tsp. freshly grated nutmeg

3 tbsp. mustard
2 tbsp. fresh, white bread
  crumbs
2 bunches fresh dill
1 bunch fresh tarragon
1 lime, sliced
⅔ cup reduced-fat sour cream
scant 2 cups plain yogurt
sprigs of fresh dill, to garnish

1 Preheat the oven to 425° F. Lightly rinse the fish and pat dry with absorbent paper towels. Season the cavity with a little salt and pepper. Make several diagonal cuts across the flesh of the fish, and season lightly.

2 Mix together the low-fat spread, garlic, lemon, orange zest and juice, nutmeg, mustard, and fresh bread crumbs. Mix well together. Spoon the bread crumb mixture into the slits with a small sprig of dill. Place the remaining herbs inside the fish cavity. Weigh the fish and calculate the cooking time. Allow 10 minutes per pound.

3 Lay the fish on a double thickness of foil. If desired, smear the fish with a little low-fat spread. Top with the lime slices and then fold the foil over to enclose the fish and to form a pocket. Chill in the refrigerator for about 15 minutes.

4 Place in a roasting pan and cook in the preheated oven for the calculated cooking time. Fifteen minutes before the end of cooking, open the foil and return until the skin begins to crisp. Remove the fish from the oven and let stand for 10 minutes.

5 Pour the juices from the roasting pan into a saucepan. Bring to a boil, and stir in the sour cream and yogurt. Simmer for about 3 minutes or until hot. Garnish with dill sprigs and serve immediately.

FOOD FACT

Wild salmon are caught in the freshwaters of North America and Northern Europe. There are many varieties: humpback (pink salmon), chinook, and sockeye. Now that they are farmed, they are more affordable.

SEARED SCALLOP SALAD

INGREDIENTS   Serves 4

12 sea (large) scallops
1 tbsp. low-fat spread or butter
2 tbsp. orange juice
2 tbsp. balsamic vinegar
1 tbsp. honey

2 ripe pears, washed
2½ cups arugula
2½ cups watercress
½ cup walnuts
freshly ground black pepper

1 Clean the scallops, removing the thin black vein from around the white meat and coral. Rinse thoroughly and dry on absorbent paper towels.

2 Cut into 2–3 thick slices, depending on the size of the scallop.

3 Heat a griddle pan or heavy skillet, then when hot, add the low-fat spread or butter, and allow to melt.

4 Once melted, sear the scallops for 1 minute on each side or until golden. Remove from the pan and set aside.

5 Briskly whisk together the orange juice, balsamic vinegar, and honey to make the dressing, and set aside.

6 With a small, sharp knife, carefully cut the pears into quarters, core, and cut into chunks.

7 Mix the arugula, watercress, pear chunks, and walnuts. Pile onto serving plates and top with the scallops.

8 Drizzle the dressing on top, and add plenty of ground black pepper. Serve immediately.

FOOD FACT

As well as the large sea scallops, which are used in this recipe, there are also the smaller bay scallops. Scallops are in season between September and March, when they will not only be at their best, but they may also be slightly cheaper in price. When buying, especially the larger sea scallops, make sure that the orange coral is left intact.

FISH ROULADES WITH RICE & SPINACH

INGREDIENTS   Serves 4

4 ½-lb. fillets of sole, skinned
salt and freshly ground black pepper
1 tsp. fennel seeds
1 cup long-grain rice, cooked
1 cup white crabmeat, fresh or canned

2½ cups baby spinach, washed and trimmed
5 tbsp. dry white wine
5 tbsp. reduced-fat sour cream
2 tbsp. freshly chopped parsley, plus extra to garnish
asparagus spears, to serve

1 Wipe each fish fillet with either a clean, damp cloth or paper towels. Place on a chopping board, skinned-side up, and season lightly with salt and black pepper.

2 Place the fennel seeds in a mortar and pestle, and crush lightly. Transfer to a small bowl, and stir in the cooked rice. Drain the crabmeat thoroughly. Add to the rice mixture and mix lightly.

3 Lay 2–3 spinach leaves over each fillet, and top with a quarter of the crabmeat mixture. Roll up and secure with a toothpick if necessary. Place into a large saucepan and pour in the wine. Cover and cook for 5–7 minutes or until cooked.

4 Remove the fish from the cooking liquid, and transfer to a serving plate and keep warm. Stir the sour cream into the cooking liquid and season to taste.

Heat for 3 minutes, then stir in the chopped parsley.

5 Spoon the sauce onto the base of a plate. Cut each roulade into slices, and arrange on top of the sauce. Serve with freshly cooked asparagus spears.

FOOD FACT

Spinach is one of the healthiest leafy green vegetables to be found. It also acts as an antioxidant, and it is believed that it can reduce the risk of certain cancers. Why not use whole-grain rice to add nutritional value and to give the dish a nuttier taste?

TRADITIONAL FISH PIE

INGREDIENTS

Serves 4

1 lb. white fish fillets, skinned
2 cups milk
1 small onion, peeled and quartered
salt and freshly ground black pepper
5 cups peeled and coarsely diced potatoes
¼ cup plus 3 tbsp. butter

¼ lb. large shrimp, peeled
2 large eggs, hard-boiled and quartered
7-oz. can corn, drained
2 tbsp. freshly chopped parsley
3 tbsp. all-purpose flour
½ cup shredded cheddar cheese

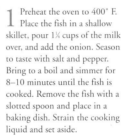

1 Preheat the oven to 400° F. Place the fish in a shallow skillet, pour 1¼ cups of the milk over, and add the onion. Season to taste with salt and pepper. Bring to a boil and simmer for 8–10 minutes until the fish is cooked. Remove the fish with a slotted spoon and place in a baking dish. Strain the cooking liquid and set aside.

2 Boil the potatoes until soft, then mash with the 3 tablespoons of butter and 2–3 tablespoons of the remaining milk. Set aside.

3 Arrange the shrimp and sliced eggs on top of the fish, then sprinkle with the corn and parsley.

4 Melt the remaining butter in a saucepan, stir in the flour, and cook gently for 1 minute, stirring. Whisk in the cooking liquid and remaining milk. Cook for 2 minutes or until thickened, then pour over the fish mixture and cool slightly.

5 Spread the mashed potato over the top of the pie and sprinkle the cheese over the top. Bake in the preheated oven for 30 minutes, until golden. Serve immediately.

TASTY TIP

Any variety of white fish may be used in this delicious dish. You could also used smoked fish, such as smoked cod or haddock, for a change. After simmering in milk, carefully remove any bones from the cooked fish. Serve with a selection of vegetables.

SEAFOOD RISOTTO

INGREDIENTS

Serves 4

¼ cup butter
2 shallots, peeled and finely
  chopped
1 garlic clove, peeled and
  crushed
2 cups Arborio rice
⅔ cup white wine
2½ cups fish or vegetable
  stock, heated

¾ cup whole cooked unpeeled
  large shrimp
10-oz. can baby clams
⅓ cup smoked salmon
  trimmings
2 tbsp. freshly chopped parsley

TO SERVE:
green salad

1 Melt the butter in a large, heavy-based saucepan, add the shallots and garlic, and cook for 2 minutes until slightly softened. Add the rice and cook for 1–2 minutes, stirring continuously, then pour in the wine and boil for 1 minute.

2 Pour in half the hot stock, bring to a boil, cover the saucepan, and simmer gently for 15 minutes, adding the remaining stock a little at a time. Continue to simmer for 5 minutes or until the rice is cooked and all the liquid is absorbed.

3 Meanwhile, prepare the seafood by peeling the shrimp, and removing their heads and tails. Drain the clams and discard the liquid. Cut the smoked salmon into thin strips.

4 When the rice has cooked, stir in the shrimp, clams, smoked salmon strips, and half the chopped parsley, then heat for 1–2 minutes until everything is piping hot. Turn into a serving dish, sprinkle with the remaining parsley and the Parmesan cheese, and serve immediately with a green salad.

TASTY TIP

A good-quality stock will make a huge difference to the finished flavor of this risotto. Rinse 2 lbs. fish bones and trimmings, and put in a large saucepan with 1 carrot, 1 onion, and 1 celery stalk, all peeled and roughly chopped, 1 bouquet garni, 4 peppercorns, and 3¾ cups cold water. Slowly bring to a boil, then skim. Cover and simmer for 30 minutes. Strain the stock through a fine sieve, cool, and chill in the refrigerator for up to 2 days. After chilling, boil vigorously before using.

SMOKED HADDOCK KEDGEREE

INGREDIENTS

Serves 4

1 lb. smoked haddock fillet
¼ cup butter
1 onion, peeled and finely
   chopped
2 tsp. mild curry powder
1 cup long-grain rice
2 cups fish or vegetable stock,
   heated

2 large eggs, hard-boiled and
   peeled
2 tbsp. freshly chopped
   parsley
2 tbsp. whipping cream
   (optional)
salt and freshly ground black
   pepper
pinch of cayenne pepper

1 Place the haddock in a shallow skillet, and cover with 1¼ cups water. Simmer gently for 8–10 minutes or until the fish is cooked. Drain, then remove all the skin and bones from the fish, and flake into a dish. Keep warm.

2 Melt the butter in a saucepan and add the chopped onion and curry powder. Cook, stirring, for 3–4 minutes, or until the onion is soft, then stir in the rice. Cook for an additional minute, stirring continuously, then stir in the hot stock.

3 Cover and simmer gently for 15 minutes or until the rice has absorbed all the liquid. Cut the eggs into quarters or eighths, and add half to the mixture with half the parsley.

4 Carefully fold the cooked fish into the mixture and add the cream, if desired. Season to taste with salt and pepper. Heat the kedgeree until piping hot.

5 Transfer the mixture to a large dish, and garnish with the remaining quartered eggs and parsley, and season with a pinch of cayenne pepper. Serve immediately.

FOOD FACT

The word *khichri* means a "mixture," in Hindi. The British in India adapted this dish of lentils, rice and spices into kedgeree by adding smoked fish and hard-boiled eggs. If smoked haddock is unavailable, use smoked salmon instead.

TUNA-FISH PATTIES

INGREDIENTS

Makes 8

2⅔ cups peeled and coarsely
  diced potatoes
¼ cup butter
2 tbsp. milk
14-oz. can tuna in oil
1 scallion, trimmed and finely
  chopped
1 tbsp. freshly chopped parsley
salt and freshly ground black
  pepper
2 medium eggs, beaten

2 tbsp. seasoned all-purpose
  flour
2 cups fresh white bread
  crumbs
4 tbsp. vegetable oil
4 hamburger buns

TO SERVE:
french fries
mixed salad
tomato chutney

1 Place the potatoes in a large saucepan, cover with boiling water, and simmer until soft. Drain, then mash with 3 tablespoons of the butter and the milk. Turn into a large bowl. Drain the tuna, discarding the oil, and flake into the bowl of potatoes. Stir well to mix.

2 Add the scallion and parsley, and season to taste with salt and pepper. Add 1 tablespoon of the beaten egg to bind the mixture together. Chill in the refrigerator for at least 1 hour.

3 Shape the chilled mixture with your hands into 4 large patties. First, coat the patties with seasoned flour, then brush them with the remaining beaten egg, allowing any excess to drip back into the bowl. Finally, coat them evenly in the bread crumbs, pressing the crumbs on with your hands, if necessary.

4 Heat a little of the oil in a skillet, and fry the patties for 2–3 minutes on each side, until golden, adding more oil if necessary. Drain on paper towels and serve hot on buns with french fries, mixed salad, and chutney.

HELPFUL HINT

Drain the potatoes thoroughly, and dry them over a very low heat before mashing with the milk and butter to ensure the mixture is not too soft to shape. If time allows, cover the patties with plastic wrap and chill in the refrigerator for 30 minutes so that they are really firm before cooking.

SALMON PATTIES

INGREDIENTS   Serves 4

1 lb. salmon fillet, skinned
salt and freshly ground black
   pepper
2⅔ cups peeled and coarsely
   diced potatoes
¼ cup butter
1 tbsp. milk
2 medium tomatoes, skinned,
   deseeded, and chopped
2 tbsp. freshly chopped
   parsley

1½ cups whole-wheat bread
   crumbs
¼ cup shredded cheddar
   cheese
2 tbsp. all-purpose flour
2 medium eggs, beaten
3–4 tbsp. vegetable oil

TO SERVE:
raita
sprigs of fresh mint

1 Place the salmon in a shallow skillet, and cover with water. Season to taste with salt and pepper, and simmer for 8–10 minutes, until the fish is cooked. Drain and flake into a bowl.

2 Boil the potatoes in lightly salted water until soft, then drain. Mash with the butter and milk until smooth. Add the potato to the bowl of fish, and stir in the tomatoes and half the parsley. Adjust the seasoning to taste. Chill the mixture in the refrigerator for at least 2 hours to firm up.

3 Mix the bread crumbs with the cheese and the remaining parsley. When the fish mixture is firm, form into 8 patties. First, lightly coat the patties in the flour, then dip into the beaten egg, allowing any excess to drip back into the bowl. Finally, press the patties into the bread-crumb mixture until well coated.

4 Heat a little of the oil in a skillet, and fry the patties in batches for 2–3 minutes on each side until golden and crisp, adding more oil if necessary. Serve with raita, garnished with sprigs of mint.

HELPFUL HINT

To remove the skins from the tomatoes, pierce each with the tip of a sharp knife, then plunge into boiling water and leave for up to 1 minute. After a cold-water rinsing, the skins should peel off easily.
Raita is a refreshing Indian condiment made of yogurt and flavored with mint.

BATTERED FISH & CHUNKY FRIES

INGREDIENTS

Serves 4

1 package yeast
1¼ cups beer
2 cups all-purpose flour
1 tsp. salt
1½ lbs. potatoes
2 cups peanut oil
4 pieces thick white fish fillet, about ½ lb. each, skinned and boned

2 tbsp. seasoned all-purpose flour

TO GARNISH:
lemon wedges
sprigs of Italian parsley

1 Dissolve the yeast in a little of the beer in a pitcher, and mix to a paste. Pour in the remaining beer, whisking all the time until smooth. Place the flour and salt in a bowl, and gradually pour in the beer mixture, whisking continuously to make a thick, smooth batter. Cover the bowl and allow the batter to stand at room temperature for 1 hour.

2 Peel the potatoes and cut into thick slices. Cut each slice lengthwise to make chunky fries. Place them in a nonstick frying pan and heat, shaking the pan until all the moisture has evaporated. Turn them onto paper towels to dry off.

3 Heat the oil to 350° F, then fry the potatoes, a few at a time, for 4–5 minutes until crisp and golden. Drain on paper towels and keep warm.

4 Pat the fish fillets dry, then coat in the flour. Dip the floured fillets into the batter. Fry for 2–3 minutes until cooked and crisp, then drain. Garnish with lemon wedges and parsley, and serve immediately with the fries.

HELPFUL HINT

Yeast is a living, microscopic organism that converts food into alcohol and carbohydrates. When mixed with warm liquid, yeast produces gases which lighten this batter. Check that the yeast is moist and creamy-colored, and has a strong yeasty smell. If it is dry, discolored, and crumbly, it is probably stale and will not work well. Active dry yeast can be used instead. Follow the manufacturer's instructions for dry yeast.

PAELLA

INGREDIENTS

Serves 6

1 lb. live mussels
4 tbsp. olive oil
6 medium chicken thighs
1 medium onion, peeled and
    finely chopped
1 garlic clove, peeled and
    crushed
¾ cup skinned, deseeded and
    chopped tomatoes
1 red bell pepper, deseeded
    and chopped
1 green bell pepper, deseeded
    and chopped

⅔ cup frozen peas
1 tsp. paprika
2⅓ cups Arborio rice
½ tsp. turmeric
3¾ cups chicken stock, warmed
1 cup large shrimp, peeled
salt and freshly ground black
    pepper
2 limes
1 lemon
1 tbsp. freshly chopped basil
whole, cooked, unpeeled
    shrimp, to garnish

1 Rinse the mussels under cold running water, scrubbing well to remove any grit and barnacles, then pull off the hairy "beards." Tap any open mussels sharply with a knife, and discard if they refuse to close.

2 Heat the oil in a paella pan or large, heavy-based skillet, and cook the chicken thighs for 10–15 minutes until golden. Remove and keep warm.

3 Fry the onion and garlic in the remaining oil in the pan for 2–3 minutes, then add the tomatoes, peppers, peas, and paprika, and cook for an additional 3 minutes.

4 Add the rice to the pan and return the chicken with the turmeric and half the stock.

Bring to a boil and simmer, gradually adding more stock as it is absorbed. Cook for 20 minutes, or until most of the stock has been absorbed and the rice is almost tender.

5 Put the mussels in a large saucepan with 2 in. salted, boiling water, cover, and steam for 5 minutes. Discard any with shells that have not opened, then stir into the rice with the shrimp. Season to taste with salt and pepper. Heat for 2–3 minutes until piping hot. Squeeze the juice from 1 of the limes over the paella.

6 Cut the remaining limes and the lemon into wedges, and arrange on top of the paella. Sprinkle with the basil, garnish with the shrimp, and serve.

RUSSIAN FISH PIE

INGREDIENTS

Serves 4–6

1 lb. white fish fillet
⅔ cup dry white wine
salt and freshly ground black
  pepper
⅓ cup butter or margarine
1 large onion, peeled and
  finely chopped
½ cup long-grain rice
1 tbsp. freshly chopped dill
¼ lb. baby button mushrooms,
  quartered

¾ cup peeled, whole, cooked
  shrimp, thawed if frozen
3 medium eggs, hard-boiled
  and chopped
1¼ lbs. ready-made puff pastry,
  thawed if frozen
1 small egg, beaten with a
  pinch of salt
assorted lettuce, to serve

1 Preheat the oven to 400° F.
Place the fish in a shallow
skillet with the wine, ⅔ cup water,
and salt and pepper. Simmer for
8–10 minutes. Strain the fish,
setting aside the liquid, and, when
cool enough to handle, flake into
a bowl.

2 Melt the butter or margarine
in a saucepan, and cook the
onions for 2–3 minutes, then add
the rice, remaining fish liquid,
and dill. Season lightly. Cover
and simmer for 10 minutes, then
stir in the mushrooms and cook
for an additional 10 minutes or
until all the liquid is absorbed.
Mix the rice with the cooked fish,
shrimps, and eggs. Let cool.

3 Roll half the pastry out on a
lightly floured surface into a
9 x 12 in. rectangle. Place on a
dampened cookie sheet and
arrange the fish mixture on top,

leaving a ½-in. border. Brush the
border with a little water.

4 Roll out the remaining pastry
to a rectangle and use to
cover the fish. Brush the edges
lightly with a little of the beaten
egg and press to seal. Roll out the
pastry trimmings and use to
decorate the top. Chill in the
refrigerator for 30 minutes. Brush
with the beaten egg and bake for
30 minutes or until golden. Serve
immediately with lettuce.

FOOD FACT

Kulebyaka, or koulubiac, is a
classic festive dish from
Russia. It is traditionally made
with a yeast dough, but puff
pastry works well as an easy
alternative.

TUNA & MUSHROOM RAGOUT

INGREDIENTS   Serves 4

1⅓ cups mixed basmati and
   wild rice
¼ cup butter
1 tbsp. olive oil
1 large onion, peeled and
   finely chopped
1 garlic clove, peeled and
   crushed
¾ lb. baby button mushrooms,
   halved
2 tbsp. all-purpose flour
14-oz. can chopped tomatoes
1 tbsp. freshly chopped parsley

dash of Worcestershire sauce
14 oz. canned tuna in oil,
   drained
salt and freshly ground black
   pepper
4 tbsp. grated Parmesan
   cheese
1 tbsp. freshly shredded basil

TO SERVE:
green salad
garlic bread

1 Cook the basmati and wild rice in a saucepan of boiling salted water for 20 minutes, then drain and return to the pan. Stir in half of the butter, cover the pan, and let stand for 2 minutes until the butter has melted.

2 Heat the oil and the remaining butter in a skillet, and cook the onion for 1–2 minutes until soft. Add the garlic and mushrooms, and continue to cook for an additional 3 minutes.

3 Stir in the flour and cook for 1 minute, then add the tomatoes and bring the sauce to a boil. Add the parsley, Worcestershire sauce, and tuna, and simmer gently for 3 minutes. Season to taste with salt and freshly ground pepper.

4 Stir the rice well, then spoon onto four serving plates, and top with the tuna and mushroom mixture. Sprinkle with a spoonful of grated Parmesan cheese and some shredded basil, and serve immediately with a green salad and chunks of garlic bread.

TASTY TIP

Fresh basil adds a wonderful flavor and fragrance to this dish, but sometimes it can be difficult to find during the winter months. If you have problems finding it, buy canned tomatoes that have basil already added to them, or use extra freshly chopped parsley instead.

COCONUT FISH CURRY

INGREDIENTS

Serves 4

2 tbsp. sunflower oil
1 medium onion, peeled and very finely chopped
1 yellow bell pepper, deseeded and finely chopped
1 garlic clove, peeled and crushed
1 tbsp. mild curry paste
1-in. piece of ginger, peeled and grated
1 red chili, deseeded and finely chopped
14-oz. can coconut milk
1½ lb. firm white fish, skinned and cut into chunks
1⅓ cups basmati rice

1 tbsp. freshly chopped cilantro
1 tbsp. mango chutney
salt and freshly ground black pepper

TO GARNISH:
lime wedges
fresh cilantro sprigs

TO SERVE:
plain yogurt
warm naan bread

1 Put 1 tablespoon of the oil into a large skillet and cook the onion, pepper, and garlic for 5 minutes or until soft. Add the remaining oil, curry paste, ginger, and chili, and cook for an additional minute.

2 Pour in the coconut milk and bring to a boil. Reduce the heat and simmer gently for 5 minutes, stirring occasionally. Add the fish to the pan and continue to simmer gently for 5–10 minutes or until the fish is tender, but not overcooked.

3 Meanwhile, cook the rice in a saucepan of salted boiling water for 15 minutes or until tender. Drain the rice thoroughly and turn out into a serving dish.

4 Stir the chopped cilantro and chutney gently into the fish curry, and season to taste with salt and pepper. Spoon the fish curry over the cooked rice, garnish with lime wedges and cilantro sprigs, and serve immediately with spoonfuls of plain yogurt and warm naan bread.

FOOD FACT

Coconut milk is the liquid extracted from grated and pressed coconut flesh, combined with a little water.

CHUNKY FISH CASSEROLE

INGREDIENTS

Serves 6

¼ cup butter or margarine
2 large onions, peeled and
   sliced into rings
1 red bell pepper, deseeded
   and roughly chopped
1 lb. potatoes, peeled
1 lb. zucchini, trimmed and
   thickly sliced
2 tbsp. all-purpose flour
1 tbsp. paprika
2 tsp. vegetable oil

1¼ cups white wine
⅔ cup fish stock
14-oz. can chopped tomatoes
2 tbsp. freshly chopped basil
salt and freshly ground black
   pepper
1 lb. firm white fish fillet,
   skinned and cut into 1-in.
   cubes
sprigs of fresh basil, to garnish
freshly cooked rice, to serve

1 Melt the butter or margarine in a large saucepan, add the onions and pepper, and cook for 5 minutes or until softened.

2 Cut the peeled potatoes into 1-in. cubes, rinse lightly, and shake dry, then add them to the onions and pepper in the saucepan. Add the zucchini and cook, stirring frequently, for an additional 2–3 minutes.

3 Sprinkle the flour, paprika, and vegetable oil into the saucepan and cook, stirring continuously, for 1 minute. Pour in ⅔ cup of the wine, with all the stock, and the chopped tomatoes, and bring to a boil.

4 Add the basil to the casserole, season to taste with salt and pepper, and cover. Simmer for 15 minutes, then add the fish and the remaining wine, and simmer very gently for an additional 5–7

minutes, or until the fish and vegetables are just tender. Garnish with basil sprigs and serve immediately with freshly cooked rice.

FOOD FACT

Halibut has firm, milky white flesh that has an almost meaty texture, making it ideal for this casserole. They can grow to an enormous size, at times weighing in at over 450 lbs., and are fished in the deep, freezing-cold waters of the North Sea.

MEDITERRANEAN CHOWDER

INGREDIENTS

Serves 6

1 tbsp. olive oil
1 tbsp. butter
1 large onion, peeled and finely sliced
4 celery stalks, trimmed and thinly sliced
2 garlic cloves, peeled and crushed
1 bird's eye chili, deseeded and finely chopped
1 tbsp. all-purpose flour
1⅓ cups peeled and diced potatoes

2½ cups fish or vegetable stock
1½ lbs. white fish fillet, cut into 1-in. cubes
2 tbsp. freshly chopped parsley
¾ cup large peeled cooked shrimp
7-oz. can corn, drained
salt and freshly ground black pepper
⅔ cup light cream
1 tbsp. freshly cut chives
warm, crusty bread, to serve

1 Heat the oil and butter together in a large saucepan. Add the onion, celery, and garlic, and cook gently for 2–3 minutes until softened. Add the chili and stir in the flour. Cook, stirring, for an additional minute.

2 Add the potatoes to the saucepan with the stock. Bring to a boil, cover, and simmer for 10 minutes. Add the fish cubes to the saucepan with the chopped parsley, and cook for an additional 5–10 minutes or until the fish and potatoes are just tender.

3 Stir in the peeled shrimp and corn, and season to taste with salt and pepper. Pour in the cream and adjust the seasoning, if necessary.

4 Sprinkle the chives over the chowder. Ladle into six large bowls and serve immediately, with plenty of warm, crusty bread.

FOOD FACT

A chowder is a classic meal-in-a-bowl soup whose name originates from the French *chaudière* (the pot used by settlers in the southern states for making soups and stews). Chowders are usually fish based and often feature corn. This version has been thickened with potatoes.

SPANISH OMELETTE WITH SMOKED FISH

INGREDIENTS

Serves 3–4

3 tbsp. sunflower oil
2 cups peeled and diced potatoes
2 medium onions, peeled and cut into wedges
2–4 large garlic cloves, peeled and thinly sliced
1 large red bell pepper, deseeded, quartered, and thinly sliced
¼ lb. smoked haddock
salt and freshly ground black pepper
2 tbsp. butter, melted

1 tbsp. heavy cream
6 medium eggs, beaten
2 tbsp. freshly chopped Italian parsley
½ cup shredded cheddar cheese

TO SERVE:
crusty bread
tossed green salad, to serve

1 Heat the oil in a large, nonstick, heavy-based skillet, add the potatoes, onions, and garlic, and cook gently for 10–15 minutes until golden brown, then add the red bell pepper and cook for 3 minutes.

2 Meanwhile, place the fish in a shallow skillet and cover with water. Season to taste with salt and pepper, and poach gently for 10 minutes. Drain and flake the fish into a bowl, toss in the melted butter and cream, adjust the seasoning, and set aside.

3 When the vegetables are cooked, drain off any excess oil, and stir in the beaten egg with the chopped parsley. Pour the fish mixture over the top and

cook gently for 5 minutes or until the eggs become firm.

4 Sprinkle with the cheese and place the pan under a preheated broiler. Cook for 2–3 minutes until the cheese is golden and bubbling. Carefully slide the omelette onto a large plate, and serve immediately with plenty of bread and salad.

HELPFUL HINT

For best results, Spanish omelettes should be cooked slowly until set. Finishing the dish under the broiler gives it a delicious golden look.

SUPREME BAKED POTATOES

INGREDIENTS

Serves 4

4 large baking potatoes
3 tbsp. butter
1 tbsp. sunflower oil
1 carrot, peeled and chopped
2 celery stalks, trimmed and finely chopped
7-oz. can white crabmeat

2 scallions, trimmed and finely chopped
salt and freshly ground black pepper
½ cup shredded cheddar cheese
tomato salad, to serve

1 Preheat the oven to 400° F. Scrub the potatoes and prick all over with a fork or insert long metal skewers. Place the potatoes in the preheated oven for 1–1½ hours, or until soft to the touch. Allow to cool a little, then cut in half.

2 Scoop out the cooked potato flesh and turn into a bowl, leaving a reasonably firm potato shell. Mash the cooked potato flesh, then mix in the butter, and mash until the butter has melted.

3 While the potatoes are cooking, heat the oil in a frying pan, and cook the carrot and celery for 2 minutes. Cover the pan tightly and continue to cook for another 5 minute or until the vegetables are tender.

4 Add the cooked vegetables to the bowl of mashed potatoes and mix well. Fold in the crabmeat and the scallions, then season to taste with salt and pepper.

5 Pile the mixture back into the potato shells and press in firmly. Sprinkle the cheese over the top and return the potato halves to the oven for 12–15 minutes until hot, golden, and bubbling. Serve immediately with a tomato salad.

TASTY TIP

Inserting metal skewers helps potatoes to cook more evenly and quickly, as heat is transferred via the metal to the centers of the potatoes during cooking. To give the skins a crunchier finish, rub them with a little oil and lightly sprinkle with salt before baking.

SMOKED SALMON QUICHE

INGREDIENTS   Serves 6

2 cups all-purpose flour
¼ cup butter
¼ cup shortening or lard
2 tsp. sunflower oil
1⅓ cup peeled and diced
   potato
1 cup shredded Gruyère
   cheese
½ cup smoked salmon
   trimmings
5 medium eggs, beaten

1¼ cups light cream
salt and freshly ground black
   pepper
1 tbsp. freshly chopped Italian
   parsley

TO SERVE:
mixed salad
baby new potatoes

1 Preheat the oven to 400° F. Blend the flour, butter, and shortening together until the mixture resembles fine bread crumbs. Blend again, adding sufficient water to make a firm, but pliable, dough. Use the dough to line a 9-in. quiche dish or pan, then chill in the refrigerator for 30 minutes. Bake blind with baking beans for 10 minutes.

4 Beat the eggs with the cream, and season to taste with salt and pepper. Whisk in the parsley and pour the mixture carefully into the dish.

5 Reduce the oven to 350° F and bake for about 30–40 minutes or until the filling is set and golden. Serve hot or cold with a mixed salad and baby new potatoes.

2 Heat the oil in a small skillet, add the diced potatoes, and cook for 3–4 minutes until lightly browned. Reduce the heat and cook for 2–3 minutes or until tender. Let cool.

3 Sprinkle the cheese evenly over the base of the pastry case, then arrange the cooled potatoes on top. Add the smoked salmon in an even layer.

TASTY TIP

Using lard or vegetable shortening with the butter makes a delicious crust, but you can use all butter if you prefer a richer flavor and color. Do not be tempted to leave out the chilling time for the pastry case. This allows the pastry to rest and helps to minimize shrinkage during baking.

SMOKED MACKEREL & POTATO SALAD

INGREDIENTS

Serves 4

½ tsp. dry mustard powder
1 large egg yolk
salt and freshly ground black pepper
⅔ cup sunflower oil
1–2 tbsp. lemon juice
1 lb. baby new potatoes
¼ cup butter
¾ lb. smoked mackerel fillets (or salmon if preferred)

4 celery stalks, trimmed and finely chopped
3 tbsp. creamed horseradish
⅔ cup crème fraîche
1 romaine lettuce, rinsed and roughly torn
8 cherry tomatoes, halved

1 Place the mustard powder and egg yolk in a small bowl with salt and pepper, and whisk until blended. Add the oil, drop by drop, into the egg mixture, whisking continuously. When the mayonnaise is thick, add the lemon juice, drop by drop, until a smooth, glossy consistency is formed. Set aside.

2 Cook the potatoes in salted, boiling water until tender, then drain. Cool slightly, then cut into halves or quarters, depending on size. Return to the saucepan and toss in the butter.

3 Remove and discard the skin from the mackerel fillets and flake into pieces. Add to the potatoes in the saucepan, together with the celery.

4 Blend 4 tablespoons of the mayonnaise with the horseradish and crème fraîche. Season to taste with salt and pepper, then add to the potato and mackerel mixture, and stir lightly.

5 Arrange the lettuce and tomatoes on four serving plates. Pile the smoked mackerel mixture on top of the lettuce, grind over a little pepper, and serve with the remaining mayonnaise.

HELPFUL HINT

When making mayonnaise, ensure that the ingredients are at room temperature, or it may curdle. For speed, it can be made in a food processor: briefly blend the mustard, yolk, seasoning, and lemon juice, then, with the motor running, slowly add the oil.

SEAFOOD RICE RING

INGREDIENTS

Serves 4

2 cups long-grain rice
½ tsp. turmeric
5 tbsp. sunflower oil
2 tbsp. white wine vinegar
1 tsp. Dijon mustard
1 tsp. granulated sugar
1 tbsp. mild curry paste
4 shallots, peeled and finely
  chopped
salt and freshly ground black
  pepper

¾ cup peeled, cooked shrimp,
  thawed if frozen
2 tbsp. freshly chopped
  cilantro
8 fresh large tiger shrimp, with
  shells on
4 sprigs of cilantro, to garnish
lemon wedges, to serve

1 Lightly oil a 5-cup ring mold, or line the mold with plastic wrap. Cook the rice in salted, boiling water with the turmeric for 15 minutes or until tender. Drain thoroughly. Whisk 4 tablespoons of the oil with the vinegar, mustard, and sugar to form a dressing, and pour over the warm rice. Set aside.

2 Heat the remaining oil in a saucepan, add the curry paste and shallots, and cook for 5 minutes or until the shallots are just softened. Fold into the dressed rice, season to taste with salt and pepper, and mix well. Let cool completely.

3 Stir in the shrimp and the chopped cilantro, and turn into the prepared ring mold. Press the mixture down firmly with a spoon, then chill in the refrigerator for at least 1 hour.

4 Invert the ring onto a serving plate, and fill the center with the tiger shrimp. Garnish with sprigs of cilantro. Serve immediately with lemon wedges.

HELPFUL HINT

Make sure that you use ordinary long-grain rice for this seafood ring—easy-cook varieties are pretreated so that the grains remain separate and do not stick together (the opposite of what you require here). A mixture of basmati and wild rice can be used, if desired.

CHEESY VEGETABLE & SHRIMP BAKE

INGREDIENTS

Serves 4

1 cup long-grain rice
salt and freshly ground black
  pepper
1 garlic clove, peeled and
  crushed
1 large egg, beaten
3 tbsp. freshly shredded basil
4 tbsp. grated Parmesan
  cheese
¼ lb. baby asparagus spears,
  trimmed

1 cup trimmed baby carrots
1 cup trimmed fine green
  beans
¼ lb. cherry tomatoes
1 cup peeled cooked shrimp,
  thawed if frozen
¼ lb. mozzarella cheese, thinly
  sliced

1 Preheat the oven to 400° F. Cook the rice in lightly salted, boiling water for 12–15 minutes or until tender and drain. Stir in the garlic, beaten egg, shredded basil, 2 tablespoons of the Parmesan cheese, and season to taste with salt, and pepper. Press this mixture into a greased 9-in. square, ovenproof dish and set aside.

2 Bring a large saucepan of water to a boil, then drop in the asparagus, carrots, and green beans. Return to a boil and cook for 3–4 minutes. Drain and let cool.

3 Quarter or halve the cherry tomatoes, and mix them into the cooled vegetables. Spread the prepared vegetables over the rice, and top with the shrimp. Season to taste with salt and pepper.

4 Cover the shrimp with the mozzarella, and sprinkle with the remaining Parmesan cheese. Bake in the preheated oven for 20–25 minutes until piping hot and golden brown in places. Serve immediately.

FOOD FACT

Mozzarella is a fresh-tasting unripened cheese, now produced throughout the world. Traditional mozzarella is made from buffalo milk, but cow's milk is commonly used or sometimes a mixture of the two. The cheese becomes stringy when cooked, so it should be sliced as thinly as possible here.

FISH CRUMBLE

INGREDIENTS

Serves 6

1 lb. white fish fillets
1¼ cups milk
salt and freshly ground black pepper
1 tbsp. sunflower oil
⅓ cup butter or margarine
1 medium onion, peeled and finely chopped
2 leeks, trimmed and sliced
1 medium carrot, peeled and diced
2 medium potatoes, peeled and cut into small pieces
1½ cups all-purpose flour

1½ cups fish or vegetable stock
2 tbsp. whipping cream
1 tsp. freshly chopped dill

FOR THE CRUMBLE TOPPING:

⅓ cup butter or margarine
1½ cups all-purpose flour
¾ cup grated Parmesan cheese
¾ tsp. cayenne pepper

1 Preheat the oven to 400° F. Grease a pie pan. Place the fish in a saucepan with the milk, salt, and pepper. Bring to a boil, cover, and simmer for 8–10 minutes until the fish is cooked. Remove with a slotted spoon, setting aside the cooking liquid. Flake the fish into the prepared dish.

2 Heat the oil and 1 tablespoon of the butter or margarine in a small skillet and gently fry the onion, leeks, carrot, and potatoes for 1–2 minutes. Cover tightly, and cook over a gentle heat for an additional 10 minutes until softened. Spoon the vegetables over the fish.

3 Melt the remaining butter or margarine in a saucepan, add the flour, and cook for 1 minute, stirring. Whisk in the cooking liquid and the stock. Cook until thickened, then stir in the cream. Remove from the heat and stir in the dill. Pour over the fish.

4 To make the crumble, rub the butter or margarine into the flour until the mixture resembles bread crumbs, then stir in the cheese and cayenne pepper. Sprinkle over the dish, and bake in the oven for 20 minutes.

TASTY TIP

Vary the taste and texture of the topping by making it with whole-wheat flour, or by adding ¼ cup chopped nuts or jumbo rolled oats.

POTATO BOULANGÈRE WITH GROUPER

INGREDIENTS

Serves 2

2½ cups peeled and thinly
    sliced potatoes
1 large onion, peeled and
    thinly sliced
salt and freshly ground black
    pepper

1¼ cups fish or vegetable stock
⅓ cup butter or margarine
¾ lb. grouper or other white
    fish fillets
sprigs of fresh Italian parsley,
    to garnish

1 Preheat the oven to 400° F. Lightly grease a shallow baking dish with oil or butter. Layer the potato slices and onions alternately in the prepared dish, seasoning each layer with salt and pepper.

2 Pour the stock over the top, then cut ¼ cup of the butter or margarine into small pieces and dot over the top layer. Bake in the preheated oven for 50–60 minutes. Do not cover the dish at this stage.

3 Lightly rinse the fish fillets and pat dry on paper towels. Cook on a griddle, or heat the remaining butter or margarine in a skillet and pan-fry the fish fillets for 3–4 minutes per side, flesh side first. Remove from the pan with a fish slice and drain on paper towels.

4 Remove the partly cooked potato and onion mixture from the oven and place the fish on the top. Cover with aluminum foil and return to the oven for 10 minutes until heated through. Garnish with sprigs of parsley and serve immediately.

FOOD FACT

The grouper family of fish includes several Atlantic and Pacific varieties. These fish generally have firm, white flesh with a mild, slightly sweet flavor. Any other white fish can be used in this dish, if desired. Serve this dish with a selection of freshly cooked green vegetables.

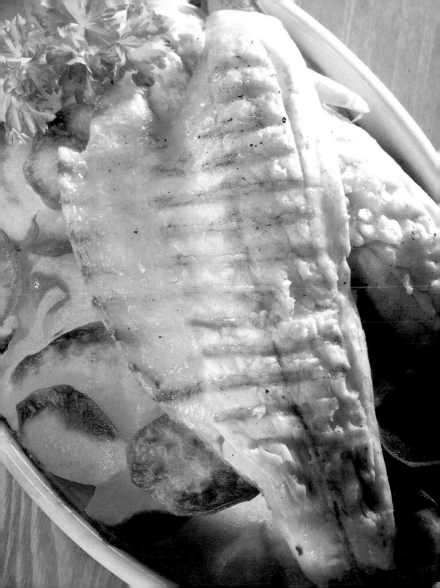

JAMAICAN JERK PORK WITH RICE & PEAS

INGREDIENTS

Serves 4

2 onions, peeled and chopped
2 garlic cloves, peeled and crushed
4 tbsp. lime juice
2 tbsp. each dark molasses, soy sauce, and chopped fresh ginger
2 jalapeño chilies, deseeded and chopped
½ tsp. ground cinnamon
¼ tsp. each ground allspice and ground nutmeg
4 pork loin chops, on the bone
1 cup dried red kidney beans, soaked overnight

FOR THE RICE:
1 tbsp. vegetable oil
1 onion, peeled and finely chopped
1 celery stalk, trimmed and finely sliced
3 garlic cloves, peeled and crushed
2 bay leaves
1⅓ cups long-grain white rice
2¼ cups chicken or ham stock
sprigs of fresh Italian parsley, to garnish

1 To make the jerk pork marinade, purée the onions, garlic, lime juice, molasses, soy sauce, ginger, chilies, cinnamon, allspice, and nutmeg together in a food processor until smooth. Put the pork chops into a plastic or nonreactive dish, and pour over the marinade, turning the chops to coat. Marinate in the refrigerator for at least 1 hour or overnight.

2 Drain the beans and place in a large saucepan with about 9 cups cold water. Bring to a boil and boil rapidly for 10 minutes. Reduce the heat, cover, and simmer gently for 1 hour until tender, adding more water if necessary. When cooked, drain well and mash roughly.

3 Heat the oil for the rice in a saucepan with a tight-fitting lid, and add the onion, celery, and garlic. Cook gently for 5 minutes until softened. Add the bay leaves, rice, and stock, and stir. Bring to a boil, cover, and cook very gently for 10 minutes. Add the beans and stir well again. Cook for an additional 5 minutes, then remove from the heat.

4 Heat a griddle until almost smoking. Remove the pork chops from the marinade, scraping off any surplus and place on the griddle. Cook for 5–8 minutes on each side, or until cooked. Garnish with parsley and serve immediately with the rice.

PORK LOIN STUFFED WITH ORANGE & HAZELNUT RICE

INGREDIENTS

Serves 4

1 tbsp. butter
1 shallot, peeled and finely chopped
⅓ cup long-grain brown rice
¾ cup vegetable stock
½ orange
⅓ cup pitted and chopped prunes
¼ cup roasted and roughly chopped hazelnuts
1 small egg, beaten

1 tbsp. freshly chopped parsley
salt and freshly ground pepper
1 lb. boneless pork tenderloin or fillet, trimmed

FOR THE RICE:
steamed zucchini
carrots

1 Preheat the oven to 375° F. Heat the butter in a small saucepan, add the shallot, and cook gently for 2–3 minutes until softened. Add the rice and stir well for 1 minute. Add the stock, stir well, and bring to a boil. Cover tightly and simmer gently for 30 minutes, until the rice is tender and all the liquid is absorbed. Let cool.

2 Grate the orange zest and set aside. Remove the white pith and chop the orange flesh finely. Mix together the orange zest and flesh, prunes, hazelnuts, cooled rice, egg, and parsley. Season to taste with salt and pepper.

3 Cut the pork in half, then, using a sharp knife, split the meat lengthwise almost in two, forming a pocket, leaving it just attached. Open out the pork and put between 2 pieces of plastic wrap. Flatten using a meat mallet until about half its original thickness. Spoon the filling into the pocket and close the fillet over. Tie along the length with kitchen string at regular intervals.

4 Put the pork fillet in a small roasting pan and cook in the top of the preheated oven for 25–30 minutes, or until the meat is just tender. Remove from the oven and allow to rest for 5 minutes. Slice into rounds and serve with steamed zucchini and carrots.

TASTY TIP

For an alternative stuffing, try adding pine nuts and thyme.

PORK GOULASH & RICE

INGREDIENTS

Serves 4

1½ lbs. boneless pork rib chops
1 tbsp. olive oil
2 onions, peeled and roughly chopped
1 red bell pepper, deseeded and thinly sliced
1 garlic clove, peeled and crushed
1 tbsp. all-purpose flour
1 rounded tbsp. paprika

14-oz. can chopped tomatoes
salt and freshly ground black pepper
1½ cups long-grain white rice
2 cups chicken stock
sprigs of fresh Italian parsley, to garnish
⅔ cup sour cream, to serve

1 Preheat the oven to 275° F. Cut the pork into large cubes, about 1½ in. square. Heat the oil in a large flameproof casserole and brown the pork in batches over a high heat, transferring the cubes to a plate as they brown.

2 Over a medium heat, add the onions and pepper, and cook for about 5 minutes, stirring regularly, until they begin to brown. Add the garlic, and return the meat to the casserole along with any juices on the plate. Sprinkle in the flour and paprika, and stir well to soak up the oil and juices.

3 Add the tomatoes and season to taste with salt and pepper. Bring slowly to a boil, cover with a tight-fitting lid, and cook in the preheated oven for 1½ hours.

4 Meanwhile, rinse the rice in several changes of water until the water remains relatively clear.

Drain well and put into a saucepan with the chicken stock or water and a little salt. Cover tightly and bring to a boil. Turn the heat down as low as possible and cook for 10 minutes, without removing the lid. After 10 minutes, remove from the heat, and leave for an additional 10 minutes, without removing the lid. Fluff with a fork.

5 When the meat is tender, lightly stir in the sour cream to create a marbled effect, or serve separately. Garnish with parsley, and serve with the rice.

FOOD FACT

Paprika is the ground red dried pepper, *Capsicum annum*; it is a vital ingredient of goulash, giving it a distinctive color and flavor.

LAMB PILAF

INGREDIENTS
Serves 4

2 tbsp. vegetable oil
¼ cup flaked or slivered
  almonds
1 medium onion, peeled and
  finely chopped
1 medium carrot, peeled and
  finely chopped
1 celery stalk, trimmed and
  finely chopped
¾ lb. lean lamb, cut into
  chunks
¼ tsp. ground cinnamon
¼ tsp. chili flakes
2 large tomatoes, skinned,
  deseeded, and chopped

grated zest of 1 orange
2 cups easy-cook brown
  basmati rice
2½ cups vegetable or lamb
  stock
2 tbsp. freshly cut chives
3 tbsp. freshly chopped
  cilantro
salt and freshly ground black
  pepper

TO GARNISH:
lemon slices
sprigs of cilantro

1 Preheat the oven to 275° F. Heat the oil in a flameproof casserole dish with a tight-fitting lid, and add the almonds. Cook, stirring often, for about 1 minute, until just browning. Add the onion, carrot, and celery, and cook gently for an additional 8–10 minutes until soft and lightly browned.

2 Increase the heat and add the lamb. Cook for an additional 5 minutes until the lamb has changed color. Add the ground cinnamon and chili flakes. Stir briefly before adding the tomatoes and orange zest.

3 Stir and add the rice, then the stock. Bring slowly to a boil and cover tightly. Transfer to the preheated oven and cook for 30–35 minutes until the rice is tender and the stock is absorbed.

4 Remove from the oven and leave for 5 minutes before stirring in the chives and cilantro. Season to taste with salt and pepper. Garnish with the lemon slices and sprigs of cilantro, and serve immediately.

TASTY TIP

The lamb in this aromatic pilaf is cooked for a relatively short time, so choose a tender cut such as leg, shoulder, or fillet. If you buy the meat on the bone, use the bones to make a stock—it will make all the difference to the final flavor of the dish.

NASI GORENG

INGREDIENTS

Serves 4

7 large shallots, peeled
1 red chili, deseeded and
  roughly chopped
2 garlic cloves, peeled and
  roughly chopped
4 tbsp. sunflower oil
2 tsp. each tomato paste and
  Indonesian sweet soy sauce
  (*katjap manis*)
1⅓ cups long-grain white rice
¾ cup trimmed green beans
3 medium eggs, beaten
pinch of sugar

salt and freshly ground black
  pepper
2½ cups shredded cooked ham
1½ cups peeled, cooked
  shrimp, thawed if frozen
6 scallions, trimmed and thinly
  sliced
1 tbsp. light soy sauce
3 tbsp. freshly chopped
  cilantro

1 Roughly chop one of the shallots and place with the red chili, garlic, 1 tablespoon of the oil, tomato paste, and sweet soy sauce in a food processor, and blend until smooth, then set aside. Boil the rice in plenty of salted water for 6–7 minutes until tender, adding the French beans after 4 minutes. Drain well and allow to cool.

2 Beat the eggs with the sugar and a little salt and pepper. Heat a little of the oil in a small nonstick skillet and add about one third of the egg mixture. Swirl to coat the base of the pan thinly, and cook for about 1 minute until golden. Flip and cook the other side briefly before removing from the pan. Roll the omelette, and slice thinly into strips. Repeat with the remaining egg to make 3 omelettes.

3 Thinly slice the remaining shallots, then heat an additional 2 tablespoons of the oil in a clean skillet. Cook the shallots for 8–10 minutes over a medium heat until golden and crisp. Drain on paper towels and set aside.

4 Add the remaining 1 tablespoon of oil to a large wok or skillet, and fry the chili paste over a medium heat for 1 minute. Add the cooked rice and beans, and stir-fry for 2 minutes. Add the ham and shrimp, and continue stir-frying for an additional 1–2 minutes. Add the omelette slices, half the fried shallots, the scallions, soy sauce, and chopped cilantro. Stir-fry for an additional minute until heated through. Spoon onto serving plates and garnish with the remaining crispy shallots. Serve immediately.

LEEK & HAM RISOTTO

INGREDIENTS   Serves 4

1 tbsp. olive oil
2 tbsp. butter
1 medium onion, peeled and
  finely chopped
4 leeks, trimmed and thinly
  sliced
1½ tbsp. freshly chopped
  thyme
2 cups Arborio rice

5½ cups vegetable or chicken
  stock, heated
½ lb. cooked ham
1¼ cups peas, thawed if frozen
½ cup grated Parmesan cheese
salt and freshly ground black
  pepper

1 Heat the oil and half the
butter together in a large
saucepan. Add the onion and
leeks, and cook over a medium
heat for 6–8 minutes, stirring
occasionally, until soft and
beginning to color. Stir in the
thyme and cook briefly.

2 Add the rice and stir well.
Continue stirring over a
medium heat for about 1 minute
until the rice is glossy. Add a
ladleful or two of the stock, and
stir well until the stock is
absorbed. Continue adding stock,
a ladleful at a time, stirring well
between additions, until about
two thirds of the stock has been
added.

3 Meanwhile, either chop or
finely shred the ham, then
add to the saucepan of rice,
together with the peas. Continue
adding ladlefuls of stock, as
described in step 2, until the rice
is tender and the ham is heated
through completely.

4 Add the remaining butter,
sprinkle with the Parmesan
cheese, and season to taste with
salt and pepper. When the butter
has melted and the cheese has
softened, stir well to incorporate.
Taste and adjust the seasoning,
then serve immediately.

HELPFUL HINT

Risotto should take about 15
minutes to cook, so taste it
after this time—the rice
should be creamy, with just a
slight bite to it. If it is not
quite ready, continue adding
the stock, a little at a time,
and cook for a few more
minutes. Stop as soon as it
tastes ready, as you do not
have to add all of the liquid.

ROAST LEG OF LAMB & BOULANGÈRE POTATOES

INGREDIENTS   Serves 6

2½ lbs. potatoes, peeled
1 large onion, peeled and
    finely sliced
salt and freshly ground black
    pepper
2 tbsp. olive oil
¼ cup butter
¼ cup lamb stock

½ cup milk
4½ lb. leg of lamb
2–3 sprigs of fresh rosemary
6 large garlic cloves, peeled
    and finely sliced
6 anchovy fillets, drained
extra sprigs of fresh rosemary,
    to garnish

1 Preheat the oven to 450° F. Finely slice the potatoes—a mandolin is the best tool for this. Layer the potatoes with the onion in a large roasting pan, seasoning each layer with salt and pepper. Drizzle about 1 tablespoon of the olive oil over the potatoes, and add the butter in small pieces. Pour in the lamb stock and milk. Set aside.

2 Make small incisions all over the lamb with the point of a small, sharp knife. Into each incision, insert a small piece of rosemary, a sliver of garlic, and a piece of anchovy fillet.

3 Drizzle the rest of the olive oil over the leg of lamb and its flavorings, and season well. Place the meat directly onto a shelf in the preheated oven. Position the roasting pan of potatoes directly underneath to catch the juices during cooking. Roast for 15 minutes per pound—about 1 hour

for a leg of this size—reducing the oven temperature to 400° F after 20 minutes.

4 When the lamb is cooked, remove from the oven and allow to rest for 10 minutes before carving. Meanwhile, increase the temperature to 450°F, and cook the potatoes for an additional 10–15 minutes to become crisp. Garnish and serve.

FOOD FACT

Leg of lamb is one of the prime roasting joints and may weigh between 4–6 lbs., so when you visit the butcher, ask for a small joint. This dish is delicious served with a selection of winter vegetables, such as freshly cooked broccoli and carrots.

LANCASHIRE HOTPOT

INGREDIENTS   Serves 4

2¼ lbs. neck slices or rib chops of lamb
2 tbsp. vegetable oil
2 large onions, peeled and sliced
2 tsp. all-purpose flour
⅔ cup vegetable or lamb stock
3¾ cups peeled and thickly sliced waxy potatoes

salt and freshly ground black pepper
1 bay leaf
2 sprigs of fresh thyme
1 tbsp. melted butter
2 tbsp. freshly chopped herbs, to garnish
freshly cooked green beans, to serve

1 Preheat the oven to 325° F. Trim any excess fat from the lamb. Heat the oil in a skillet, and brown the pieces of lamb in batches for 3–4 minutes each. Remove with a slotted spoon and set aside. Add the onions to the pan and cook for 6–8 minutes until softened and just beginning to brown, then set aside.

2 Stir in the flour and cook for a few seconds, then gradually pour in the stock, stirring well, and bring to a boil. Remove from the heat.

3 Spread the bottom of a large casserole dish with half the potato slices. Top with half the onions and season well with salt and pepper. Arrange the browned meat in a layer. Season again and add the remaining onions, bay leaf, and thyme. Pour in the remaining liquid from the onions and top with remaining potatoes so that they overlap in a single layer. Brush the potatoes with the melted butter and season again.

4 Cover and cook in the preheated oven for 2 hours. Uncover for the last 30 minutes to brown the potatoes. Garnish with chopped herbs and serve immediately with green beans.

FOOD FACT

This classic British dish is named after the old tradition of taking stews to be cooked in the local baker's. To keep the dish hot until lunchtime, the "hotpot" was wrapped in blankets. Dozens of versions claim to be authentic. Some include lamb's kidneys to enrich the gravy, but whatever the ingredients, it is important to season well and cook it slowly.

SHEPHERD'S PIE

INGREDIENTS

Serves 4

2 tbsp. vegetable or olive oil
1 onion, peeled and finely chopped
1 carrot, peeled and finely chopped
1 celery stalk, trimmed and finely chopped
1 tbsp. sprigs of fresh thyme
5 cups finely chopped leftover roast lamb
⅔ cup red wine
⅔ cup lamb or vegetable stock

2 tbsp. tomato paste
salt and freshly ground black pepper
4 cups roughly chopped potatoes
2 tbsp. butter
6 tbsp. milk
1 tbsp. freshly chopped parsley
fresh herbs, to garnish

1 Preheat the oven to 400° F about 15 minutes before cooking. Heat the oil in a large saucepan and add the onion, carrot, and celery. Cook over a medium heat for 8–10 minutes, until softened and starting to brown.

2 Add the thyme and cook briefly, then add the cooked lamb, wine, stock, and tomato paste. Season to taste with salt and pepper, and simmer gently for 25–30 minutes or until reduced and thickened. Remove from the heat to cool slightly and season again.

3 Meanwhile, boil the potatoes in plenty of salted water for 12–15 minutes until tender. Drain and return to the saucepan over a low heat to dry out. Remove from the heat and add the butter, milk, and parsley.

Mash until creamy, adding a little more milk if necessary. Season.

4 Transfer the lamb mixture to a shallow ovenproof dish. Spoon the mashed potatoes over the filling, spreading evenly to cover completely. Fork the surface, then cook in the preheated oven for 25–30 minutes until the potato topping is browned and the filling is piping hot. Garnish and serve.

TASTY TIP

A traditional Shepherd's pie is always made from cold roast lamb, but you can make it with fresh ground lamb if desired. Simply fry 1 lb. lean meat in a nonstick skillet over a high heat until well-browned, then follow the recipe.

CORNISH PASTIES

INGREDIENTS

Makes 8

FOR THE PASTRY:
3 cups self-rising flour
⅓ cup butter or margarine
⅓ cup shortening or lard
salt and freshly ground black
  pepper

FOR THE FILLING:
1¼ lbs. braising steak, chopped
  very finely
1 large onion, peeled and

finely chopped
1 large potato, peeled and diced
heaping 1 cup peeled and
  diced rutabaga
3 tbsp. Worcestershire sauce
1 small egg, beaten, to glaze

TO GARNISH:
tomato slices or wedges
sprigs of fresh parsley

1 Preheat the oven to 350° F. To make the pastry, sift the flour into a large bowl and add the fats, chopped into little pieces. Rub the fats and flour together until the mixture resembles coarse bread crumbs. Season to taste with salt and pepper, and mix again.

2 Add about 2 tablespoons of cold water, a little at a time, and mix until the crumbs come together to form a firm, but pliable, dough. Turn onto a lightly floured surface, knead until smooth, then wrap, and chill in the refrigerator.

3 To make the filling, put the braising steak in a large bowl with the onion. Add the potatoes and rutabaga to the bowl, along with the Worcestershire sauce, and salt and pepper. Mix well.

4 Divide the dough into 8 balls and roll each ball into a circle about 10 in. across. Divide the filling among the circles of pastry. Wet the edge of the pastry, then fold over the filling. Pinch the edges to seal.

5 Transfer the pasties to a lightly greased cookie sheet. Make a couple of small holes in each pasty and brush with beaten egg. Cook in the preheated oven for 15 minutes, remove, and brush again with the egg. Return to the oven for an additional 30—40 minutes until golden. Cool slightly, garnish with tomato and parsley, and serve.

TASTY TIP

The pastry for these pasties is made with self-rising flour, which gives it a softer, lighter texture.

SEARED CALF'S LIVER WITH ONIONS & MUSTARD MASH

INGREDIENTS

Serves 2

2 tbsp. olive oil
7 tbsp. butter
3 large onions, peeled and finely sliced
pinch of sugar
salt and freshly ground black pepper
1 tbsp. sprigs of fresh thyme
1 tbsp. balsamic vinegar

4 cups peeled and roughly chopped potatoes
6–8 tbsp. milk
1 tbsp. whole-grain mustard
3–4 fresh sage leaves
1¼ lbs. thinly sliced calf's liver
1 tsp. lemon juice

1 Preheat the oven to 300° F. Heat half the oil and 2 tablespoons of the butter in a flameproof casserole dish. When foaming, add the onions. Cover and cook over a low heat for 20 minutes until softened and beginning to collapse. Add the sugar, and season with salt and pepper. Stir in the thyme. Cover and transfer to the preheated oven. Cook for an additional 30–45 minutes until softened completely, but not browned. Remove from the oven and stir in the balsamic vinegar.

2 Meanwhile, cook the potatoes in salted, boiling water for 15–18 minutes until tender. Drain well, then return to the pan. Place over a low heat to dry completely, remove from the heat, and stir in 4 tablespoons of the butter, the milk, mustard, and salt and pepper to taste. Mash until creamy and keep warm.

3 Heat a large skillet and add the remaining butter and oil. When the fat is foaming, add the mustard and sage leaves, and stir for a few seconds, then add the liver. Cook over a high heat for 1–2 minutes on each side. It should remain slightly pink—do not overcook. Remove the liver from the pan. Add the lemon juice and swirl it around to deglaze the pan.

4 To serve, place a large spoonful of the mashed potatoes on each plate. Top with some of the onions, the liver, and finally the pan juices.

HELPFUL HINT

Calf's liver is mild and tender, and needs only brief cooking over a high heat to sear the outside, but keep it moist and juicy within.

RED WINE RISOTTO WITH LAMB'S KIDNEYS & CARAMELIZED SHALLOTS

INGREDIENTS   Serves 4

8 lamb's kidneys, halved and
  cores removed
⅔ cup milk
2 tbsp. olive oil
¼ cup butter
¾ lb. shallots, peeled and
  halved if large
1 onion, peeled and finely
  chopped
2 garlic cloves, peeled and
  finely chopped

2 cups Arborio rice
1 cup red wine
4¼ cups chicken or vegetable
  stock, heated
1 tbsp. sprigs of fresh thyme
½ cup grated Parmesan cheese
salt and freshly ground black
  pepper
fresh herbs, to garnish

1 Place the lamb's kidneys in a bowl and pour the milk over. Let soak for 15–20 minutes, then drain and pat dry on paper towels. Discard the milk.

2 Heat 1 tablespoon of the oil with half of the butter in a medium saucepan. Add the shallots, cover, and cook for 10 minutes over a gentle heat. Remove the lid and cook for an additional 10 minutes or until tender and golden.

3 Meanwhile, heat the remaining oil with the remaining butter in a deep-sided skillet. Add the onion and cook over a medium heat for 5–7 minutes until starting to brown. Add the garlic and cook briefly.

4 Stir in the rice and cook for a minute until glossy and well coated in oil and butter. Add half the red wine and stir until absorbed. Add a ladleful or two of the stock and stir well until the stock is absorbed. Continue adding the stock, a ladleful at a time, stirring well between additions, until all of it is added and the rice is just tender, but still firm. Remove from the heat.

5 Meanwhile, when the rice is nearly cooked, increase the heat under the shallots, and add the thyme and kidneys. Cook for 3–4 minutes, then add the wine.

6 Bring to a boil, then simmer rapidly until the red wine is reduced and syrupy. Stir the cheese into the rice with the caramelized shallots and kidneys. Season to taste, garnish and serve.

MARINATED LAMB CHOPS WITH GARLIC FRIED POTATOES

INGREDIENTS

Serves 4

4 thick lamb chops
3 tbsp. olive oil
3 cups peeled and diced
   potatoes
6 unpeeled garlic cloves
mixed salad or freshly cooked
   vegetables, to serve

FOR THE MARINADE:
1 small bunch of fresh thyme,
   leaves removed
1 tbsp. freshly chopped
   rosemary
1 tsp. salt
2 garlic cloves, peeled and
   crushed
zest and juice of 1 lemon
2 tbsp. olive oil

1 Trim the chops of any excess fat, wipe with a clean, damp cloth, and set aside. To make the marinade, pound the thyme leaves and rosemary with the salt until pulpy. Add the garlic and continue pounding until crushed. Stir in the lemon zest and juice, and the olive oil.

2 Pour the marinade over the lamb chops, turning them until they are well coated. Cover lightly and marinate in the refrigerator for about 1 hour.

3 Heat the oil in a large nonstick skillet. Add the potatoes and garlic, and cook over a low heat for about 20 minutes, stirring occasionally. Increase the heat and cook for an additional 10–15 minutes until golden. Drain on paper towels, and add salt to taste. Keep the mixture warm.

4 Heat a griddle until almost smoking. Add the lamb chops and cook for 3–4 minutes on each side until golden, but still pink in the middle. Serve with the potatoes and either a mixed salad or freshly cooked vegetables.

TASTY TIP

Marinating the chops not only adds flavor, but it also tenderizes them, due to the acids in the lemon juice. If time allows, marinate the chops for slightly longer. Try other citrus juices in this recipe. Both orange and lime juice would be delicious.

PORK SAUSAGES WITH ONION GRAVY & BEST-EVER MASH

INGREDIENTS

Serves 4

¼ cup butter
1 tbsp. olive oil
2 large onions, peeled and thinly sliced
pinch of sugar
1 tbsp. freshly chopped thyme
1 tbsp. all-purpose flour
½ cup Madeira
¾ cup vegetable stock
8–12 good-quality pork sausages, depending on size

FOR THE MASHED POTATOES:
2 lbs. floury potatoes, peeled
⅓ cup butter
4 tbsp. crème fraîche or sour cream
salt and freshly ground black pepper

1 Melt the butter with the oil and add the onions. Cover and cook gently for about 20 minutes until the onions have collapsed. Add the sugar and stir well. Uncover and continue to cook, stirring often, until the onions are very soft and golden. Add the thyme, stir well, then add the flour while stirring. Gradually add the Madeira and the stock. Bring to a boil and simmer gently for 10 minutes.

2 Meanwhile, put the sausages in a large skillet, and cook over a medium heat for about 15–20 minutes, turning often, until golden brown and slightly sticky all over.

3 For the mashed potatoes, boil the potatoes in plenty of lightly salted water for 15–18 minutes until tender. Drain well and return to the saucepan. Put over a low heat to allow to dry. Remove from the heat and add the butter, crème fraîche or sour cream, and salt and pepper. Mash thoroughly. Serve the mashed potatoes topped with the sausages and onion gravy.

HELPFUL HINT

Sausages should always be cooked slowly over a gentle heat to ensure that they are cooked through and evenly browned on the outside. The skins should be slightly crisp and the insides firm. If the sausages are pink on the inside, do not eat them; cook until they are an even color. Serve hot.

CHILI CON CARNE WITH CRISPY-SKINNED POTATOES

INGREDIENTS

Serves 4

2 tbsp. vegetable oil, plus extra for brushing
1 large onion, peeled and finely chopped
1 garlic clove, peeled and finely chopped
1 red chili, deseeded and finely chopped
1 lb. chuck steak, finely chopped, or lean ground beef
1 tbsp. chili powder

14-oz. can chopped tomatoes
2 tbsp. tomato paste
14-oz. can red kidney beans, drained and rinsed
4 large baking potatoes
coarse salt and freshly ground black pepper

TO SERVE:
guacamole
sour cream

1 Preheat the oven to 300° F. Heat the oil in a large flameproof casserole and add the onion. Cook gently for 10 minutes until soft and lightly browned. Add the garlic and chili, and cook briefly. Increase the heat. Add the steak or ground beef and cook for an additional 10 minutes, stirring occasionally, until browned.

4 To serve, remove the chili from the oven and stir in the kidney beans. Return to the oven for an additional 15 minutes. Cut a cross in each potato, then squeeze to open slightly, and season to taste with salt and pepper. Serve with the chili, guacamole, and sour cream.

2 Add the chili powder and stir well. Cook for about 2 minutes, then add the chopped tomatoes and tomato paste. Bring slowly to a boil. Cover and cook in the preheated oven for 1½ hours.

3 Meanwhile, brush a little vegetable oil all over the potatoes and rub on some coarse salt. Put the potatoes in the oven alongside the chili.

TASTY TIP

Make your own guacamole by peeling, pitting, and mashing 1 large avocado in a bowl with 2 tablespoons each of lemon juice and crème fraîche, ¼ teaspoon hot sauce, 1 crushed garlic clove, and salt and pepper. Push the avocado pit into the dip to keep it from discoloring.

ROAST CURED PORK LOIN WITH BAKED, SLICED POTATOES

INGREDIENTS
Serves 4

2 tbsp. whole-grain mustard
2 tbsp. honey
1 tsp. coarsely crushed black pepper
2 lb. piece of smoked, cured pork loin
5 cups peeled and thinly sliced potatoes

⅓ cup butter, diced
1 large onion, peeled and finely chopped
¼ cup all-purpose flour
salt and freshly ground black pepper
2½ cups milk
fresh green salad, to serve

1 Preheat the oven to 375° F. Mix together the mustard, honey, and black pepper. Spread evenly over the pork loin. Place in the center of a large square of aluminum foil and wrap loosely. Cook in the preheated oven for 15 minutes per pound, plus an additional 15 minutes (total cooking time 45 minutes). Unwrap the joint for the last 30 minutes of cooking time.

2 Meanwhile, layer one third of the potatoes, one third of the butter, half the onions, and half the flour in a large gratin dish. Add half the remaining potatoes and butter, and the remaining onions and flour. Finally, cover with the remaining potatoes. Season well with salt and pepper between layers. Pour in the milk, and dot with the remaining butter. Cover loosely with foil. Put in the oven below the pork. Cook for 1½ hours.

3 Uncover the potatoes and cook for an additional 20 minutes until tender and golden. Remove the pork loin from the oven and let rest for 10 minutes before carving thinly. Serve with the potatoes and a fresh green salad.

HELPFUL HINT

Delicately flavored, smoked, cured pork loin can be found at specialty meat markets. If you are unable to find it, a regular piece of pork loin can be used instead. It usually has a good layer of rind, so remove it for this recipe. Sprinkle with a little salt, and cook separately under the broiler.

GRILLED STEAKS WITH SAFFRON POTATOES & ROAST TOMATOES

INGREDIENTS

Serves 4

1½ lbs. halved new potatoes
few strands of saffron
1¼ cups vegetable or beef stock
1 small onion, peeled and finely chopped
⅓ cup butter
salt and freshly ground black pepper
2 tsp. balsamic vinegar

2 tbsp. olive oil
1 tsp. granulated sugar
8 plum tomatoes, halved
4 boneless steaks, each weighing ½ lb.
2 tbsp. freshly chopped parsley

1 Cook the potatoes in salted, boiling water for 8 minutes and drain well. Return the potatoes to the saucepan, along with the saffron, stock, onion, and one third of the butter. Season to taste with salt and pepper, and simmer uncovered for 10 minutes until the potatoes are tender.

2 Meanwhile, turn on the broiler. Mix together the vinegar, olive oil, sugar, and seasoning. Arrange the tomatoes cut-side up in a broiler pan lined with aluminum foil, and drizzle over the dressing. Broil for 12–15 minutes, basting occasionally, until tender.

3 Melt the remaining butter in a large skillet. Add the steaks and cook for 4–8 minutes, to taste.

4 Arrange the potatoes and tomatoes on the middles of four serving plates. Top with the steaks, along with any pan juices. Sprinkle over the parsley and serve immediately.

HELPFUL HINT

You can tell how well a steak is cooked by lightly pressing with your fingertips—the less the resistance, the rarer the meat. Timing depends on the thickness rather than the weight of the steak. As a rough guide, a ¾-in. thick steak will take about 2 minutes on each side for rare, 3–4 minutes on each side for medium, and 6–7 minutes on each side for well-done.

OSSO BUCO WITH SAFFRON RISOTTO

INGREDIENTS

Serves 4

½ cup butter
2 tbsp. olive oil
4 large pieces of veal shank
2 onions, peeled and roughly chopped
2 garlic cloves, peeled and finely chopped
1¼ cups white wine
5 plum tomatoes, peeled and chopped
1 tbsp. tomato paste

salt and freshly ground black pepper
2 tbsp. freshly chopped parsley
grated zest of 1 small lemon
few strands of saffron, crushed
2 cups Arborio rice
5½ cups chicken stock, heated
½ cup grated Parmesan cheese

1 Heat half the butter with half the oil in a large saucepan, and add the pieces of veal. Brown lightly on both sides, then transfer to a plate. Add half the onion and the garlic, and cook gently for about 10 minutes until the onion is just golden.

2 Return the veal to the pan, and add the white wine, tomatoes, and tomato paste. Season lightly with salt and pepper, cover, and bring to a gentle simmer. Cook very gently for 1 hour. Uncover and cook for an additional 30 minutes until the meat is cooked and the sauce is reduced and thickened. Season to taste. Mix together the remaining garlic, parsley, and lemon zest, and set aside.

3 Meanwhile, slowly melt the remaining butter and oil in a large deep-sided skillet. Add the remaining onion and cook gently for 5–7 minutes until just brown. Add the saffron and stir for a few seconds, then add the rice. Cook for an additional minute until the rice is well coated in oil and butter.

4 Begin adding the stock a ladleful at a time, stirring well after each addition and waiting until it is absorbed before adding the next. Continue in this way until all the stock is used. Remove from the heat and stir in the grated Parmesan cheese and seasoning.

5 Spoon a little of the saffron risotto onto each of four serving plates. Top with the osso buco and sauce, and sprinkle with the garlic and parsley mixture. Serve immediately.

SPANISH-STYLE PORK STEW WITH SAFFRON RICE

INGREDIENTS

Serves 4

2 tbsp. olive oil
2 lbs. lean boneless pork, diced
1 large onion, peeled and sliced
2 garlic cloves, peeled and finely chopped
1 tbsp. all-purpose flour
1 lb. plum tomatoes, peeled and chopped
¾ cup red wine
1 tbsp. freshly chopped basil
1 green bell pepper, deseeded and sliced
½ cup pimiento-stuffed olives, cut in half crosswise

salt and freshly ground black pepper
fresh basil leaves, to garnish

FOR THE SAFFRON RICE:
1 tbsp. olive oil
2 tbsp. butter
1 small onion, peeled and finely chopped
few strands of saffron, crushed
1½ cups long-grain white rice
2½ cups chicken stock

1 Preheat the oven to 300° F. Heat the oil in a large flameproof casserole and add the pork in batches. Fry over a high heat until browned. Transfer each batch to a plate until all the pork is browned.

2 Reduce the heat and add the onion to the casserole. Cook for an additional 5 minutes until soft and starting to brown. Add the garlic. Stir briefly before returning the pork to the casserole. Add the flour and stir.

3 Add the tomatoes. Gradually stir in the red wine and add the basil. Bring to simmering point and cover. Transfer the casserole

to the lower part of the preheated oven and cook for 1½ hours. Stir in the green pepper and olives, and cook for 30 minutes. Season to taste with salt and pepper.

4 To make the saffron rice, heat the oil with the butter in a saucepan. Add the onion and cook for 5 minutes over a medium heat until softened. Add the saffron and rice, and stir well. Add the stock, bring to a boil, cover, and reduce the heat as much as possible. Cook for 15 minutes, covered, until the rice is tender and the stock is absorbed. Adjust the seasoning and serve with the stew, garnished with fresh basil.

BEEF TERIYAKI WITH GREEN & BLACK RICE

INGREDIENTS   Serves 4

3 tbsp. sake (Japanese rice
  wine)
3 tbsp. dry sherry
3 tbsp. dark soy sauce
1½ tbsp. brown sugar
4 trimmed steaks, each
  weighing 6 oz.
2 cups mixed long-grain and
  wild rice

1-in. piece ginger
½ lb. snow peas
salt
6 scallions, trimmed and cut
  into fine strips

1 In a small saucepan, gently heat the sake, dry sherry, dark soy sauce, and sugar until the sugar has dissolved. Increase the heat and bring to a boil. Remove from the heat and leave until cold. Lightly wipe the steaks, place in a shallow dish, and pour the sake mixture over. Cover loosely and marinate in the refrigerator for at least 1 hour, spooning the marinade over the steaks occasionally.

2 Cook the rice with the ginger, according to the package's instructions. Drain well, then remove and discard the piece of ginger.

3 Slice the snow peas thinly lengthwise into fine shreds. Plunge into a saucepan of salted, boiling water, return the water to a boil, and drain immediately. Stir the drained snow peas and scallions into the hot rice.

4 Meanwhile, heat a griddle until almost smoking. Remove the steaks from the marinade and cook on the hot griddle for 3–4 minutes each side, depending on the thickness.

5 Place the remaining marinade in a saucepan and bring to a boil. Simmer rapidly for 2 minutes and remove from the heat. When the steaks are cooked as desired, allow to rest for 2–3 minutes, then slice thinly and serve with the rice and the hot marinade.

FOOD FACT

Before 1867, meat was prohibited in Japan to try to prevent aggression. The Japanese still eat a relatively small amount of meat and tend to use quick-cook tender cuts in dishes.

CHICKEN WITH ROASTED FENNEL & CITRUS RICE

INGREDIENTS   Serves 4

2 tsp. fennel seeds
1 tbsp. freshly chopped
   oregano
1 garlic clove, peeled and
   crushed
salt and freshly ground
   black pepper
4 chicken quarters, about ½ lb.
   each
½ lemon, finely sliced
1 fennel bulb, trimmed
2 tsp. olive oil
4 plum tomatoes
2 tbsp. pitted green olives

TO GARNISH:
fennel leaves
orange slices

FOR THE CITRUS RICE:
1 cup long-grain rice
2 tsp. finely grated lemon rind
1 tbsp. lemon juice
⅔ cup orange juice
2 cups boiling chicken or
   vegetable stock

1 Preheat the oven to 400° F. Lightly crush the fennel seeds and mix with the oregano, garlic, salt, and pepper. Place between the skin and flesh of the chicken breasts, being careful not to tear the skin. Arrange the lemon slices on top of the chicken.

2 Cut the fennel into 8 wedges. Place in a roasting pan with the chicken. Brush the fennel with the oil. Cook the chicken and fennel on the top shelf of the preheated oven for 10 minutes.

3 Meanwhile, put the rice in a large ovenproof dish. Stir in the lemon rind and juice, orange juice, and stock. Cover with a tight-fitting lid and put on the center shelf of the oven.

4 Reduce the oven temperature to 350° F. Cook the chicken for an additional 40 minutes, turning the fennel wedges and lemon slices once. Seed and chop the tomatoes. Add to the tray and cook for 5–10 minutes. Remove from the oven.

5 When cooled slightly, remove the chicken skin and discard. Fluff the rice, then sprinkle with olives. Garnish with fennel leaves and orange slices, and serve.

HELPFUL HINT

Check that the chicken is cooked thoroughly by piercing the thickest part with a skewer. The juices should run clear.

BRAISED CHICKEN IN BEER

INGREDIENTS   Serves 4

4 chicken joints, skinned
⅔ cup pitted dried prunes
2 bay leaves
12 shallots
2 tsp. olive oil
1¾ cups small button
   mushrooms, wiped
1 tsp. dark brown sugar
½ tsp. mustard
2 tsp. tomato paste
⅔ cup light beer

⅔ cup chicken stock
salt and freshly ground
   black pepper
2 tsp. cornstarch
2 tsp. lemon juice
2 tbsp. freshly chopped parsley
Italian parsley, to garnish

TO SERVE:
mashed potatoes
seasonal green vegetables

1 Preheat the oven to 325° F. Cut each chicken joint in half and put in an ovenproof casserole dish with the prunes and bay leaves.

2 To peel the shallots, put in a small bowl and cover with boiling water.

3 After 2 minutes, drain the shallots and rinse under cold water until cool enough to handle. The skins should then peel away easily from the shallots.

4 Heat the oil in a large nonstick skillet. Add the shallots and cook gently for about 5 minutes until beginning to brown.

5 Add the mushrooms to the skillet and cook for an additional 3–4 minutes until both the mushrooms and onions are softened.

6 Sprinkle the sugar over the shallots and mushrooms, then add the mustard, tomato paste, beer, and chicken stock. Season to taste with salt and pepper, and bring to a boil, stirring to combine. Carefully pour over the chicken.

7 Cover the casserole and cook in the preheated oven for 1 hour. Blend the cornstarch with the lemon juice and 1 tablespoon of cold water, and stir into the chicken casserole.

8 Return to the oven for an additional 10 minutes or until the chicken is cooked and the vegetables are tender.

9 Remove the bay leaves and stir in the chopped parsley. Garnish the chicken with the Italian parsley. Serve with the mashed potatoes and fresh green vegetables.

CHICKEN BAKED IN A SALT CRUST

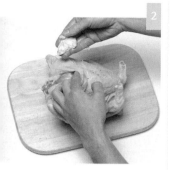

INGREDIENTS

Serves 4

4-lb. oven-ready chicken
salt and freshly ground
 black pepper
1 medium onion, peeled
sprig of fresh rosemary
sprig of fresh thyme
1 bay leaf
1 tbsp. butter, softened
1 garlic clove, peeled and
 crushed
pinch of paprika
2 tsp. finely grated lemon rind

TO GARNISH:
fresh herbs
lemon slices

FOR THE SALT CRUST:
8 cups all-purpose flour
3⅔ cups fine cooking salt
3⅔ cups coarse sea salt
2 tbsp. oil

1 Preheat the oven to 325° F. Remove the giblets if necessary, and rinse the chicken with cold water. Sprinkle the inside with salt and pepper. Put the onion inside, along with the rosemary, thyme, and bay leaf.

2 Mix the butter, garlic, paprika, and lemon rind together. Starting at the neck end, gently ease the skin from the chicken and push the mixture under.

3 To make the salt crust, put the flour and salts in a large bowl, and stir together. Make a well in the center. Pour in 2 cups of cold water and the oil. Mix to a stiff dough, then knead on a lightly floured surface for 2–3 minutes. Roll out the dough to a 20-inch circle. Place the chicken breast-side down in

the center. Lightly brush the edges with water, then fold over to enclose. Pinch the joints together to seal.

4 Put the chicken joint-side down in a roasting pan, and cook in the preheated oven for 2¾ hours. Remove from the oven and let stand for 20 minutes.

5 Break open the hard crust and remove the chicken. Discard the crust. Remove the skin from the chicken, and garnish with the fresh herbs and lemon slices. Serve the chicken immediately.

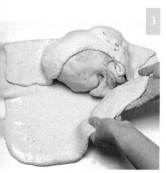

HELPFUL HINT

It is best to avoid eating the skin from the chicken. It is high in fat and absorbs a lot of salt from the crust.

SPICY CHICKEN SKEWERS WITH MANGO TABBOULEH

INGREDIENTS

Serves 4

¾ lb. chicken breast fillet
1 cup low-fat plain yogurt
1 garlic clove, peeled and
  crushed
1 small red chili, seeded and
  finely chopped
½ tsp. turmeric
2 tsp. finely grated lemon rind
2 tsp. lemon juice
sprigs of fresh mint, to garnish

FOR THE TABBOULEH:
1 cup bulgur
1 tsp. olive oil
1 tbsp. lemon juice
½ red onion, finely chopped
1 ripe mango, halved, pitted,
  peeled, and chopped
¼ cucumber, finely diced
2 tbsp. freshly chopped parsley
2 tbsp. freshly torn mint
salt and finely ground
  black pepper

1 If using wooden skewers, presoak them in cold water for 30 minutes. This keeps them from burning during broiling.

2 Cut the chicken into 2 x ½ inch strips, and place in a shallow dish.

3 Mix together the yogurt, garlic, chili, turmeric, lemon rind, and juice. Pour over the chicken and toss to coat. Cover and leave to marinate in the refrigerator for up to 8 hours.

4 To make the tabbouleh, put the bulgur in a bowl. Pour in enough boiling water to cover. Put a plate over the bowl. Allow to soak for 20 minutes.

5 Whisk together the oil and lemon juice in a bowl. Add

the red onion and leave to marinate for 10 minutes.

6 Drain the bulgur and squeeze out any excess moisture in a clean dishtowel. Add to the red onion with the mango, cucumber, herbs, and season to taste with salt and pepper. Toss together to mix thoroughly.

7 Thread the chicken strips onto 8 wooden or metal skewers. Cook under a hot broiler for 8 minutes. Turn and brush with the marinade until the chicken is lightly browned and cooked through.

8 Spoon the tabbouleh onto individual plates. Arrange the chicken skewers on top, and garnish with the sprigs of mint. Serve warm or cold.

PAN-COOKED CHICKEN WITH THAI SPICES

INGREDIENTS

Serves 4

4 kaffir lime leaves
2-in. piece fresh ginger, peeled and chopped
1¼ cups chicken stock, boiling
4 ½-lb. chicken breasts
2 tsp. peanut oil
5 tbsp. coconut milk
1 tbsp. fish sauce
2 red chilies, seeded and finely chopped
1 cup Thai jasmine rice
1 tbsp. lime juice

3 tbsp. freshly chopped cilantro
salt and freshly ground black pepper

TO GARNISH:
lime wedges
freshly chopped cilantro

1 Lightly bruise the kaffir lime leaves and put in a bowl with the chopped ginger. Pour in the chicken stock, cover, and allow to infuse for 30 minutes.

2 Meanwhile, cut each chicken breast into 2 pieces. Heat the oil in a large nonstick skillet or flameproof casserole dish, and brown the chicken pieces for 2–3 minutes on each side.

3 Strain the infused chicken stock into the skillet. Half-cover the skillet with a lid, and gently simmer for 10 minutes.

4 Stir in the coconut milk, fish sauce, and chopped chilies. Simmer uncovered for 5–6 minutes or until the chicken is tender and cooked through, and the sauce has reduced slightly.

5 Meanwhile, cook the rice in boiling, salted water according to the package instructions. Drain the rice thoroughly.

6 Stir the lime juice and chopped cilantro into the sauce. Season to taste with salt and pepper. Serve the dish on a bed of rice. Garnish with wedges of lime and freshly chopped cilantro and serve immediately.

FOOD FACT

Fresh kaffir lime leaves can be found in Asian food stores. Most supermarkets now stock dried kaffir lime leaves. If using dried, crumble lightly and use as above.

SAUVIGNON CHICKEN & MUSHROOM PHYLLO PIE

INGREDIENTS

Serves 4

1 onion, peeled and chopped
1 leek, trimmed and chopped
1 cup chicken stock
1 ½ lbs. chicken breast
⅔ cup dry white wine
1 bay leaf
2½ cups button mushrooms
2 tbsp. all-purpose flour
1 tbsp. freshly chopped tarragon

salt and freshly ground black pepper
sprig of fresh parsley, to garnish
seasonal vegetables, to serve

TOPPING:

5–6 sheets phyllo pastry
1 tbsp. corn oil
1 tsp. sesame seeds

1 Preheat the oven to 375° F. Put the chopped onion and leek in a heavy saucepan with ½ cup of the stock.

2 Bring to a boil, cover, and simmer for 5 minutes, then uncover and cook until all the stock has evaporated, and the vegetables are tender.

3 Cut the chicken into bite-size cubes. Add to the saucepan with the remaining stock, wine, and bay leaf. Cover and gently simmer for about 5 minutes. Add the baby button mushrooms, and simmer for an additional 5 minutes.

4 Blend the flour with 3 tablespoons of cold water. Stir into the saucepan and cook, stirring all the time, until the sauce has thickened.

5 Stir the tarragon into the sauce, and season to taste with salt and pepper.

6 Spoon the mixture into a large, deep pie plate, discarding the bay leaf.

7 Brush a sheet of phyllo pastry with a little of the oil.

8 Crumple the pastry slightly. Arrange on top of the filling. Repeat with the remaining phyllo sheets and oil, then sprinkle the top of the pie with the sesame seeds.

9 Cook the pie on the center shelf of the preheated oven for 20 minutes until the phyllo pastry topping is golden and crisp. Garnish with a sprig of parsley. Serve the pie immediately with the seasonal vegetables.

CHILI ROAST CHICKEN

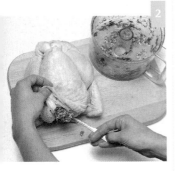

INGREDIENTS

Serves 4

3 medium-hot, fresh red
 chilies, seeded
½ tsp. turmeric
1 tsp. cumin seeds
1 tsp. coriander seeds
2 garlic cloves, peeled and
 crushed
1-in. piece fresh ginger, peeled
 and chopped
1 tbsp. lemon juice
1 tbsp. olive oil
2 tbsp. coarsely chopped
 fresh cilantro

½ tsp. salt
freshly ground black pepper
3 lbs. oven-ready chicken
1 tbsp. unsalted butter, melted
1¼ lbs. butternut squash
sprigs of fresh parsley and
 cilantro, to garnish

TO SERVE:
4 baked potatoes
seasonal green vegetables

1 Preheat the oven to 375° F. Coarsely chop the chilies, and put in a food processor with the turmeric, cumin seeds, coriander seeds, garlic, ginger, lemon juice, olive oil, cilantro, salt, pepper, and 2 tablespoons of cold water. Blend to a paste, leaving the ingredients still slightly chunky.

2 Starting at the neck end of the chicken, gently ease up the skin to loosen it from the breast. Set aside 3 tablespoons of the paste. Push the remaining paste over the chicken breast, spreading it evenly under the skin.

3 Put the chicken in a large roasting pan. Mix the chili paste with the melted butter. Use 1 tablespoon to brush evenly over the chicken. Roast in the oven for 20 minutes.

4 Meanwhile, halve, peel, and scoop out the seeds from the butternut squash. Cut into large chunks, and mix in the remaining chili paste and butter mixture.

5 Arrange the butternut squash around the chicken. Roast for an additional hour, basting with the cooking juices about every 20 minutes until the chicken is fully cooked and the squash is tender. Garnish with parsley and cilantro. Serve hot with baked potatoes and green vegetables.

HELPFUL HINT

Chilies vary considerably in heat. A good guide is the smaller the chili, the hotter it is. Red chilies are sweeter than green ones.

AROMATIC CHICKEN CURRY

INGREDIENTS
Serves 4

⅔ cup red lentils
2 tsp. ground coriander
½ tsp. cumin seeds
2 tsp. mild curry paste
1 bay leaf
small strip of lemon rind
2½ cups chicken or
  vegetable stock
8 chicken thighs, skinned
¾ cup spinach leaves, rinsed
  and shredded

1 tbsp. freshly chopped
  cilantro
2 tsp. lemon juice
salt and freshly ground
  black pepper

TO SERVE:
freshly cooked rice
low-fat plain yogurt

1 Put the lentils in a sieve and rinse thoroughly under cold running water.

2 Fry the ground coriander and cumin seeds in a large saucepan over a low heat for about 30 seconds. Stir in the curry paste.

3 Add the lentils to the saucepan with the bay leaf and lemon rind, then pour in the stock.

4 Stir, then slowly bring to a boil. Turn down the heat, half-cover the saucepan with a lid, and simmer gently for 5 minutes, stirring occasionally.

5 Secure the chicken thighs with toothpicks to hold their shape. Place in the saucepan and half-cover. Simmer for 15 minutes.

6 Stir in the shredded spinach, and cook for an additional

25 minutes or until the chicken is very tender, and the sauce is thick.

7 Remove the bay leaf and lemon rind. Stir in the cilantro and lemon juice, then season to taste with salt and pepper. Serve immediately with the rice and some plain yogurt.

HELPFUL HINT

Frying spices really releases the flavor of the spices and is a technique that can be used in many dishes. It is a particularly good way to flavor lean meat or fish. Try mixing fried spices with a little water or oil to make a paste. Spread the paste on meat or fish before cooking to make a spicy crust.

CHEESY CHICKEN BURGERS

INGREDIENTS

Serves 6

1 tbsp. corn oil
1 small onion, peeled and finely chopped
1 garlic clove, peeled and crushed
½ red bell pepper, seeded and finely chopped
1 lb. fresh ground chicken
2 tbsp. nonfat plain yogurt
½ cup whole-wheat bread crumbs
1 tbsp. freshly chopped herbs, such as parsley or tarragon
½ cup cheddar cheese, crumbled
salt and freshly ground black pepper

FOR THE CORN AND CARROT RELISH:
7-oz. can corn, drained
1 carrot, peeled, and grated
½ green chili, seeded and finely chopped
2 tsp. cider vinegar
2 tsp. light brown sugar

TO SERVE:
whole-wheat rolls
lettuce
sliced tomatoes
mixed lettuce leaves

1 Preheat the broiler. Heat the oil in a skillet and gently cook the onion and garlic for 5 minutes. Add the red bell pepper and cook for 5 minutes. Transfer into a bowl and set aside.

2 Add the chicken, yogurt, bread crumbs, herbs, and cheese, and season to taste with salt and pepper. Mix well.

3 Divide and shape the mixture into 6 burgers. Cover and chill in the refrigerator for at least 20 minutes.

4 To make the relish, put all the ingredients in a small saucepan with 1 tablespoon of water, and heat gently, stirring occasionally, until all the sugar has dissolved.

5 Cover and cook over a low heat for 2 minutes, then uncover and cook for an additional minute or until the relish is thick.

6 Place the burgers on a lightly greased broiler pan, and broil under a medium heat for 8–10 minutes on each side or until browned and cooked through.

7 Warm the rolls, if desired, then split in half and fill with the burgers, lettuce, sliced tomatoes, and relish.

CHICKEN CACCIATORE

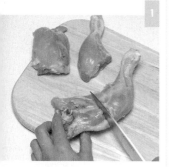

INGREDIENTS

Serves 4

4 chicken legs
1 tbsp. olive oil
1 red onion, peeled and cut
  into very thin wedges
1 garlic clove, peeled and
  crushed
sprig of fresh thyme
sprig of fresh rosemary
⅔ cup dry white wine
1 cup chicken stock

14-oz. can chopped tomatoes
¼ cup pitted ripe olives,
2 tbsp. capers, drained
salt and freshly ground
  black pepper
freshly cooked fettuccine,
  linguine, or pasta shells

1 Skin the chicken pieces and cut each one into 2 pieces to make 4 thighs and 4 drumsticks.

2 Heat 2 teaspoons of the oil in a flameproof casserole dish and cook the chicken for 2–3 minutes on each side until lightly browned. Remove the chicken from the dish and set aside.

3 Add the remaining 1 teaspoon of oil to the juices in the dish.

4 Add the red onion and gently cook for 5 minutes, stirring occasionally.

5 Add the garlic and cook for an additional 5 minutes until soft and beginning to brown. Return the chicken to the casserole dish.

6 Add the herbs, then pour in the wine, and let it boil for 1–2 minutes.

7 Add the stock and tomatoes, cover, and gently simmer for 15 minutes.

8 Stir in the olives and capers. Cook uncovered for an additional 5 minutes or until the chicken is cooked and the sauce is thickened. Remove the herbs and season to taste with salt and pepper.

9 Place the chicken on a bed of pasta, allowing 1 thigh and 1 drumstick per person. Spoon the sauce on top, and serve.

HELPFUL HINT

When watching your saturated fat intake, it is essential to remove the skin from the chicken before eating. Any fat is deposited directly underneath the skin.

CHICKEN & SUMMER VEGETABLE RISOTTO

INGREDIENTS

Serves 4

4 cups chicken or vegetable
  stock
1¼ cups baby asparagus
  spears
¾ cup fine green beans
1 tbsp. butter
1 small onion, peeled and
  finely chopped
⅔ cup dry white wine

1¼ cups risotto rice
pinch of saffron strands
¾ cup frozen peas, defrosted
2½ cups cooked chicken,
  skinned and diced
1-2 tbsp. lemon juice
salt and freshly ground
  black pepper
¼ cup Parmesan cheese, shaved

1 Bring the stock to a boil in a large saucepan. Trim the asparagus and cut into 1½-inch lengths.

2 Blanch the asparagus in the stock for 1–2 minutes or until tender, then remove with a slotted spoon, and set aside.

3 Halve the fine green beans and cook in the boiling stock for 4 minutes. Remove and set aside. Turn down the heat and keep the stock barely simmering.

4 Melt the butter in a heavy saucepan. Add the onion and cook gently for about 5 minutes.

5 Pour the wine into the saucepan and boil rapidly until the liquid has almost reduced. Add the rice and cook, stirring, for 1 minute until the grains are coated and look translucent.

6 Add the saffron and a ladle of the stock. Simmer, stirring all the time, until the stock has been absorbed. Continue adding the stock, a ladle at a time, until it is all absorbed.

7 After 15 minutes, the risotto should be creamy with a slight bite to it. If not, add a little more stock and cook for a few more minutes or until it is of the correct texture and consistency.

8 Add the peas, the remaining vegetables, chicken, and lemon juice. Season to taste with salt and pepper, and cook for 3-4 minutes or until the chicken is heated thoroughly and piping hot.

9 Spoon the risotto onto warmed serving plates. Sprinkle each portion with a few shavings of Parmesan cheese and serve immediately.

MEXICAN CHICKEN

INGREDIENTS

Serves 4

3 lbs. oven-ready chicken, jointed
3 tbsp. all-purpose flour
½ tsp. paprika
salt and freshly ground black pepper
2 tsp. corn oil
1 small onion, peeled and chopped
1 red chili, seeded and finely chopped
½ tsp. ground cumin
½ tsp. dried oregano
1¼ cups chicken or vegetable stock

1 green bell pepper, seeded and sliced
2 tsp. cocoa
1 tbsp. lime juice
2 tsp. honey
3 tbsp. nonfat plain yogurt

TO GARNISH:
sliced limes
red chili slices
sprig of fresh oregano

TO SERVE:
freshly cooked rice
fresh green lettuce leaves

1 Using a knife, remove the skin from the chicken joints.

2 In a shallow dish, mix together the flour, paprika, salt, and pepper. Coat the chicken on both sides with flour, and shake off any excess if necessary.

3 Heat the oil in a large nonstick skillet. Add the chicken and brown on both sides. Transfer to a plate and set aside.

4 Add the onion and red chili to the skillet, and gently cook for 5 minutes or until the onion is soft. Stir occasionally.

5 Stir in the cumin and oregano, and cook for an additional minute. Pour in the stock and bring to a boil.

6 Return the chicken to the skillet, cover, and cook for 40 minutes. Add the green bell pepper and cook for 10 minutes until the chicken is cooked. Using a slotted spoon, remove the chicken and pepper, and keep warm in a serving dish.

7 Blend the cocoa with 1 tablespoon of warm water. Stir into the sauce, then boil rapidly until the sauce has thickened and reduced by about one-third. Stir in the lime juice, honey, and yogurt.

8 Pour the sauce over the chicken and pepper, and garnish with the lime slices, chili, and oregano. Serve immediately with the freshly cooked rice and green salad.

TURKEY & TOMATO TAGINE

INGREDIENTS

Serves 4

FOR THE MEATBALLS:
1 lb. fresh ground turkey
1 small onion, peeled and
  very finely chopped
1 garlic clove, peeled and
  crushed
1 tbsp. freshly chopped
  cilantro
1 tsp. cumin
1 tbsp. olive oil
salt and freshly ground
  black pepper

FOR THE SAUCE:
1 onion, peeled and finely
  chopped
1 garlic clove, peeled and
  crushed
⅔ cup turkey stock
14-oz. can chopped tomatoes
½ tsp. ground cumin
½ tsp. ground cinnamon
pinch of cayenne pepper
freshly chopped parsley
freshly chopped herbs,
  to garnish
couscous or rice, to serve

1 Preheat the oven to 375° F.
Put all the ingredients (except
for the oil) for the meatballs in a
bowl, and mix well. Season to
taste with salt and pepper. Shape
into 20 balls, about the size of
walnuts.

2 Put on a tray, cover lightly,
and chill in the refrigerator
while making the sauce.

3 Put the onion and garlic in a
saucepan with ½ cup of the
stock. Cook over a low heat until
all the stock has evaporated.
Continue cooking for 1 minute
or until the onions start to brown.

4 Add the remaining stock to
the pan with the tomatoes,
cumin, cinnamon, and cayenne
pepper. Simmer for 10 minutes

until slightly thickened and
reduced. Stir in the parsley and
season to taste.

5 Heat the oil in a large
nonstick skillet, and cook the
meatballs in 2 batches until
lightly browned all over.

6 Using a slotted spoon, lift the
meatballs out, and drain on
absorbent paper towels.

7 Pour the sauce into a tagine
or an ovenproof casserole
dish. Top with the meatballs,
cover, and cook in the preheated
oven for 25–30 minutes or until
the meatballs are cooked through
and the sauce is bubbling. Garnish
with freshly chopped herbs, and
serve immediately with couscous
or plain boiled rice.

TURKEY ESCALOPES WITH APRICOT CHUTNEY

INGREDIENTS

Serves 4

4 turkey steaks, ¼ lb. each
1 tbsp. all-purpose flour
salt and freshly ground
 black pepper
1 tbsp. olive oil
sprigs of Italian parsley,
 to garnish
orange wedges, to serve

FOR THE APRICOT CHUTNEY:

⅔ cup dried apricots, chopped
1 red onion, peeled and
 finely chopped
1 tsp. freshly grated ginger
2 tbsp. sugar
½ tbsp. grated orange rind
½ cup fresh orange juice
½ cup ruby port
1 whole clove
1 tbsp. freshly chopped
 cilantro

1 Put a turkey steak onto a sheet of plastic wrap or nonstick baking parchment. Cover with a second sheet.

2 Using a rolling pin, gently pound the turkey until the meat is flattened to about ¼ inch thick. Repeat to make 4 escalopes.

3 Mix the flour with the salt and pepper, and use to lightly dust the turkey escalopes.

4 Put the turkey escalopes on a board or cookie sheet, and cover with a piece of plastic wrap or nonstick baking parchment. Chill in the refrigerator until ready to cook.

5 For the apricot chutney, put the apricots, onion, ginger,

sugar, orange rind, orange juice, port, and clove into a saucepan.

6 Slowly bring to a boil and simmer uncovered for 10 minutes, stirring occasionally, until thick and syrupy.

7 Remove the clove and stir in the chopped cilantro.

8 Heat the oil in a griddle pan, and cook the turkey escalopes (in 2 batches if necessary) for 3–4 minutes on each side until golden brown and tender.

9 Spoon the chutney onto 4 individual serving plates. Place a turkey escalope on top of each spoonful of chutney. Garnish with sprigs of parsley, and serve immediately with orange wedges.

SMOKED TURKEY TAGLIATELLE

INGREDIENTS

Serves 4

2 tsp. olive oil
1 bunch scallions, trimmed
  and diagonally sliced
1 garlic clove, peeled and
  crushed
1 small zucchini, trimmed,
  sliced, and cut in half
4 tbsp. dry white wine
14-oz. can chopped tomatoes
2 tbsp. freshly torn basil

salt and freshly ground
  black pepper
2 cups spinach and egg
  tagliatelle
¼ lb. smoked turkey breast, cut
  into strips
small fresh basil leaves,
  to garnish

1 Heat the oil in a large saucepan. Add the scallions and garlic, and gently cook for 2–3 minutes until beginning to soften. Stir in the sliced zucchini and cook for 1 minute.

2 Add the wine and let it boil for 1–2 minutes. Stir in the chopped tomatoes, bring to a boil, and simmer, uncovered, over a low heat for 15 minutes or until the zucchini is tender and the sauce slightly reduced. Stir the shredded basil into the sauce, and season to taste with salt and pepper.

3 Meanwhile, bring a large saucepan of salted water to a boil. Add the tagliatelle and cook for 10 minutes until al dente, or according to the package instructions. Drain thoroughly.

4 Return the tagliatelle to the saucepan, add half the tomato sauce, and toss together to coat the pasta thoroughly in the sauce. Cover and set aside.

5 Add the strips of turkey to the remaining sauce and heat gently for 2–3 minutes until piping hot.

6 Divide the tagliatelle among 4 serving plates. Spoon the sauce on top, garnish with basil leaves, and serve immediately.

TASTY TIP

Many stores and supermarkets now stock flavored pasta, as well as the plain traditional type. Why not try using a garlic and herb or sun-dried tomato tagliatelle in this recipe?

TURKEY & MIXED MUSHROOM LASAGNA

INGREDIENTS

Serves 4

1 tbsp. olive oil
2 cups mixed mushrooms,
   such as button, chestnut,
   and portobello, wiped
   and sliced
1 tbsp. butter
¼ cup all-purpose flour
1¼ cups nonfat milk
1 bay leaf
2½ cups cooked turkey, cubed
¼ tsp. freshly grated nutmeg
salt and freshly ground
   black pepper

14-oz. can plum tomatoes,
   drained and chopped
1 tsp. dried mixed herbs
9 lasagna sheets

FOR THE TOPPING:
1 cup nonfat plain yogurt
1 medium egg, lightly beaten
1 tbsp. finely shredded
   Parmesan cheese
mixed lettuce leaves, to serve

1 Preheat the oven to 350° F. Heat the oil and cook the mushrooms until tender and the juices have evaporated. Remove and set aside.

2 Put the butter, flour, milk, and bay leaf in the saucepan. Slowly bring to a boil, stirring until thickened. Simmer for 2–3 minutes. Remove the bay leaf, and stir in the mushrooms, turkey, nutmeg, salt, and pepper.

3 Mix together the tomatoes and mixed herbs, and season with salt and pepper. Spoon half into the base of a large ovenproof dish. Top with 3 sheets of lasagna, then with half the turkey mixture. Repeat the layers, then arrange the remaining 3 sheets of pasta on top.

4 Mix together the yogurt and egg. Spoon over the lasagna, spreading the mixture into the corners. Sprinkle with the Parmesan, and cook in the preheated oven for 45 minutes. Serve with the mixed salad.

TASTY TIP

Garlic bread is the perfect accompaniment to lasagna. Preheat the oven to 350° F. Finely chop 2–3 garlic cloves. Mix with a little chopped parsley and ½ cup of low-fat spread. Make cuts almost to the base of a loaf of French bread. Spread with the flavored, low-fat spread. Wrap in foil. Cook in the preheated oven for 15 minutes.

TERIYAKI TURKEY WITH ASIAN VEGETABLES

INGREDIENTS   Serves 4

1 red chili
1 garlic clove, peeled and
  crushed
1-in. piece ginger, peeled and
  grated
3 tbsp. dark soy sauce
1 tsp. corn oil
¾ lb. skinless, boneless turkey
  breast
1 tbsp. vegetable oil
1 tbsp. sesame seeds
2 carrots, peeled and cut
  into matchsticks

1 leek, trimmed and shredded
1¼ cups broccoli, cut into
  tiny florets
1 tsp. cornstarch
3 tbsp. dry sherry
1 cup snow peas, cut into
  thin strips

TO SERVE:
freshly cooked egg noodles
sprinkling of sesame seeds

1 Halve, seed, and thinly slice the chili. Put into a small bowl with the garlic, ginger, soy sauce, and corn oil.

2 Cut the turkey into thin strips. Add to the mixture and mix until well coated. Cover with plastic wrap and marinate in the refrigerator for at least 30 minutes.

3 Heat a wok or large skillet. Add 2 teaspoons of the vegetable oil. When hot, remove the turkey from the marinade. Stir-fry for 2–3 minutes until browned and cooked. Remove from the wok and set aside.

4 Heat the remaining 1 teaspoon of oil in the wok. Add the sesame seeds and stir-fry for a few seconds until they start to brown.

5 Add the carrots, leek, and broccoli, and continue stir-frying for 2–3 minutes.

6 Blend the cornstarch with 1 tablespoon of cold water to make a smooth paste. Stir in the sherry and marinade. Add to the wok with the snow peas, and cook for 1 minute, stirring all the time, until thickened.

7 Return the turkey to the wok and continue cooking for 1–2 minutes or until the turkey is hot, the vegetables are tender, and the sauce is bubbling. Serve the turkey and vegetables immediately with the egg noodles. Sprinkle with the sesame seeds.

GAME HEN WITH CALVADOS & APPLES

INGREDIENTS

Serves 4

4 game hen breasts, each about ¼ lb., skinned
1 tbsp. all-purpose flour
1 tbsp. corn oil
1 onion, peeled and finely sliced
1 garlic clove, peeled and crushed
1 tsp. freshly chopped thyme
⅔ cup dry cider

salt and freshly ground black pepper
3 tbsp. Calvados brandy
sprigs of fresh thyme, to garnish

CARAMELIZED APPLES:
1 tbsp. unsalted butter
2 red-skinned apples, quartered, cored, and sliced
1 tsp. sugar

1 Lightly dust the game hen breasts with the flour.

2 Heat 2 teaspoons of the oil in a large nonstick skillet and cook the breasts for 2–3 minutes on each side until browned. Remove the breasts from the skillet and set aside.

3 Heat the remaining teaspoon of oil in the skillet, and add the onion and garlic. Cook over a medium heat for 10 minutes, stirring occasionally, until soft and just beginning to brown.

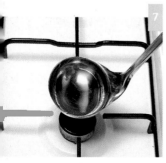

4 Stir in the chopped thyme and cider. Return the game hens to the skillet, season with salt and pepper, and bring to a very gentle simmer. Cover and cook over a low heat for 15–20 minutes or until the game hens are tender.

5 Remove the game hens and keep warm. Turn up the heat and boil the sauce until thickened and reduced by half.

6 Meanwhile, prepare the caramelized apples. Melt the butter in a small nonstick saucepan, add the apple slices in a single layer, and sprinkle with the sugar. Cook until the apples are tender and beginning to caramelize, turning once.

7 Put the Calvados in a metal ladle or small saucepan, and gently heat until warm. Carefully set aflame with a match, let the flames die down, then stir into the sauce.

8 Serve the game hens with the sauce spooned on top and garnished with the caramelized apples and sprigs of fresh thyme.

DUCK WITH BERRY SAUCE

INGREDIENTS

Serves 4

4 boneless duck breasts,
  ½ lb. each
salt and freshly ground
  black pepper
1 tsp. corn oil

FOR THE SAUCE:
⅓ cup orange juice
1 bay leaf
3 tbsp. red currant jelly
¾ cup fresh or frozen
  mixed berries

2 tbsp. dried cranberries
  or cherries
½ tsp. light brown sugar
1 tbsp. balsamic vinegar
1 tsp. freshly chopped mint
sprigs of fresh mint, to garnish

TO SERVE:
freshly cooked potatoes
freshly cooked green beans

1 Remove the skins from the duck breasts and season with a little salt and pepper. Brush a griddle pan with the oil, then heat on the stove until smoking hot.

2 Place the duck skinned-side down in the pan. Cook over a medium-high heat for 5 minutes or until well browned. Turn the duck and cook for 2 minutes. Lower the heat and cook for an additional 5–8 minutes or until cooked, but still slightly pink in the center. Remove from the pan and keep warm.

3 While the duck is cooking, make the sauce. Put the orange juice, bay leaf, red currant jelly, fresh or frozen and dried berries, and sugar in a small griddle pan. Add any juices left in the griddle pan to the small pan. Slowly bring to a boil, lower the

heat, and simmer uncovered for 4–5 minutes or until the fruit is soft.

4 Remove the bay leaf. Stir in the vinegar and chopped mint, and season to taste with salt and pepper.

5 Slice the duck breasts diagonally, and arrange on serving plates. Spoon the berry sauce on top, and garnish with sprigs of fresh mint. Serve immediately with the potatoes and green beans.

HELPFUL HINT

Duck breasts are best served slightly pink in the center. Whole ducks, however, should be cooked thoroughly.

STICKY-GLAZED GAME HENS

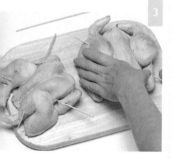

INGREDIENTS

Serves 4

2 game hens, each about
  1½ lbs.
salt and freshly ground
  black pepper
4 kumquats, thinly sliced
assorted lettuce leaves, crusty
  bread, and/or new potatoes,
  to serve

FOR THE GLAZE:
2 tbsp. finely grated
  lemon zest
1 tbsp. lemon juice
1 tbsp. dry sherry
2 tbsp. honey
2 tbsp. dark soy sauce
2 tbsp. mustard
1 tsp. tomato paste
½ tsp. Chinese five spice
  powder

1 Preheat the broiler just before cooking. Place one of the game hens breast-side down on a board. Using poultry shears, cut down one side of the backbone. Cut down the other side of the backbone. Remove the bone.

2 Open up the game hen and press down hard on the breastbone with the heel of your hand to break it and to flatten the game hen.

3 Thread 2 skewers crosswise through the bird to keep it flat, ensuring that each skewer goes through a wing and out through the leg on the opposite side. Repeat with the other bird. Season both sides of the bird with salt and pepper.

4 To make the glaze, mix together the lemon zest and

juice, sherry, honey, soy sauce, mustard, tomato paste, and Chinese five spice powder, and use to brush over the game hens.

5 Place the game hens skin-side down on a broiler rack and broil under a medium heat for 15 minutes, brushing halfway through with more glaze.

6 Turn the game hens over and broil for 10 minutes. Brush again with glaze and arrange the kumquat slices on top. Broil for an additional 15 minutes until well browned and cooked through. If they brown too quickly, turn down the broiler.

7 Remove the skewers and cut each game hen in half along the breastbone. Serve immediately with the salad, crusty bread, and/or new potatoes.

CHICKEN BASQUAISE

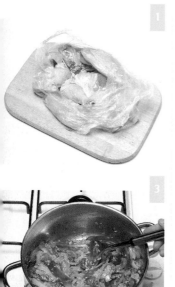

INGREDIENTS

Serves 4–6

3 lb. chicken, cut into 8 pieces
2 tbsp. all-purpose flour
salt and freshly ground black pepper
3 tbsp. olive oil
1 large onion, peeled and sliced
2 red bell peppers, deseeded and cut into thick strips
2 garlic cloves, peeled and crushed
¼ lb. spicy chorizo sausage, cut into ½-in. pieces

heaping 1 cup long-grain white rice
2 cups chicken stock
1 tsp. crushed dried chilies
½ tsp. dried thyme
1 tbsp. tomato paste
1¼ cups diced Spanish ham
12 black olives
2 tbsp. freshly chopped parsley

1 Dry the chicken pieces well with paper towels. Put the flour in a plastic bag, season with salt and pepper, and add the chicken pieces. Twist the bag to seal, then shake to coat the chicken pieces thoroughly.

2 Heat 2 tablespoons of the oil in a large heavy-based saucepan over a medium-high heat. Add the chicken pieces and cook for about 15 minutes, turning on all sides, until well browned. Using a slotted spoon, transfer to a plate.

3 Add the remaining olive oil to the saucepan, then add the onion and bell peppers. Reduce the heat to medium and cook, stirring frequently, until starting to brown and soften. Stir in the garlic and chorizo, and continue

cooking for an additional 3 minutes. Add the rice and cook for about 2 minutes, stirring to coat with the oil, until the rice is translucent and golden.

4 Stir in the stock, crushed chilies, thyme, tomato paste, and salt and pepper, and bring to a boil. Return the chicken to the saucepan, pressing it gently into the rice. Cover and cook over a very low heat for about 45 minutes until the chicken and rice are cooked and tender.

5 Gently stir in the ham, black olives, and half the parsley. Cover and heat for an additional 5 minutes. Sprinkle with the remaining parsley and serve immediately.

PAD THAI

INGREDIENTS

Serves 4

½ lb. flat rice noodles
2 tbsp. vegetable oil
½ lb. boneless chicken breast, skinned and thinly sliced
4 shallots, peeled and thinly sliced
2 garlic cloves, peeled and finely chopped
4 scallions, trimmed and cut diagonally into 2-in. pieces
¾ lb. fresh white crabmeat or tiny shrimp
1½ cups fresh bean sprouts, rinsed and drained
2 tbsp. preserved or fresh radish, chopped

2–3 tbsp. roasted peanuts, chopped (optional)

FOR THE SAUCE:
3 tbsp. Thai fish sauce
2–3 tbsp. rice vinegar or cider vinegar
1 tbsp. oyster sauce
1 tbsp. toasted sesame oil
1 tbsp. light brown sugar
1 red chili, deseeded and thinly sliced

1 To make the sauce, whisk all the sauce ingredients in a bowl and set aside. Put the rice noodles in a large bowl and pour over enough hot water to cover. Let stand for about 15 minutes until softened. Drain and rinse, then drain again.

2 Heat the oil in a wok over a high heat until hot, but not smoking. Add the chicken strips and stir-fry constantly until they begin to color. Using a slotted spoon, transfer to a plate. Reduce the heat to medium-high.

3 Add the shallots, garlic, and scallions, and stir-fry for 1 minute. Stir in the rice noodles, then the sauce; mix well.

4 Add the chicken strips with the crabmeat, bean sprouts, and radish, and stir well. Cook for about 5 minutes, stirring frequently, until heated through. If the noodles begin to stick, add a little water.

5 Turn into a large shallow serving dish and sprinkle with the chopped peanuts, if desired. Serve immediately.

HELPFUL HINT

Rice noodles are usually sold dried, but fresh noodles are sometimes available. Check package instructions on use.

FRIED GINGER RICE WITH SOY GLAZED DUCK

INGREDIENTS

Serves 4–6

2 duck breasts, skinned and cut diagonally into thin slices
2–3 tbsp. Japanese soy sauce
1 tbsp. mirin (sweet rice wine) or sherry
2 tbsp. brown sugar
2-in. piece of ginger, peeled and finely chopped
4 tbsp. peanut or vegetable oil
2 garlic cloves, peeled and crushed
1¼ cups long-grain brown rice
3¾ cups chicken stock
freshly ground black pepper

⅔ cup diced, lean, cooked ham
1 cup snow peas, cut in half diagonally
8 scallions, trimmed and thinly sliced diagonally
1 tbsp. freshly chopped cilantro
sweet or hot chili sauce, to taste (optional)
sprigs of cilantro, to garnish

1 Put the duck slices in a bowl with 1 tablespoon of the soy sauce, the mirin, 1 teaspoon of the sugar, and one third of the ginger; stir. Set aside.

2 Heat 2 tablespoons of the oil in a large heavy-based saucepan. Add the garlic and half the remaining ginger, and stir-fry for 1 minute. Add the rice and cook for 3 minutes, stirring constantly, until translucent.

3 Stir in all but ½ cup of the stock, along with 1 teaspoon of the soy sauce, and bring to a boil. Season with pepper. Reduce the heat to very low and simmer, covered, for 25–30 minutes until the rice is tender and the liquid is absorbed. Cover and let stand.

4 Heat the remaining oil in a large skillet or wok. Drain the duck strips and add to the frying pan. Stir-fry for 2–3 minutes until just colored. Add 1 tablespoon of soy sauce and the remaining sugar, and cook for 1 minute until glazed. Transfer to a plate and keep warm.

5 Stir in the ham, snow peas, scallions, the remaining ginger, and the chopped cilantro. Add the remaining stock and duck marinade, and cook until the liquid is almost reduced. Fork in the rice and a little chili sauce to taste; stir well. Turn into a serving dish and top with the duck. Garnish with cilantro and serve immediately.

PERSIAN CHICKEN PILAF

INGREDIENTS

Serves 4–6

2–3 tbsp. vegetable oil
1½ lbs. boneless skinless chicken pieces (breast and thighs), cut into 1-in. pieces
2 medium onions, peeled and coarsely chopped
1 tsp. ground cumin
heaping 1 cup long-grain white rice
1 tbsp. tomato paste
1 tsp. saffron strands

salt and freshly ground black pepper
1 cup pomegranate juice
3¾ cups chicken stock
1 cup halved and pitted dried apricots or prunes
2 tbsp. raisins
2 tbsp. freshly chopped mint or parsley
pomegranate seeds, to garnish (optional)

1 Heat the oil in a large, heavy-based saucepan over a medium-high heat. Cook the chicken pieces in batches until lightly browned. Return all the browned chicken to the saucepan.

2 Add the onions to the saucepan, reduce the heat to medium, and cook for 3–5 minutes, stirring frequently, until the onions begin to soften. Add the cumin and rice, and stir to coat the rice. Cook for about 2 minutes until the rice is golden and translucent. Stir in the tomato paste and the saffron strands, then season to taste with salt and pepper.

3 Add the pomegranate juice and stock, and bring to a boil, stirring once or twice. Add the apricots and raisins, and stir gently. Reduce the heat to low and cook for 30 minutes until

the chicken and rice are tender and the liquid is absorbed.

4 Turn into a shallow serving dish and sprinkle with the chopped mint or parsley. Serve immediately, garnished with pomegranate seeds, if desired.

HELPFUL HINT

Pomegranate juice is available from Middle-Eastern groceries and some specialty stores. You can extract juice from fresh pomegranates by separating the seeds from the bitter pith and membranes, then crushing the seeds in a sieve placed over a bowl. Substitute unsweetened grape or apple juice if you cannot get pomegranates.

CHICKEN & SEAFOOD RISOTTO

INGREDIENTS

Serves 6–8

½ cup olive oil

3 lbs. chicken, cut into 8 pieces

¾ lbs. spicy chorizo sausage, cut into ½-in. pieces

⅔ cup diced cooked ham

1 onion, peeled and chopped

2 red or yellow bell peppers, deseeded and cut into 1-in. pieces

4 garlic cloves, peeled and finely chopped

4⅓ cups short-grain Spanish rice or Arborio rice

2 bay leaves

1 tsp. dried thyme

1 tsp. saffron strands, lightly crushed

¾ cup dry white wine

6½ cups chicken stock

salt and freshly ground black pepper

⅔ cup fresh shelled peas

1 lb. uncooked shrimp

36 clams and/or mussels, well scrubbed

2 tbsp. freshly chopped parsley

TO GARNISH:

lemon wedges

fresh parsley sprigs

1 Heat half the oil in an 18-in. paella pan or deep, wide skillet. Add the chicken pieces and fry for 15 minutes, turning constantly until golden. Remove from the pan and set aside. Add the chorizo and ham to the pan and cook for 6 minutes until crisp, stirring occasionally. Remove and add to the chicken.

2 Add the onion to the pan and cook for 3 minutes or until beginning to soften. Add the peppers and garlic, and cook for 2 minutes; add to the chicken, chorizo, and ham.

3 Add the remaining oil to the pan and stir in the rice until well coated. Stir in the bay leaves, thyme, and saffron, then pour in the wine, and bubble until evaporated. Stir in the stock and bring to a boil, stirring occasionally.

4 Return the chicken, chorizo, ham, and vegetables to the pan, burying them in the rice. Season to taste with salt and pepper. Reduce the heat, and simmer for 10 minutes, stirring occasionally.

5 Add the peas and seafood, pushing them gently into the rice. Cover, and cook over a low heat for 5 minutes, or until the rice and shrimp are tender and the clams and mussels open (discard any that do not open). Let stand for 5 minutes. Sprinkle with the parsley, garnish, and serve.

NEW ORLEANS JAMBALAYA

INGREDIENTS   Serves 6–8

FOR THE SEASONING MIX:
2 dried bay leaves
1 tsp. salt
2 tsp. cayenne pepper
2 tsp. dried oregano
1 tsp. each ground white and
   black pepper, or to taste

3 tbsp. vegetable oil
1¼ cups diced cooked ham
½ lb. smoked pork sausage, cut
   into chunks
2 large onions, peeled and
   chopped
4 celery stalks, trimmed and
   chopped

2 green bell peppers,
   deseeded and chopped
2 garlic cloves, peeled and
   finely chopped
¾ lb. raw chicken, diced
14 oz. can chopped tomatoes
2½ cups fish stock
2½ cups long-grain white rice
4 scallions, trimmed and
   coarsely chopped
¾ lb. raw shrimp, peeled
½ lb. white crabmeat

1 Mix all the seasoning ingredients together in a small bowl and set aside.

2 Heat 2 tablespoons of the oil in a large flameproof casserole over a medium heat. Add the ham and sausage, and cook, stirring often, for 7–8 minutes until golden. Remove from the pan and set aside.

3 Add the remaining onions, celery, and peppers to the casserole and cook for about 4 minutes or until softened, stirring occasionally. Stir in the garlic, then, using a slotted spoon, transfer all the vegetables to a plate and set aside with the sausage.

4 Add the chicken pieces to the casserole and cook for about 4 minutes or until beginning to brown, turning once. Stir in the seasoning mix and turn the pieces to coat well. Return the sausage and vegetables to the casserole and stir well. Add the chopped tomatoes with their juice and the stock, and bring to a boil.

5 Stir in the rice and reduce the heat to low. Cover and simmer for 12 minutes. Uncover, stir in the scallions and shrimp, and cook, covered, for an additional 4 minutes. Add the crab and gently stir in. Cook for 2–3 minutes or until the rice is tender. Remove from the heat, cover, and let stand for 5 minutes before serving.

RICE-STUFFED POUSSINS

INGREDIENTS

Serves 6

FOR THE RICE STUFFING:

1 cup port
¾ cup raisins
1 cup chopped dried apricots
2 tbsp. olive oil
1 medium onion, peeled and finely chopped
1 celery stalk, trimmed and finely sliced
2 garlic cloves, peeled and finely chopped
1½ tsp. mixed spice
1 tsp. each dried oregano and mint or basil
2 cups chopped, unsweetened, canned chestnuts
heaping 1 cup cooked long-grain white rice

grated zest and juice of 2 oranges
1½ cups chicken stock
½ cup lightly toasted and chopped walnut halves
2 tbsp. each freshly chopped mint and parsley
salt and freshly ground black pepper

6 oven-ready game hens
¼ cup butter, melted

TO GARNISH:

fresh herbs
orange wedges

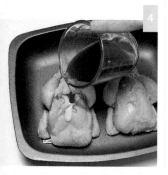

1 Preheat the oven to 350° F. For the stuffing, place the port, raisins, and apricots in a bowl and let stand for 15 minutes. In an oiled pan, add the onion and celery, and cook for 3–4 minutes. Add the garlic, mixed spices, herbs, and chestnuts, and cook for 4 minutes, stirring often. Add the rice, half the orange zest and juice, and the stock. Simmer for 5 minutes until the liquid is absorbed.

2 Drain the raisins and apricots, setting aside the port. Stir into the rice with the walnuts, mint, parsley, and seasoning, and cook for 2 minutes. Remove.

3 Rinse the game hen cavities, pat dry, and season with salt and pepper. Lightly fill the cavities with the stuffing. Tie the legs together, tucking in the tails. Form extra stuffing into balls.

4 Place in roasting pan with stuffing balls, and brush with melted butter. Drizzle over the remaining butter, remaining orange zest and juice, and port. Roast in the preheated oven for 50 minutes or until golden and cooked, basting every 15 minutes. Transfer to a platter, cover with foil, and rest. Pour over any pan juices. Garnish with herbs and orange wedges. Serve with the stuffing.

CREAMY CHICKEN & RICE PILAF

INGREDIENTS

Serves 4–6

2 cups basmati rice
salt and freshly ground black
  pepper
¼ cup butter
1 cup flaked almonds
⅔ cup unsalted shelled
  pistachio nuts
4–6 skinless chicken breast
  fillets, each cut into 4 pieces
2 tbsp. vegetable oil
2 medium onions, peeled and
  thinly sliced
2 garlic cloves, peeled and
  finely chopped
1-in. piece of ginger, finely
  chopped

6 green cardamom pods,
  lightly crushed
4–6 whole cloves
2 bay leaves
1 tsp. ground coriander
½ tsp. cayenne pepper, or to
  taste
1 cup plain yogurt
1 cup heavy cream
½ lb. seedless green grapes,
  halved if large
2 tbsp. freshly chopped
  cilantro or mint

1 Bring a saucepan of lightly salted water to a boil. Pour in the rice, return to boil, then simmer for about 12 minutes until tender. Drain, rinse under cold water, and set aside.

2 Heat the butter in a large deep skillet over a medium-high heat. Add the almonds and pistachios, and cook for about 2 minutes, stirring constantly, until golden. Using a slotted spoon, transfer to a plate.

3 Add the chicken pieces to the pan and cook for 5 minutes or until golden, turning once. Remove from the pan and set aside. Add the oil to the pan. Cook the onions for 10 minutes or until golden, stirring frequently. Stir in the garlic, ginger, and spices, and cook for 2–3 minutes, stirring.

4 Add 2–3 tablespoons of the yogurt, and cook, stirring, until the moisture evaporates. Continue adding the yogurt in this way until it is used up.

5 Return the chicken and nuts to the pan and stir. Stir in ½ cup of boiling water, and season to taste with salt and pepper. Cook, covered, over a low heat for 10 minutes, until the chicken is tender. Stir in the cream, grapes, and half the herbs. Gently fold in the rice. Heat for 5 minutes, sprinkle with herbs, then serve.

WILD RICE & BACON SALAD WITH SMOKED CHICKEN

INGREDIENTS

Serves 4

heaping ¾ cup wild rice
½ cup pecan or walnut halves
1 tbsp. vegetable oil
4 slices smoked bacon, diced
3–4 shallots, peeled and finely
   chopped
5 tbsp. walnut oil

2–3 tbsp. sherry or cider
   vinegar
2 tbsp. freshly chopped dill
salt and freshly ground black
   pepper
1½ cups thinly sliced smoked
   chicken or duck breast
dill sprigs, to garnish

1 Put the wild rice in a medium saucepan with 2½ cups water and bring to a boil, stirring once or twice. Reduce the heat, cover, and simmer gently for 30–50 minutes, depending on the texture you prefer, chewy or tender. Using a fork, gently fluff into a large bowl and allow to cool slightly.

2 Meanwhile, toast the nuts in a skillet over a medium heat for 2 minutes or until they are fragrant and lightly colored, stirring and tossing frequently. Cool, then chop coarsely, and add to the rice.

3 Heat the oil in the skillet over a medium heat. Add the bacon and cook, stirring from time to time, for 3–4 minutes or until crisp and brown. Remove from the pan and drain on paper towels. Add the shallots to the pan and cook for 4 minutes or until just softened, stirring from

time to time. Stir into the rice and nuts, along with the drained bacon pieces.

4 Whisk the walnut oil, vinegar, half the dill, and salt and pepper in a small bowl until combined. Pour the dressing over the rice mixture and toss well to combine. Mix the chicken and the remaining chopped dill into the rice, then spoon into bowls and garnish each serving with a dill sprig. Serve slightly warm or at room temperature.

FOOD FACT

Both smoked chicken and duck have a delicate smoky flavor which comes from being first cold-smoked, then briefly hot-smoked. You can, of course, use plain roasted chicken or duck if desired.

CHICKEN & WHITE WINE RISOTTO

INGREDIENTS   Serves 4–6

2 tbsp. oil
½ cup butter
2 shallots, peeled and finely
  chopped
1¾ cups Arborio rice
2½ cups dry white wine
3¼ cups chicken stock, heated
¾ lb. skinless chicken breast
  fillets, thinly sliced
½ cup grated Parmesan cheese

2 tbsp. freshly chopped dill or
  parsley
salt and freshly ground black
  pepper

1 Heat the oil and half the butter in a large heavy-based saucepan over a medium-high heat. Add the shallots and cook for 2 minutes or until softened, stirring frequently. Add the rice and cook for 2–3 minutes, stirring frequently, until the rice is translucent and well coated.

2 Pour in half the wine; it will bubble and steam rapidly. Cook, stirring constantly, until the liquid is absorbed. Add a ladleful of the hot stock and cook until the liquid is absorbed. Carefully stir in the chicken.

3 Continue adding the stock, about half a ladleful at a time, allowing each addition to be absorbed before adding the next; never allow the rice to cook dry. This process should take about 20 minutes. The risotto should have a creamy consistency, and the rice should be tender, but firm to the bite.

4 Stir in the remaining wine and cook for 2–3 minutes. Remove from the heat and stir in the remaining butter with the Parmesan cheese and half the chopped herbs. Season to taste with salt and pepper. Spoon into warmed shallow bowls and sprinkle each with the remaining chopped herbs. Serve immediately.

HELPFUL HINT

Keep the stock to be added to the risotto at a low simmer in a separate saucepan, so that it is piping hot when added to the rice. This will ensure that the dish is kept at a constant heat during cooking, which is important to achieve a perfect creamy texture.

POTATO-STUFFED ROAST POUSSIN

INGREDIENTS

Serves 4

4 oven-ready game hens
salt and freshly ground black
  pepper
1 lemon, cut into quarters
1 lb. floury potatoes, peeled
  and cut into 1½-in. pieces
1 tbsp. freshly chopped thyme
  or rosemary
3–4 tbsp. olive oil

4 garlic cloves, unpeeled and
  lightly smashed
8 slices bacon or prosciutto
  ham
½ cup white wine
2 scallions, trimmed and thinly
  sliced
2 tbsp. heavy cream or crème
  fraîche
lemon wedges, to garnish

1 Preheat the oven to 425° F. Place a roasting pan in the oven to heat. Rinse the cavities of the game hens and pat dry with paper towels. Season the cavities with salt and pepper, and a squeeze of lemon. Push a lemon quarter into each cavity.

2 Put the potatoes in a saucepan of lightly salted water and bring to a boil. Reduce the heat to low and simmer until just tender; do not overcook. Drain and cool slightly. Sprinkle the chopped herbs over the potatoes, and drizzle with 2–3 tablespoons of the oil.

3 Spoon half the seasoned potatoes into the game hen cavities; do not pack too tightly. Rub each hen with a little more oil, and season with pepper. Carefully spoon 1 tablespoon of oil into the hot roasting pan and arrange the game hens in the pan. Spoon the remaining potatoes

around the edge. Sprinkle over the garlic.

4 Roast the hens in the preheated oven for 30 minutes, or until the skin is golden and beginning to crisp. Carefully lay the bacon slices over the breast of each hen, and continue to roast for 15–20 minutes until the hens are cooked through and crisp.

5 Transfer the game hens and potatoes to a serving platter and cover loosely with aluminum foil. Skim off the fat from the juices. Place the pan over a medium heat, and add the wine and scallions. Cook briefly, scraping the bits from the bottom of the pan. Whisk in the cream or crème fraîche, and bubble for 1 minute or until thickened. Garnish the hens with lemon wedges, and serve with the creamy gravy.

TURKEY HASH WITH POTATOES & BEETS

INGREDIENTS

Serves 4–6

2 tbsp. vegetable oil
¼ cup butter
4 slices bacon, diced or sliced
1 medium onion, peeled and
   finely chopped
2¼ cups diced cooked turkey
2½ cups finely chopped cooked
   potatoes

2–3 tbsp. freshly chopped
   parsley
2 tbsp. all-purpose flour
1¾ cups diced, cooked beets
green salad, to serve

1 In a large, heavy-based skillet, heat the oil and half the butter over a medium heat until sizzling. Add the bacon and cook for 4 minutes or until crisp and golden, stirring occasionally. Using a slotted spoon, transfer to a large bowl. Add the onion to the pan and cook for 3–4 minutes or until soft and golden, stirring frequently.

2 Meanwhile, add the turkey, potatoes, parsley, and flour to the cooked bacon in the bowl. Stir and toss gently, then fold in the diced beet.

3 Add half the remaining butter to the skillet and then the turkey-vegetable mixture. Stir, then spread the mixture to evenly cover the bottom of the pan. Cook for 15 minutes or until the underside is crisp and brown, pressing the hash firmly with a spatula. Remove from the heat.

4 Place a large plate over the skillet and, holding the plate and pan together with an oven mitt, invert the hash out onto the plate. Heat the remaining butter in the pan, slide the hash back into the pan, and cook for 4 minutes or until crisp and brown on the other side. Invert onto the plate again and serve immediately with a green salad.

TASTY TIP

A hash is usually made just with potatoes, but here they are combined with ruby red beets, which add vibrant color and a sweet earthy flavor to the dish. Make sure that you buy plain beets, rather than the pickled variety.

CHICKEN & NEW POTATOES ON ROSEMARY SKEWERS

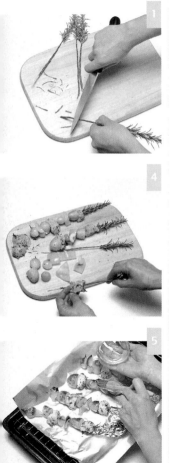

INGREDIENTS   Serves 4

8 thick, fresh rosemary stems, at least 9 in. long
3–4 tbsp. extra-virgin olive oil
2 garlic cloves, peeled and crushed
1 tsp. freshly chopped thyme
grated zest and juice of 1 lemon
salt and freshly ground black pepper

4 skinless chicken breast fillets
16 small new potatoes, peeled or scrubbed
8 very small onions or shallots, peeled
1 large yellow or red bell pepper, deseeded
lemon wedges, to garnish
parsley-flavored cooked rice, to serve

1 Preheat the broiler and line the broiler pan with aluminum foil just before cooking. If using a barbecue, light at least 20 minutes before needed. Strip the leaves from the rosemary stems, leaving about 2 in. of soft leaves at the top. Chop the leaves coarsely and set aside. Using a sharp knife, cut the thicker, woody ends of the stems to a sharp point for piercing the chicken and potatoes. Blend the chopped rosemary, oil, garlic, thyme, and lemon zest and juice in a shallow dish. Season to taste with salt and pepper.

2 Cut the chicken into ½-in. cubes, add to the flavored oil, and stir well. Cover, and refrigerate for at least 30 minutes, turning occasionally.

3 Cook the potatoes in lightly salted, boiling water for 10–12 minutes until just tender. Add the onions to the potatoes 2 minutes before the end of the cooking time. Drain, rinse under cold running water, and let cool. Cut the pepper into 1-in. squares.

4 Beginning with a piece of chicken and starting with the pointed end of the skewer, alternately thread equal amounts of chicken, potato, pepper, and onion onto each rosemary skewer. Cover the leafy ends of the skewers with foil to keep them from burning. Do not thread the chicken and vegetables too closely together on the skewer or the chicken may not cook completely.

5 Cook the kabobs for 15 minutes or until tender and golden, turning and brushing with either extra oil or the marinade. Remove the foil, garnish with lemon wedges, and serve on rice.

AROMATIC DUCK PATTIES ON POTATO PANCAKES

INGREDIENTS

Serves 4

1½ lbs. boneless duck breasts
2 tbsp. hoisin sauce
1 garlic clove, peeled and finely chopped
4 scallions, trimmed and finely chopped
2 tbsp. Japanese soy sauce
½ tsp. Chinese five-spice powder
salt and freshly ground black pepper

freshly chopped cilantro, to garnish
extra hoisin sauce, to serve

FOR THE POTATO PANCAKES:

1 lb. floury potatoes
1 small onion, peeled and grated
1 small egg, beaten
1 heaping tbsp. all-purpose flour

1 Peel off the thick layer of skin and fat from the duck breasts, and cut into small pieces. Put in a small dry saucepan, and set over a low heat for 10–15 minutes or until the fat runs clear and the crackling goes crisp. Set aside.

2 Cut the duck meat into pieces and blend in a food processor until coarsely chopped. Spoon into a bowl and add the hoisin sauce, garlic, half the scallions, soy sauce, and Chinese five-spice powder. Season to taste with salt and pepper, and shape into 4 patties. Cover and chill in the refrigerator for 1 hour.

3 To make the potato pancakes, shred the potatoes into a large bowl, squeeze out the water with your hands, then put on a clean dishtowel. Twist the ends to squeeze out any remaining water.

Return the potato to the bowl, add the onion and egg, and mix well. Add the flour and salt and pepper. Stir to blend.

4 Heat about 2 tablespoons of the duck fat in a large skillet. Spoon the potato mixture into 2–4 patty shapes, and cook for 6 minutes or until golden and crisp, turning once. Keep warm in the oven. Repeat with the remaining mixture, adding duck fat as needed.

5 Preheat the broiler and line the pan with aluminum foil. Brush the patties with a little of the duck fat and broil for 6–8 minutes, longer if desired, turning once. Arrange 1–2 potato pancakes on a plate and top with a patty. Spoon over a little hoisin sauce, and garnish with the remaining scallions and cilantro.

CHICKEN PIE WITH SWEET POTATO TOPPING

INGREDIENTS

Serves 4

4 cups peeled and coarsely diced sweet potatoes

1½ cups peeled and coarsely diced potatoes

salt and freshly ground black pepper

⅔ cup milk

2 tbsp. butter

2 tsp. brown sugar

grated zest of 1 orange

4 skinless chicken breast fillets, diced

1 medium onion, peeled and coarsely chopped

¼ lb. baby mushrooms, stems trimmed

2 leeks, trimmed and thickly sliced

⅔ cup dry white wine

1 chicken bouillon cube

1 tbsp. freshly chopped parsley

¼ cup crème fraîche or thick heavy cream

green vegetables, to serve

1 Preheat the oven to 375° F. Cook the sweet and regular potatoes together in lightly salted, boiling water until tender. Drain well, then return to the saucepan, and mash until creamy, gradually adding the milk, then the butter, sugar, and orange zest. Season to taste and set aside.

2 Place the chicken in a saucepan with the onion, mushrooms, leeks, wine, bouillon cube, and seasoning to taste. Simmer covered until the chicken and vegetables are tender. Using a slotted spoon, transfer the chicken and vegetables to a pie dish. Add the parsley and crème fraîche to the liquid in the pan, and bring to a boil. Simmer until thickened and smooth, stirring constantly. Pour over the chicken in the pie dish, mix, and cool.

3 Spread the mashed potatoes over the chicken filling, and swirl the surface into decorative peaks. Bake in the preheated oven for 35 minutes or until the top is golden and the chicken is heated through. Serve immediately with fresh green vegetables.

HELPFUL HINT

There are two types of sweet potatoes; one has a cream-colored flesh, the other orange. Both are good for mashing, as in this recipe, but the cream-colored variety has a drier texture, so you may need a little more milk.

WARM CHICKEN & POTATO SALAD WITH PEAS & MINT

INGREDIENTS

Serves 4–6

1 lb. new potatoes, peeled or scrubbed and cut into bite-sized pieces

salt and freshly ground black pepper

2 tbsp. cider vinegar

1¼ cups frozen peas, thawed

1 small ripe avocado

4 cooked chicken breasts, about 1 lb. in weight, skinned and diced

2 tbsp. freshly chopped mint

2 heads romaine lettuce

fresh mint sprigs, to garnish

FOR THE DRESSING:

2 tbsp. raspberry or sherry vinegar

2 tsp. Dijon mustard

1 tsp. honey

¼ cup sunflower oil

¼ cup extra-virgin olive oil

1 Cook the potatoes in lightly salted, boiling water for 15 minutes or until just tender when pierced with the tip of a sharp knife; do not overcook. Rinse under cold running water to cool slightly, then drain and turn into a large bowl. Sprinkle with the cider vinegar and toss gently.

2 Run the peas under hot water to ensure that they are thawed, pat dry with paper towels, and add to the potatoes.

3 Cut the avocado in half lengthwise and remove the pit. Peel and cut the avocado into cubes, and add to the potatoes and peas. Add the chicken and stir together lightly.

4 To make the dressing, place all the ingredients in a

screw-top jar with a little salt and pepper. Shake well to mix; add a little more oil if the flavor is too sharp. Pour over the salad and toss gently to coat. Sprinkle in half the mint and stir lightly.

5 Separate the lettuce leaves and spread onto a large shallow serving plate. Spoon the salad on top and sprinkle with the remaining mint. Garnish with mint sprigs and serve.

FOOD FACT

Cider vinegar, made from cider as the name suggests, has a strong, sharp flavor with a hint of apples. Raspberry vinegar has a wine-vinegar base, macerated with fresh raspberries.

BROWN RICE & LENTIL SALAD WITH DUCK

INGREDIENTS

Serves 6

1¼ cups Puy lentils, rinsed
4 tbsp. olive oil
1 medium onion, peeled and finely chopped
1¼ cups long-grain brown rice
½ tsp. dried thyme
2 cups chicken stock
salt and freshly ground black pepper
¾ lb. shiitake or portabella mushrooms, trimmed and sliced
¾ lb. cooked Chinese-style spicy duck or roasted duck, sliced into large chunks
2 garlic cloves, peeled and finely chopped
1¼ cups diced, cooked, smoked ham

2 small zucchini, trimmed, diced, and blanched
6 scallions, trimmed and thinly sliced
2 tbsp. freshly chopped parsley
2 tbsp. walnut halves, toasted and chopped

FOR THE DRESSING:

2 tbsp. red or white wine vinegar
1 tbsp. balsamic vinegar
1 tsp. Dijon mustard
1 tsp. honey
⅓ cup extra-virgin olive oil
2–3 tbsp. walnut oil

1 Bring a large saucepan of water to a boil, sprinkle in the lentils, return to a boil, then simmer over a low heat for 30 minutes, or until tender; do not overcook. Drain and rinse under cold running water, then drain again, and set aside.

2 Heat 2 tablespoons of the oil in a saucepan. Add the onion and cook for 2 minutes until it begins to soften. Stir in the rice with the thyme and stock. Season to taste with salt and pepper, and bring to a boil. Cover and simmer for 40 minutes or until tender and the liquid is absorbed.

3 Heat the remaining oil in a large skillet and add the mushrooms. Cook for 5 minutes until golden. Stir in the duck and garlic, and cook for 2–3 minutes to heat through. Season well.

4 To make the dressing, whisk the vinegars, mustard, and honey in a large serving bowl, then gradually whisk in the oils. Add the lentils and the rice, then stir lightly together. Gently stir in the ham, blanched zucchini, scallions, and parsley. Season to taste and sprinkle with the walnuts. Serve topped with the duck and mushrooms.

CHINESE-STYLE FRIED RICE

INGREDIENTS   Serves 4–6

2–3 tbsp. peanut oil or
   vegetable oil
2 small onions, peeled and cut
   into wedges
2 garlic cloves, peeled and
   thinly sliced
1-in. piece of ginger, peeled
   and cut into thin slivers
2½ cups shredded, cooked
   chicken
1¼ cups shredded, cooked ham
1⅓ cups long-grain white rice,
   cooked and cooled
½ cup canned water chestnuts,
   sliced
1½ cups cooked peeled shrimp
3 large eggs

3 tsp. sesame oil
salt and freshly ground black
   pepper
6 scallions, trimmed and sliced
   into ½-in. pieces
2 tbsp. dark soy sauce
1 tbsp. sweet chili sauce
2 tbsp. freshly chopped
   cilantro

TO GARNISH:
2 tbsp. chopped roasted
   peanuts
sprig of fresh cilantro

1 Heat a wok or large deep skillet until very hot, add the oil, and heat for 30 seconds. Add the onions and stir-fry for 2 minutes. Stir in the garlic and ginger, and cook for 1 minute. Add the cooked chicken and ham, and stir-fry for an additional 2–3 minutes.

2 Add the rice, water chestnuts, and shrimp, if using, with 2 tablespoons of water, and stir-fry for 2 minutes until the rice is heated through.

3 Beat the eggs with 1 teaspoon of the sesame oil, and season to taste with salt and pepper. Make a well in the center of the rice, then pour in the egg mixture

and stir immediately, gradually drawing the rice mixture into the egg until the egg is cooked.

4 Add the scallions, soy and chili sauces, cilantro, and a little water, if necessary. Adjust the seasoning and drizzle with the remaining sesame oil. Sprinkle with the nuts and serve.

HELPFUL HINT

Long-grain white rice absorbs
about 3 times its weight
during cooking, so if cooking
rice specially for this dish you
will need 8 oz. raw rice. Add
extra flavor by cooking in
vegetable or chicken stock.

TURKEY & PESTO RICE ROULADES

INGREDIENTS
Serves 4

cooked white rice, at room temperature
1 garlic clove, peeled and crushed
1–2 tbsp. grated Parmesan cheese
2 tbsp. prepared pesto sauce
2 tbsp. pine nuts, lightly toasted and chopped
4 turkey steaks, each weighing about 5 oz.

salt and freshly ground black pepper
4 slices prosciutto
2 tbsp. olive oil
¼ cup white wine
2 tbsp. butter, chilled

TO SERVE:
freshly cooked spinach
freshly cooked pasta

1 Put the rice in a bowl and add the garlic, Parmesan cheese, pesto, and pine nuts. Stir to combine the ingredients, then set aside.

2 Place the turkey steaks on a chopping board and, using a sharp knife, slice horizontally through each steak, without cutting all the way through. Fold back the top slice and cover with baking parchment. Flatten slightly by pounding with a meat mallet or rolling pin.

3 Season each steak with salt and pepper. Divide the stuffing equally among the steaks, spreading evenly over one half. Fold the steaks in half to enclose the filling, then wrap each steak in a slice of prosciutto and secure with wooden toothpicks.

4 Heat the oil in a large skillet over medium heat. Cook the steaks for 5 minutes or until golden on one side. Turn and cook for an additional 2 minutes. Push the steaks to the side and pour in the wine. Allow the wine to bubble and evaporate. Add the butter a little at a time, whisking constantly until the sauce is smooth. Discard the toothpicks, then serve the steaks, drizzled with the sauce, with spinach and pasta.

FOOD FACT

Prosciutto, the classic Italian ham, is dry-cured, rubbed with salt for about a month, then hung up to dry for a year. Carved very thinly, it's often served raw, but is also good when lightly fried.

SLOW-ROAST CHICKEN WITH POTATOES & OREGANO

INGREDIENTS

Serves 6

3–4 lb. oven-ready chicken
1 lemon, halved
1 onion, peeled and quartered
¼ cup butter, softened
salt and freshly ground black
  pepper
2¼ lb. potatoes, peeled and
  quartered

3–4 tbsp. extra-virgin olive oil
1 tbsp. dried oregano,
  crumbled
1 tsp. fresh thyme leaves
2 tbsp. freshly chopped thyme
fresh sage leaves, to garnish

1 Preheat the oven to 400° F. Rinse the chicken and dry well, inside and out, with paper towels. Rub the chicken all over with the lemon halves, then squeeze the juice over it and into the cavity. Put the squeezed halves into the cavity with the quartered onion.

2 Rub the softened butter all over the chicken, and season to taste with salt and pepper, then put it in a large roasting pan, breast-side down.

3 Toss the potatoes in the oil, season with salt and pepper to taste, and add the oregano and fresh thyme. Arrange the potatoes, along with the oil, around the chicken, and carefully pour ⅔ cup water into one end of the pan (not over the oil).

4 Roast in the preheated oven for 25 minutes. Reduce the oven temperature to 375° F, and turn the chicken breast-side up. Turn the potatoes, sprinkle with half the fresh herbs, and baste the chicken and potatoes with the juices. Continue roasting for 1 hour or until the chicken is cooked, basting occasionally. If the liquid evaporates completely, add a little more water. The chicken is cooked when the juices run clear when the thigh is pierced with a skewer.

5 Transfer the chicken to a carving dish and let rest for 5 minutes, covered with aluminum foil. Meanwhile, return the potatoes to the oven.

6 Carve the chicken into serving pieces and arrange on a large, heatproof serving dish. Arrange the potatoes around the chicken and drizzle over any remaining juices. Sprinkle with the remaining herbs and serve.

THAI NOODLES & VEGETABLES WITH TOFU

INGREDIENTS

Serves 4

¼ lb. firm tofu
2 tbsp. soy sauce
2 tsp. grated lime rind
2 lemongrass stalks
1 red chili
4 cups vegetable stock
2 slices fresh ginger, peeled
2 garlic cloves, peeled
2 sprigs of fresh cilantro
2½ cups dried egg noodles
1¾ cups shiitake or button mushrooms, sliced if large

2 carrots, peeled and cut into matchsticks
1 cup snow peas
2½ cups bok choy or other Chinese cabbage
1 tbsp. freshly chopped cilantro
salt and freshly ground black pepper
sprigs of fresh cilantro, to garnish

1 Drain the tofu well and cut into cubes. Put into a shallow dish with the soy sauce and lime rind. Stir well to coat, and leave to marinate for 30 minutes.

2 Meanwhile, put the lemongrass and chili on a chopping board and bruise with the side of a large knife, ensuring the blade is pointing away from your body. Put the vegetable stock in a large saucepan, and add the lemongrass, chili, ginger, garlic, and cilantro. Bring to a boil, cover, and simmer gently for 20 minutes.

3 Strain the stock into a clean saucepan. Return to a boil and add the noodles, tofu and its marinade, and the mushrooms. Simmer gently for 4 minutes.

4 Add the carrots, snow peas, bok choy, and cilantro, and simmer for an additional 3–4 minutes until the vegetables are just tender. Season to taste with salt and pepper. Garnish with cilantro sprigs and serve immediately.

FOOD FACT

Tofu is a curd derived from soybeans, and is an extremely protein-rich food that is virtually fat-free. Recent studies suggest that there are many health benefits to incorporating soy into your diet, not least of which are its cancer-prevention properties.

TAGLIATELLE WITH BROCCOLI & SESAME

INGREDIENTS

Serves 2

2⅔ cups broccoli, cut into florets
1 cup baby corn
1½ cups dried tagliatelle
1½ tbsp. tahini paste
1 tbsp. dark soy sauce
1 tbsp. dark brown sugar
1 tbsp. red wine vinegar
1 tbsp. corn oil

1 garlic clove, peeled and finely chopped
1-in. piece fresh ginger, peeled and shredded
½ tsp. dried chili flakes
salt and freshly ground black pepper
1 tbsp. toasted sesame seeds
slices of radish, to garnish

1 Bring a large saucepan of salted water to a boil, and add the broccoli and corn. Return the water to a boil, then using a slotted spoon, remove the vegetables at once, saving the water. Plunge them into cold water and drain well. Dry on paper towels and set aside.

2 Return the water to a boil. Add the tagliatelle and cook until al dente, or according to the package instructions. Drain well. Run under cold water, then drain well again.

3 Place the tahini, soy sauce, sugar, and vinegar into a bowl. Mix well, then set aside. Heat the oil in a wok or large skillet over a high heat and add the garlic, ginger, and chili flakes, and stir-fry for about 30 seconds. Add the broccoli and baby corn, and continue to stir-fry for about 3 minutes.

4 Add the tagliatelle to the wok along with the tahini mixture, and stir together for an additional 1–2 minutes until heated through. Season to taste with salt and pepper. Sprinkle with sesame seeds, garnish with the radish slices, and serve immediately.

FOOD FACT

Tahini is made from ground sesame seeds and is generally available in large supermarkets and Middle Eastern groceries. It is most often used in hummus.

PAD THAI NOODLES WITH MUSHROOMS

INGREDIENTS   Serves 4

2 cups flat rice noodles or rice
   vermicelli
1 tbsp. vegetable oil
2 garlic cloves, peeled and
   finely chopped
1 medium egg, lightly beaten
2 cups mixed mushrooms,
   such as shiitake, oyster, field,
   brown, and wild mushrooms
2 tbsp. lemon juice
1½ tbsp. Thai fish sauce

½ tsp. sugar
½ tsp. cayenne pepper
2 scallions, trimmed and cut
   into 1-in. pieces
¼ cup fresh bean sprouts

TO GARNISH:
chopped roasted peanuts
freshly chopped cilantro

1 Cook the noodles according
to the package instructions.
Drain well and set aside.

2 Heat a wok or large skillet.
Add the oil and garlic. Cook
until just golden. Add the egg
and stir quickly to break it up.

3 Cook for a few seconds
before adding the noodles
and mushrooms. Scrape down
the sides of the skillet to ensure
they mix with the egg and garlic.

4 Add the lemon juice, fish
sauce, sugar, cayenne pepper,
scallions, and half of the bean
sprouts, stirring quickly all the
time.

5 Cook over a high heat for an
additional 2–3 minutes until
everything is heated through.

6 Turn onto a serving plate.
Sprinkle with the remaining
bean sprouts. Garnish with the
chopped peanuts and cilantro,
and serve immediately.

TASTY TIP

Far Eastern cooking is low-fat
and often based around its
fragrant spices. An aromatic
alternative to this dish is to
replace the lemon used in
this dish with lemongrass.
Discard the outer leaves,
finely chop, and add with
the other ingredients
in Step 4.

PASTA WITH ZUCCHINI, ROSEMARY, & LEMON

INGREDIENTS

Serves 4

4½ cups dried pasta shapes, such as rigatoni
1½ tbsp. extra-virgin olive oil
2 garlic cloves, peeled and finely chopped
4 medium zucchini, thinly sliced
1 tbsp. freshly chopped rosemary
1 tbsp. freshly chopped parsley
2 tbsp. lemon zest

5 tbsp. lemon juice
2 tbsp. pitted ripe olives, coarsely chopped
2 tbsp. pitted green olives, coarsely chopped
salt and freshly ground black pepper

TO GARNISH:
lemon slices
sprigs of fresh rosemary

1 Bring a large saucepan of salted water to a boil and add the dried pasta.

2 Return to a boil and cook until al dente or according to the package instructions.

3 Meanwhile, when the pasta is almost done, heat the oil in a large skillet and add the garlic.

4 Cook over a medium heat until the garlic just begins to brown. Be careful not to overcook the garlic at this stage or it will become bitter.

5 Add the zucchini, rosemary, parsley, lemon zest, and juice. Cook for 3–4 minutes until the zucchini are just tender.

6 Add the olives to the skillet and stir well. Season to taste

with salt and pepper, and remove from the heat.

7 Drain the pasta well and add to the skillet. Stir until combined thoroughly. Garnish with lemon and sprigs of fresh rosemary, and serve immediately.

TASTY TIP

Look for pattypan squashes—small yellow or green squashes, shaped a little like flying saucers. They would make a good substitute for the zucchini in this recipe, as they have a similar flavor. Cut them in half vertically and cook as above.

VEGETARIAN SPAGHETTI BOLOGNESE

INGREDIENTS

Serves 4

2 tbsp. olive oil
1 onion, peeled and
  finely chopped
1 carrot, peeled and
  finely chopped
1 celery stick, trimmed and
  finely chopped
¼ lb. soy meat substitute, such
  as seitan

½ cup red wine
1¼ cups vegetable stock
1 tsp. ketchup
4 tbsp. tomato paste
4 cups dried spaghetti
4 tbsp. reduced-fat sour cream
salt and freshly ground
  black pepper
1 tbsp. freshly chopped parsley

1 Heat the oil in a large saucepan, and add the onion, carrot, and celery. Cook gently for 10 minutes, adding a little water if necessary, until softened and starting to brown.

2 Add the soy and cook an additional 2–3 minutes before adding the red wine. Increase the heat and simmer gently until nearly all the wine has evaporated.

3 Mix the vegetable stock and ketchup together, and add about half to the soy mixture, along with the tomato paste. Cover and simmer gently for about 45 minutes, adding the remaining stock as necessary.

4 Meanwhile, bring a large saucepan of salted water to a boil and add the spaghetti. Cook until al dente or according to the package instructions. Drain well.

Remove from the heat, add the sour cream, and season to taste with salt and pepper. Stir in the parsley, and serve immediately with the pasta.

HELPFUL HINT

Quorn is a flavorful texturized vegetable protein high in fiber and low in fat. It is derived from the mushroom family and readily takes on any flavor it is cooked with. Use an equal portion of quorn and soy meat substitute for a change.

SPRING VEGETABLE & HERB RISOTTO

INGREDIENTS

Serves 2–3

4 cups vegetable stock
½ cup asparagus tips, trimmed
1 cup baby carrots, scrubbed
½ cup peas, fresh or frozen
½ cup fine green beans, trimmed
1 tbsp. olive oil
1 onion, peeled and finely chopped

1 garlic clove, peeled and finely chopped
2 tsp. freshly chopped thyme
1 cup risotto rice
⅔ cup white wine
1 tbsp. each freshly chopped basil, chives, and parsley
1 tbsp. lemon zest
3 tbsp. reduced-fat sour cream
salt and freshly ground black pepper

1 Bring the vegetable stock to a boil in a large saucepan and add the asparagus, baby carrots, peas, and beans. Bring the stock back to a boil, and using a slotted spoon, remove the vegetables at once. Rinse under cold running water. Drain again and set aside. Keep the stock hot.

2 Heat the oil in a large, deep skillet and add the onion. Cook over a medium heat for 4–5 minutes until starting to brown. Add the garlic and thyme, and cook for a few seconds. Add the rice and stir well for a minute until the rice is hot and coated in oil.

3 Add the white wine and stir constantly until the wine is almost completely absorbed by the rice. Begin adding the stock,

a ladleful at a time, stirring well and waiting until the last ladleful has been absorbed before stirring in the next. Add the vegetables after using about half of the stock. Continue until all the stock is used. This will take 20–25 minutes. The rice and vegetables should both be tender.

4 Remove the skillet from the heat. Stir in the herbs, lemon zest, and sour cream. Season to taste with salt and pepper, and serve immediately.

FOOD FACT

In Italy, they use different types of rice, such as Arborio and Carnaroli, depending on whether the risotto is vegetable- or meat-based.

BABY ONION RISOTTO

INGREDIENTS   Serves 4

FOR THE BABY ONIONS:
1 tbsp. olive oil
18 baby onions, peeled and
  halved if large
pinch of sugar
1 tbsp. freshly chopped thyme

FOR THE RISOTTO:
1 tbsp. olive oil
1 small onion, peeled
  and finely chopped
2 garlic cloves, peeled
  and finely chopped

1½ cups risotto rice
⅔ cup red wine
4 cups hot vegetable stock
½ cup reduced-fat goat cheese
salt and freshly ground
  black pepper
sprigs of fresh thyme,
  to garnish
arugula, to serve

1 For the baby onions, heat the olive oil in a saucepan and add the onions with the sugar. Cover and cook over a low heat, stirring occasionally, for 20–25 minutes until caramelized. Uncover during the last 10 minutes of cooking.

2 Meanwhile, for the risotto, heat the oil in a large skillet and add the onion. Cook over a medium heat for 5 minutes until softened. Add the garlic and cook for an additional 30 seconds.

3 Add the risotto rice and stir well. Add the red wine and stir constantly until the wine is almost completely absorbed by the rice. Begin adding the stock, a ladleful at a time, stirring well and waiting until the last ladleful has been absorbed before stirring in the next. It will take 20–25 minutes to add all the stock, by

which time the rice should be just cooked but still firm. Remove from the heat.

4 Add the thyme to the onions and cook briefly. Increase the heat and allow the onion mixture to boil for 2–3 minutes until almost evaporated. Add the onion mixture to the risotto along with the goat cheese. Stir well and season to taste with salt and pepper. Garnish with sprigs of fresh thyme. Serve immediately with the arugula.

FOOD FACT

To peel baby onions, put them into a saucepan of water and bring to a boil. Drain and run under cold water. The skins will loosen and peel easily.

VEGETABLE BIRYANI

INGREDIENTS

Serves 4

2 tbsp. vegetable oil, plus a
  little extra for brushing
2 large onions, peeled and
  thinly sliced lengthwise
2 garlic cloves, peeled and
  finely chopped
1-in. piece fresh ginger, peeled
  and finely grated
1 small carrot, peeled and cut
  into sticks
1 small parsnip, peeled and
  diced
1 small sweet potato, peeled
  and diced
1 tbsp. medium curry paste

1 cup basmati rice
4 ripe tomatoes, peeled,
  seeded and diced
2½ cups vegetable stock
2 cups cauliflower florets
½ cup peas, defrosted if frozen
salt and freshly ground
  black pepper

TO GARNISH:
roasted cashews
raisins
fresh cilantro leaves

1 Preheat the oven to 400° F.
Put 1 tablespoon of the
vegetable oil in a large bowl with
the onions and toss to coat.
Lightly brush or spray a nonstick
baking sheet with a little more
oil. Spread half the onions on
the baking sheet and cook on
the top rack of the preheated
oven for 25–30 minutes, stirring
regularly until golden and crisp.
Remove from the oven and set
aside for the garnish.

2 Meanwhile, heat a large
flameproof casserole dish
over a medium heat, and add the
remaining oil and onions. Cook
for 5–7 minutes until softened
and starting to brown. Add a
little water if they start to stick.
Add the garlic and ginger, and
cook for another minute, then

add the carrots, parsnips, and
sweet potatoes. Cook the
vegetables for an additional 5
minutes. Add the curry paste and
stir for a minute until everything
is coated, then stir in the rice and
tomatoes. After 2 minutes, add
the stock and stir well. Bring to a
boil, cover, and simmer over a very
gentle heat for about 10 minutes.

3 Add the cauliflower and peas,
and cook for 8–10 minutes
or until the rice is tender. Season
to taste with salt and pepper. Serve
garnished with the crispy onions,
cashews, raisins, and cilantro.

TASTY TIP

Biryani is a dry dish. It is best
served with a moist side dish.

BROWN RICE SPICED PILAF

INGREDIENTS
Serves 4

1 tbsp. vegetable oil
1 tbsp. blanched almonds, slivered or chopped
1 onion, peeled and chopped
1 carrot, peeled and diced
2 cups flat mushrooms, sliced thickly
¼ tsp. ground cinnamon
large pinch dried chili flakes
½ cup dried apricots, coarsely chopped
2 tbsp. currants
1 tbsp. orange zest
1½ cups brown basmati rice

3¾ cups vegetable stock
2 tbsp. freshly chopped cilantro
2 tbsp. freshly cut chives
salt and freshly ground black pepper
cut chives, to garnish

1 Preheat the oven to 400° F. Heat the oil in a large flameproof casserole dish and add the almonds. Cook for 1–2 minutes until just browning. Be very careful, as the nuts will burn easily.

2 Add the onion and carrot. Cook for 5 minutes until softened and starting to turn brown. Add the mushrooms and cook for an additional 5 minutes, stirring often.

3 Add the cinnamon and chili flakes, and cook for about 30 seconds before adding the apricots, currants, orange zest, and rice.

4 Stir together well and add the stock. Bring to a boil, cover tightly, and transfer to the preheated oven. Cook for 45 minutes until the rice and vegetables are tender.

5 Stir the cilantro and chives into the pilaf, and season to taste with salt and pepper. Garnish with the extra chives and serve immediately.

FOOD FACT

The less processed or refined the food, the higher the nutritional content. Brown basmati rice, in particular, is one of the best rices to eat, releasing carbohydrate slowly into the blood, thereby maintaining the body's energy levels, as well as supplying the body with fiber.

SPICED COUSCOUS & VEGETABLES

INGREDIENTS

Serves 4

1 tbsp. olive oil
1 large shallot, peeled and finely chopped
1 garlic clove, peeled and finely chopped
1 small red bell pepper, seeded and cut into strips
1 small yellow bell pepper, seeded and cut into strips
1 small eggplant, diced
1 tsp. each ground turmeric, cumin, ground cinnamon, and paprika
2 tsp. ground coriander

large pinch of saffron strands
2 tomatoes, peeled, seeded, and diced
2 tbsp. lemon juice
1¼ cups couscous
1 cup vegetable stock
2 tbsp. raisins
2 tbsp. whole almonds
2 tbsp. freshly chopped parsley
2 tbsp. freshly chopped cilantro
salt and freshly ground black pepper

1 Heat the oil in a large skillet, add the shallot and garlic, and cook for 2–3 minutes until softened. Add the bell peppers and eggplant, and reduce the heat.

2 Cook for 8–10 minutes until the vegetables are tender, adding a little water if necessary.

3 Test a piece of eggplant to ensure it is cooked through. Add all the spices and cook for an additional minute, stirring.

4 Increase the heat and add the tomatoes and lemon juice. Cook for 2–3 minutes until the tomatoes have started to break down. Remove from the heat and allow to cool slightly.

5 Meanwhile, put the couscous into a large bowl. Bring the stock to a boil in a saucepan, then pour over the couscous. Stir well and cover with a clean dishtowel.

6 Allow to stand for 7–8 minutes until all the stock is absorbed and the couscous is tender.

7 Uncover the couscous and fluff with a fork. Stir in the vegetable and spice mixture along with the raisins, almonds, parsley, and cilantro. Season to taste with salt and pepper, and serve.

TASTY TIP

Although substantial enough to have as a main course, this dish would also be very nice served as a side dish.

BLACK BEAN CHILI WITH AVOCADO SALSA

INGREDIENTS

Serves 4

1½ cups black beans and black-eye peas, soaked overnight
2 tbsp. olive oil
1 large onion, peeled and finely chopped
1 red bell pepper, seeded and diced
2 garlic cloves, peeled and finely chopped
1 red chili, seeded and finely chopped
2 tsp. chili powder
1 tsp. ground cumin
2 tsp. ground coriander
14-oz. can tomatoes
2 cups vegetable stock
1 small ripe avocado, diced

½ small red onion, peeled and finely chopped
2 tbsp. freshly chopped cilantro
1 tbsp. lime juice
1 small tomato, peeled, seeded, and diced
salt and freshly ground black pepper
1 square unsweetened chocolate

TO GARNISH:
reduced-fat sour cream
lime slices
sprigs of cilantro

1 Drain the beans and place in a large saucepan with at least twice their volume of fresh water.

2 Bring slowly to a boil, skimming off any froth that rises to the surface. Boil rapidly for 10 minutes, then reduce the heat and simmer for about 45 minutes, adding more water if necessary. Drain and set aside.

3 Heat the oil in a large saucepan and add the onion and pepper. Cook for 3–4 minutes until softened. Add the garlic and chili. Cook for 5 minutes or until the onion and pepper have softened. Add the chili powder,

cumin, and coriander, and cook for 30 seconds. Add the beans along with the tomatoes and stock.

4 Bring to a boil and simmer uncovered for 40–45 minutes until the beans and vegetables are tender and the sauce has reduced.

5 Mix together the avocado, onion, cilantro, lime juice, and tomato. Season with salt and pepper, and set aside. Remove the chili from the heat. Break the chocolate into pieces. Sprinkle over the chili. Let stand for 2 minutes. Stir well. Garnish with sour cream, lime, and cilantro. Serve with the avocado salsa.

BOSTON-STYLE BAKED BEANS

INGREDIENTS

Serves 8

2 cups mixed dried beans, such as kidney beans, lima beans, chickpeas, or pinto beans
1 large onion, peeled and finely chopped
5 tbsp. molasses
2 tbsp. mustard
2 tbsp. light brown sugar
1 cup all-purpose flour
1 cup fine cornmeal

2 tbsp. sugar
2½ tsp. baking powder
½ tsp. salt
2 tbsp. freshly chopped thyme
2 medium eggs
1 cup milk
2 tbsp. melted butter
salt and freshly ground black pepper
sprigs of fresh parsley, to garnish

1 Preheat the oven to 250° F. Put the beans into a large saucepan and cover with at least twice their volume of water. Bring to a boil, and simmer for 2 minutes. Allow to stand for 1 hour. Return to a boil, and boil rapidly for about 10 minutes. Drain and set aside.

2 Mix together the onion, molasses, mustard, and sugar in a large bowl. Add the drained beans and 1¼ cups fresh water. Stir well, bring to a boil, cover, and transfer to the preheated oven for 4 hours in an ovenproof dish, stirring once every hour and adding more water if necessary.

3 When the beans are cooked, remove from the oven and keep warm. Increase the oven temperature to 400° F. Mix together the all-purpose flour, cornmeal, sugar, baking powder, salt, and most of the thyme. Set

aside about one third for the garnish. In a separate bowl, beat the eggs, then stir in the milk and butter. Pour the wet ingredients onto the dry ones and stir just enough to combine.

4 Pour into a buttered 7-inch square cake pan. Sprinkle with the remaining thyme. Cook for 30 minutes until golden and risen, or until a toothpick inserted into the center comes out clean. Cut into squares, then reheat the beans. Season to taste with salt and pepper, and serve immediately, garnished with parsley sprigs.

TASTY TIP

For those who are not vegetarians, add 1¼ cups cooked bacon to the beans as a tasty alternative.

PUMPKIN & CHICKPEA CURRY

INGREDIENTS

Serves 4

1 tbsp. vegetable oil
1 small onion, peeled
  and sliced
2 garlic cloves, peeled and
  finely chopped
1-in. piece ginger, peeled and
  grated
1 tsp. ground coriander
½ tsp. ground cumin
½ tsp. ground turmeric
¼ tsp. ground cinnamon
2 tomatoes, chopped
2 red bird's eye chilies, seeded
  and finely chopped

2½ cups pumpkin or butternut
  squash flesh, cubed
1 tbsp. hot curry paste
1¼ cups vegetable stock
1 large, firm banana
14-oz. can chickpeas, drained
  and rinsed
salt and freshly ground
  black pepper
1 tbsp. freshly chopped
  cilantro
sprigs of fresh cilantro,
  to garnish
rice or naan bread, to serve

1 Heat 1 tablespoon of the oil in a saucepan and add the onion. Cook gently for 5 minutes until softened.

2 Add the garlic, ginger, and spices, and cook for an additional minute. Add the chopped tomatoes and chilies, and cook for another minute.

3 Add the pumpkin and curry paste and cook for 3–4 minutes before adding the stock.

4 Stir well, bring to a boil, and simmer for 20 minutes until the pumpkin is tender.

5 Thickly slice the banana and add to the pumpkin along with the chickpeas. Simmer for an additional 5 minutes.

6 Season to taste with salt and pepper, and add the chopped cilantro. Serve immediately, garnished with cilantro sprigs and some rice or naan bread.

HELPFUL HINT

Curry pastes come in mild, medium, and hot varieties. Although hot curry paste is recommended in this recipe, use whichever one you prefer.

ROASTED MIXED VEGETABLES WITH GARLIC & HERB SAUCE

INGREDIENTS

Serves 4

1 large garlic bulb
1 large onion, peeled and cut into wedges
4 small carrots, peeled and quartered
4 small parsnips, peeled
6 small potatoes, scrubbed and halved
1 fennel bulb, sliced thickly
4 sprigs of fresh rosemary

4 sprigs of fresh thyme
2 tbsp. olive oil
salt and freshly ground black pepper
1 cup low-fat cream cheese with herbs and garlic
4 tbsp. milk
1 tbsp. lemon zest
sprigs of thyme, to garnish

1 Preheat the oven to 425° F. Cut the garlic in half horizontally. Put into a large roasting pan with all the vegetables and herbs.

2 Add the oil, season well with salt and pepper, and toss together to coat lightly in the oil.

3 Cover with foil and roast in the preheated oven for 50 minutes. Remove the foil and cook for an additional 30 minutes until all the vegetables are tender and slightly charred.

4 Remove the pan from the oven and allow to cool.

5 In a small saucepan, melt the low-fat cream cheese together with the milk and lemon zest.

6 Remove the garlic from the roasting pan and squeeze the flesh into a bowl. Mash thoroughly, then add to the sauce. Heat through gently. Season the vegetables to taste. Pour some sauce into small ramekins and garnish with 4 sprigs of thyme. Serve immediately with the roasted vegetables and the sauce to dip.

TASTY TIP

This dish can also be served as a delicious accompaniment to any broiled or roasted fish, seafood, or chicken dish. Following the Mediterranean theme, marinate or drizzle the fish with a little olive oil, lemon juice, lemon rind, and mixed herbs.

ROASTED BUTTERNUT SQUASH

INGREDIENTS   Serves 4

2 small butternut squash
4 garlic cloves, peeled and
   crushed
1 tbsp. olive oil
salt and freshly ground
   black pepper
1 tbsp. oil
4 medium leeks, trimmed,
   cleaned, and thinly sliced
1 tbsp. black mustard seeds
11-oz. can lima beans, drained
   and rinsed

¾ cup fine green beans, halved
⅔ cup vegetable stock
1¼ cups arugula
2 tbsp. freshly cut chives

TO SERVE:
4 tbsp. reduced-fat sour cream
mixed salad

1 Preheat the oven to 400° F.
Cut the butternut squash in
half lengthwise and scoop out all
of the seeds.

2 Cut the squash in a diamond
pattern with a sharp knife.
Mix the garlic with the olive oil,
and brush over the cut surfaces of
the squash. Season well with salt
and pepper. Put on a baking
sheet and roast for 40 minutes
until tender.

3 Heat the oil in a saucepan
and cook the leeks and
mustard seeds for 5 minutes.

4 Add the drained lima beans,
green beans, and vegetable
stock. Bring to a boil, and
simmer gently for 5 minutes until
the green beans are tender.

5 Remove from the heat and
stir in the arugula and chives.

Season well. Remove the squash
from the oven and allow to cool
for 5 minutes. Spoon in the bean
mixture. Garnish with a few cut
chives and serve immediately
with the sour cream and a mixed
salad.

HELPFUL HINT

If preferred, use dried lima
beans instead of the canned
variety. To cook dried beans,
soak ⅔ cup dried lima beans
in plenty of water overnight.
Drain and put into a saucepan
with at least twice their
volume of fresh water. Bring
to a boil and boil
rapidly for 10 minutes, reduce
the heat, and simmer gently
for an additional 45–50
minutes until tender. Drain
and use as above.

VEGETABLE CASSOULET

INGREDIENTS

Serves 6

⅔ cup dried kidney beans, soaked overnight
2 tbsp. olive oil
2 garlic cloves, peeled and chopped
9 baby onions, peeled and halved
2 carrots, peeled and diced
2 celery stalks, trimmed and finely chopped
1 red bell pepper, seeded and chopped

1½ cups mixed mushrooms, sliced
1 tbsp. each freshly chopped rosemary, thyme, and sage
⅔ cup red wine
4 tbsp. tomato paste
1 tbsp. dark soy sauce
salt and freshly ground black pepper
½ cup fresh bread crumbs
1 tbsp. freshly chopped parsley
sprigs of basil, to garnish

1 Preheat the oven to 375° F. Drain the kidney beans and place in a saucepan with 1 quart of fresh water. Bring to a boil, and boil rapidly for 10 minutes. Reduce the heat and simmer gently for 45 minutes. Drain the beans, setting aside 1¼ cups of the liquid.

2 Heat 1 tablespoon of the oil in a flameproof casserole dish and add the garlic, onions, carrot, celery, and red bell pepper. Cook gently for 10–12 minutes until tender and starting to brown. Add more water if the vegetables start to stick. Add the mushrooms and cook for an additional 5 minutes until softened. Add the herbs and stir briefly.

3 Stir in the red wine and boil rapidly for about 5 minutes until reduced and syrupy. Stir in the beans and their liquid, the

tomato paste, and soy sauce. Season to taste with salt and pepper.

4 Mix together the bread crumbs and parsley with the remaining 1 tablespoon of oil. Sprinkle this mixture evenly over the top of the stew. Cover loosely with foil and transfer to the preheated oven. Cook for 30 minutes. Carefully remove the foil and cook for an additional 15–20 minutes until the topping is crisp and golden. Garnish with basil sprigs and serve immediately.

HELPFUL HINT

If cooking dried kidney beans is too time consuming, then use canned beans instead.

CREAMY LENTILS

INGREDIENTS

Serves 4

1¼ cups lentils
1 tbsp. olive oil
1 garlic clove, peeled and
finely chopped
1 tbsp. lemon zest
2 tbsp. lemon juice
1 tsp. mustard
1 tbsp. freshly chopped
tarragon
3 tbsp. reduced-fat sour cream

salt and freshly ground
black pepper
2 small tomatoes, seeded and
chopped
5 tbsp. pitted ripe olives
1 tbsp. freshly chopped
parsley

TO GARNISH:
sprigs of fresh tarragon
lemon wedges

1 Put the lentils in a saucepan with plenty of cold water, and bring to a boil.

2 Boil rapidly for 10 minutes, reduce the heat, and simmer gently for an additional 20 minutes until tender. Drain well.

3 Meanwhile, prepare the dressing. Heat the oil in a skillet over a medium heat.

4 Add the garlic and cook for about a minute until just beginning to brown. Add the lemon zest and juice.

5 Add the mustard and cook for an additional 30 seconds.

6 Add the tarragon and sour cream, and season to taste with salt and pepper.

7 Simmer and add the drained lentils, tomatoes, and olives.

8 Transfer to a serving dish and sprinkle the chopped parsley on top.

9 Garnish the lentils with the tarragon sprigs and the lemon wedges, and serve immediately.

FOOD FACT

Puy lentils are smaller and fatter than green lentils, and have a mottled coloring, ranging from gold to green. They keep their shape and firm texture when cooked. They may not always be French, however, as this type of lentil is also grown extensively in Canada.

PEPERONATA

INGREDIENTS   Serves 6

2 red bell peppers
2 yellow bell peppers
1 lb. waxy potatoes
1 large onion
2 tbsp. good-quality virgin
   olive oil
2¼ cups tomatoes, peeled,
   seeded, and chopped

2 small zucchini
5 tbsp. pitted ripe olives,
   quartered
small handful basil leaves
salt and freshly ground
   black pepper
crusty bread, to serve

1 Prepare the bell peppers by halving them lengthwise and removing the stems, seeds, and membranes.

2 Cut the peppers lengthwise into strips about ½ inch wide. Peel the potatoes and cut into rough dice, about 1–1¼ inch across. Cut the onion lengthwise into 8 wedges.

3 Heat the olive oil in a large saucepan over a medium heat.

4 Add the onion and cook for about 5 minutes or until starting to brown.

5 Add the bell peppers, potatoes, tomatoes, zucchini, ripe olives, and about 4 torn basil leaves. Season to taste with salt and pepper.

6 Stir the mixture, cover, and cook over a very low heat for about 40 minutes or until the vegetables are tender but still hold their shape. Garnish with the remaining basil. Transfer to a serving bowl and serve immediately with chunks of crusty bread.

FOOD FACT

This dish is delicious served with Parmesan melba toasts. To make, simply remove the crusts from 4 slices of thin white bread. Lightly toast and allow to cool before splitting each piece in half by slicing horizontally. Cut diagonally into triangles, place under a hot broiler, and toast each side for a few minutes until golden and curling at the edges. Sprinkle with finely shredded Parmesan cheese, and melt under the broiler.

MUSHROOM STEW

INGREDIENTS

Serves 4

¼ cup dried porcini
  mushrooms
2 lbs. assorted fresh
  mushrooms, wiped
2 tbsp. good-quality virgin
  olive oil
1 onion, peeled and finely
  chopped
2 garlic cloves, peeled and
  finely chopped
1 tbsp. fresh thyme leaves

pinch of ground cloves
salt and freshly ground
  black pepper
2¼ cups tomatoes, peeled,
  seeded, and chopped
2 cups instant polenta
2½ cups vegetable stock
3 tbsp. freshly chopped
  mixed herbs
sprigs of parsley, to garnish

1 Soak the porcini mushrooms in a small bowl of hot water for 20 minutes.

2 Drain and set aside the porcini mushrooms and their soaking liquid. Cut the fresh mushrooms in half and set aside.

3 In a saucepan, heat the oil and add the onion.

4 Cook gently for 5–7 minutes until softened. Add the garlic, thyme, and cloves, and continue cooking for 2 minutes.

5 Add all the mushrooms and cook for 8–10 minutes until the mushrooms have softened, stirring often. Season to taste with salt and pepper, and add the tomatoes and the soaking liquid.

6 Simmer, partly covered, over a low heat for about 20 minutes until thickened. Adjust the seasoning to taste.

7 Meanwhile, cook the polenta according to the package instructions using the vegetable stock. Stir in the herbs and divide among 4 dishes.

8 Spoon the mushrooms over the polenta, garnish with the parsley, and serve immediately.

TASTY TIP

For a dinner party version of this recipe, add a generous splash of red wine with the soaking liquid in step 5, and just before serving, remove from the heat and stir in 2 tablespoons of low-fat plain yogurt.

HUEVOS RANCHEROS

INGREDIENTS

Serves 4

2 tbsp. olive oil
1 large onion, peeled and
    finely chopped
1 red bell pepper, seeded and
    finely chopped
2 garlic cloves, peeled and
    finely chopped
2–4 green chilies, seeded and
    finely chopped
1 tsp. ground cumin
1 tsp. chili powder
2 tsp. ground coriander
2 tbsp. freshly chopped
    cilantro

2¼ cups ripe plum tomatoes,
    peeled, seeded, and coarsely
    chopped
¼ tsp. sugar
8 small eggs
4–8 flour tortillas
salt and freshly ground
    black pepper
sprigs of fresh cilantro,
    to garnish
refried beans, to
    serve (optional)

1 Heat the oil in a large, heavy saucepan. Add the onion and bell pepper, and cook over a medium heat for 10 minutes.

2 Add the garlic, chilies, ground cumin, chili powder, and chopped cilantro, and cook for an additional minute.

3 Add the tomatoes and sugar. Stir well, cover, and cook for 20 minutes. Uncover and cook for an additional 20 minutes.

4 Lightly poach the eggs in a large skillet filled with gently simmering water. Drain well and keep warm.

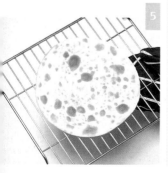

5 Place the tortillas briefly under a hot broiler. Turn once, then remove from the broiler when crisp.

6 Add the freshly chopped cilantro to the tomato sauce and season to taste with salt and pepper.

7 To serve, arrange 2 tortillas on each serving plate, then place 2 eggs on the top and spoon the sauce over. Garnish with sprigs of fresh cilantro, and serve immediately with warm refried beans, if desired.

HELPFUL HINT

Although eggs are rich in protein, they also contain high levels of cholesterol and fat, so it is best to eat no more than 2–4 eggs per week.

EGGPLANT & YOGURT DIP

INGREDIENTS

Makes 2 cups

2 eggplants
1 tbsp. light olive oil
1 tbsp. lemon juice
2 garlic cloves, peeled and crushed
9-oz. jar pimientos, drained
⅔ cup low-fat plain yogurt

salt and freshly ground black pepper
2 tbsp. pitted ripe olives, chopped
1½ cups cauliflower florets
2⅔ cups broccoli florets
½ cup carrots, peeled and cut into 2-in. strips

1 Preheat the oven to 400° F. Pierce the skin of the eggplants with a fork and place on a baking sheet. Cook in the preheated oven for 40 minutes or until very soft.

2 Cool the eggplants, then cut in half and scoop out the flesh and tip into a bowl.

3 Mash the eggplant with the olive oil, lemon juice, and garlic for a few seconds in a food processor until blended.

4 Dice the pimientos and add to the eggplant mixture.

5 When blended, add the yogurt. Stir well and season to taste with salt and pepper.

6 Add the chopped olives and leave in the refrigerator to chill for at least 30 minutes.

7 Place the cauliflower and broccoli florets and carrot strips into a saucepan, and cover with boiling water. Simmer for 2 minutes, then rinse in cold water. Drain and serve as hors d'oeuvres to accompany the dip.

TASTY TIP

Following the Middle Eastern style of this dish, why not also serve pieces of warmed, unleavened bread such as naan or pita with this dip? To warm the bread, preheat the oven to 400° F, wrap in preheated foil, and place in the oven for 5–7 minutes, depending on the size of the bread.

BULGUR SALAD WITH MINTY LEMON DRESSING

INGREDIENTS
Serves 4

⅔ cup bulgur
4-in. piece cucumber
2 shallots, peeled
1 cup baby corn
3 ripe but firm tomatoes

FOR THE DRESSING:
1 tbsp. lemon rind
3 tbsp. lemon juice

3 tbsp. freshly chopped mint
2 tbsp. freshly chopped parsley
1–2 tsp. honey
2 tbsp. corn oil
salt and freshly ground
   black pepper

1 Place the bulgur in a large saucepan and cover with boiling water.

2 Simmer for about 10 minutes, then drain thoroughly and turn into a serving bowl.

3 Cut the cucumber into small dice, chop the shallots finely, and set aside. Steam the corn over a saucepan of boiling water for 10 minutes or until tender. Drain and slice into thick chunks.

4 Cut a cross on the top of each tomato, and place in boiling water until their skins start to peel away.

5 Remove the skins and the seeds, and cut the tomatoes into small dice.

6 Make the dressing by briskly whisking all the ingredients in a small bowl until mixed well.

7 When the bulgur has cooled a little, add all the prepared vegetables and stir in the dressing. Season to taste with salt and pepper, and serve.

FOOD FACT

This dish is loosely based on the Middle Eastern dish tabbouleh, a type of salad in which all the ingredients are mixed together and served cold.

CARROT & PARSNIP TERRINE

INGREDIENTS

Serves 8–10

3¾ cups carrots, peeled and
  chopped
2 cups parsnips, peeled and
  chopped
6 tbsp. reduced-fat sour cream
10 cups spinach, rinsed
1 tbsp. brown sugar
1 tbsp. freshly chopped parsley
½ tsp. freshly grated nutmeg
salt and freshly ground
  black pepper

6 medium eggs
sprigs of fresh basil,
  to garnish

FOR THE TOMATO COULIS:

1½ cups ripe tomatoes, seeded
  and chopped
1 medium onion, peeled and
  finely chopped

1 Preheat the oven to 400° F. Grease and line a 3 x 9 inch loaf pan with nonstick baking parchment. Cook the carrots and parsnips in boiling, salted water for 10–15 minutes or until very tender. Drain and purée separately. Add 2 tablespoons of sour cream to both the carrots and the parsnips.

2 Steam the spinach for 5–10 minutes or until very tender. Drain and squeeze out as much liquid as possible, then stir in the remaining sour cream.

3 Add the brown sugar to the carrot purée, the parsley to the parsnip mixture, and the nutmeg to the spinach. Season all to taste with salt and pepper.

4 Beat 2 eggs, add to the spinach, and turn into the prepared pan. Add another 2 beaten eggs to the carrot mixture and layer carefully on top of the spinach. Beat the remaining eggs into the parsnip purée and layer on top of the terrine.

5 Place the pan in a baking dish and pour in enough hot water to come halfway up the sides of the pan. Cook for 1 hour until a toothpick inserted into the center comes out clean.

6 Let the terrine cool for at least 30 minutes. Run a sharp knife around the edges. Turn out onto a dish and set aside.

7 Make the tomato coulis by simmering the tomatoes and onions together for 5–10 minutes until thickened slightly.

8 Season to taste. Blend well in a blender or food processor and serve as an accompaniment to the terrine. Garnish with sprigs of basil and serve.

CHINESE SALAD WITH SOY & GINGER DRESSING

INGREDIENTS

Serves 4

1 head of Chinese cabbage
7-oz. can water chestnuts, drained
6 scallions, trimmed
4 ripe but firm cherry tomatoes
1 cup snow peas
¾ cup bean sprouts
2 tbsp. freshly chopped cilantro

FOR THE DRESSING:
2 tbsp. corn oil
4 tbsp. light soy sauce
1-in. piece ginger, peeled and grated
2 tbsp. lemon zest
1 tbsp. lemon juice
salt and freshly ground black pepper
crusty white bread, to serve

1 Rinse and finely shred the Chinese cabbage and place in a serving dish.

2 Slice the water chestnuts into small slivers and cut the scallions diagonally into 1-inch lengths, then split lengthwise into thin strips.

3 Cut the tomatoes in half, then slice each half into 3 wedges, and set aside.

4 Simmer the snow peas in boiling water for 2 minutes until beginning to soften, drain, and cut in half diagonally.

5 Arrange the water chestnuts, scallions, snow peas, tomatoes, and bean sprouts on top of the shredded Chinese cabbage. Garnish with the freshly chopped cilantro.

6 Make the dressing by whisking all the ingredients together in a small bowl until mixed thoroughly. Serve with the bread and the salad.

TASTY TIP

A delicious alternative is to add some chicken. Cut 2 skinless chicken breasts into strips, place in a dish, and add 1 finely chopped clove of garlic, 2 tablespoons of light soy sauce, and 1 tablespoon of oil. Leave for 30 minutes, then cook in a hot skillet or wok for 5–10 minutes, stirring frequently. Serve on top of the salad with a sprinkling of sesame seeds.

CURLY ENDIVE & SEAFOOD SALAD

INGREDIENTS

Serves 4

1 head of curly endive
2 green bell peppers
5-in. piece cucumber
1 cup squid, cleaned and cut
   into thin rings
2 cups baby asparagus spears
4 thin smoked salmon slices,
   cut into wide strips
2 cups fresh cooked mussels,
   in their shells

FOR THE LEMON DRESSING:

2 tbsp. corn oil
1 tbsp. white wine vinegar
5 tbsp. fresh lemon juice
1–2 tsp. sugar
1 tsp. mild mustard
salt and freshly ground
   black pepper

TO GARNISH:

slices of lemon
sprigs of fresh cilantro

1 Rinse and tear the endive into small pieces and arrange on a serving platter.

2 Remove the seeds from the bell peppers and dice the peppers and cucumber. Sprinkle over the endive.

3 Bring a saucepan of water to a boil and add the squid rings. Bring the saucepan up to a boil again, then turn off the heat and let stand for 5 minutes. Drain and rinse thoroughly in cold water.

4 Cook the asparagus in boiling water for 5 minutes or until tender but just crisp. Arrange with the squid, smoked salmon, and mussels on top of the salad.

5 To make the lemon dressing, put all the ingredients into a screw-topped jar or into a small bowl, and mix thoroughly until the ingredients are combined.

6 Spoon 3 tablespoons of the dressing over the salad and serve the remainder in a small jug. Garnish the salad with slices of lemon and sprigs of cilantro, and serve.

TASTY TIP

Why not substitute a 1¼ cups diced cooked turkey breast for the seafood? Add 10 cooked baby new potatoes to the salad. Peel and halve 12 hard-boiled eggs, and use as a garnish. Pour the lemon dressing over the salad and serve.

WARM FRUITY RICE SALAD

INGREDIENTS

Serves 4

¾ cup mixed basmati and wild rice
¼ lb. skinless chicken breast
1¼ cups chicken or vegetable stock
¾ cup dried apricots
½ cup dried dates
3 celery stalks

FOR THE DRESSING:
2 tbsp. corn oil
1 tbsp. white wine vinegar
4 tbsp. lemon juice
1–2 tsp. honey, warmed
1 tsp. mustard
freshly ground black pepper

TO GARNISH:
6 scallions
sprigs of fresh cilantro

1 Place the rice in a saucepan of boiling, salted water and cook for 15–20 minutes or until tender. Rinse thoroughly with boiling water and set aside.

2 Meanwhile, wipe the chicken and place in a shallow saucepan with the stock.

3 Bring to a boil, cover, and simmer for about 15 minutes or until the chicken is cooked thoroughly and the juices run clear.

4 Leave the chicken in the stock until cool enough to handle, then cut into thin slices.

5 Chop the apricots and dates into small pieces. Peel any tough membranes from the outside of the celery and dice. Fold the apricots, dates, celery, and sliced chicken into the warm rice.

6 Make the dressing by whisking all the ingredients together in a small bowl until mixed thoroughly. Pour 2–3 tablespoons over the rice and stir in gently and evenly. Serve the remaining dressing separately.

7 Trim and chop the scallions. Sprinkle the scallions over the top of the salad, and garnish with the sprigs of cilantro. Serve while still warm.

HELPFUL HINT

It is very important that the chicken is cooked properly in Step 3. Some chicken breasts can be denser than others, so the best way to test is to cut into the thickest part of the meat and check that there is no pinkness.

FUSILLI PASTA WITH SPICY TOMATO SALSA

INGREDIENTS

Serves 4

6 large, ripe tomatoes
2 tbsp. lemon juice
2 tbsp. lime juice
2 tsp. grated lime rind
2 shallots, peeled and finely chopped
2 garlic cloves, peeled and finely chopped

1–2 red chilies
1–2 green chilies
6 cups fresh fusilli pasta
4 tbsp. reduced-fat sour cream
2 tbsp. freshly chopped basil
sprig of oregano, to garnish

1 Place the tomatoes in a bowl and cover with boiling water. Allow to stand until the skins start to peel away.

2 Remove the skins from the tomatoes, quarter each, and remove all the seeds. Dice the flesh and put in a small saucepan. Add the lemon and lime juice and the lime rind, and stir well.

3 Add the chopped shallots and garlic. Remove the seeds carefully from the chilies, chop finely, and add to the saucepan.

4 Bring to a boil, and simmer gently for 5–10 minutes until the salsa has thickened slightly.

5 Set the salsa aside to allow the flavors to develop while the pasta is cooking.

6 Bring a large saucepan of water to a boil and add the pasta. Simmer for 3–4 minutes or until the pasta is just tender.

7 Drain the pasta and rinse in boiling water. Top with a large spoonful of salsa and a small spoonful of sour cream. Garnish with the chopped basil and oregano, and serve immediately.

FOOD FACT

Pasta is an excellent source of complex carbohydrates and can be a part of a healthy diet. Complex carbohydrates are broken down by the body more slowly than simple carbohydrates (contained in cakes, sweets, and cookies), and provide a sustained source of energy.

HOT & SPICY RED CABBAGE WITH APPLES

INGREDIENTS   Serves 8

7 cups red cabbage, cored and shredded
2½ cups onions, peeled and finely sliced
2¾ cups apples, peeled, cored and finely sliced
½ tsp. mixed spices
1 tsp. ground cinnamon
2 tbsp. golden brown sugar
salt and freshly ground black pepper
2 tbsp. grated orange rind

1 tbsp. fresh orange juice
¼ cup medium-sweet apple cider (or apple juice)
2 tbsp. wine vinegar

TO SERVE:
reduced-fat sour cream
freshly ground black pepper

1 Preheat the oven to 300° F. Put just enough cabbage in a large casserole dish to cover the base evenly.

2 Place a layer of the onions and apples on top of the cabbage.

3 Sprinkle a little of the mixed spice, cinnamon, and sugar over the top. Season with salt and pepper.

4 Spoon over a small portion of the orange rind, orange juice, and the cider.

5 Continue to layer the casserole dish with the ingredients in the same order until used up.

6 Pour the vinegar as evenly as possible over the top layer of the ingredients.

7 Cover the casserole dish with a close-fitting lid, and cook in the preheated oven, stirring occasionally, for 2 hours until the cabbage is moist and tender. Serve immediately with the sour cream and black pepper.

TASTY TIP

This recipe uses wine vinegar, but this can be substituted with balsamic vinegar, which has a soft, sweet and sour, slightly fuller taste, and which will work well with the spices in this recipe. Balsamic vinegar is widely available and can be purchased in most supermarkets.

MARINATED VEGETABLE KABOBS

INGREDIENTS

Serves 4

2 small zucchini, cut into
¾-in. pieces
½ green bell pepper, seeded
and cut into 1-in. pieces
½ red bell pepper, seeded and
cut into 1-in. pieces
½ yellow bell pepper, seeded
and cut into 1-in. pieces
8 baby onions, peeled
8 button mushrooms
8 cherry tomatoes
freshly chopped parsley,
to garnish
couscous, to serve

FOR THE MARINADE:
1 tbsp. light olive oil
4 tbsp. dry sherry
2 tbsp. light soy sauce
1 red chili, seeded and finely
chopped
2 garlic cloves, peeled and
crushed
1-in. piece ginger, peeled and
finely grated

1 Place the zucchini, bell peppers, and baby onions in a saucepan of just-boiled water. Bring back to a boil, and simmer for about 30 seconds.

2 Drain and rinse the cooked vegetables in cold water, and dry on absorbent paper towels.

3 Thread the cooked vegetables, mushrooms, and tomatoes alternately onto skewers and place in a large, shallow dish.

4 Make the marinade by beating all the ingredients together until blended thoroughly. Pour the marinade evenly over the kabobs, then chill in the refrigerator for at least 1 hour. Spoon the marinade over the kabobs occasionally during this time.

5 Place the kabobs in a hot griddle pan or on a hot barbecue, and cook gently for 10–12 minutes. Turn the kabobs frequently, and brush with the marinade when needed. When the vegetables are tender, sprinkle with chopped parsley, and serve immediately with couscous.

TASTY TIP

If using wooden skewers and cooking over a barbecue, soak in cold water for 30 minutes before using. Although these kabobs use only vegetables, large chunks of fish, such as cod or jumbo shrimp, could be added alternately between the vegetables and cooked as in Step 5.

PUMPKIN PÂTÉ

INGREDIENTS

Serves 8–10

1 lb. fresh pumpkin flesh (when in season), peeled, or 15-oz. can pumpkin purée
1 tsp. corn oil
1 small onion, peeled and finely chopped
½ orange bell pepper, seeded and finely chopped
2 medium eggs, beaten
3 tbsp. low-fat plain yogurt
1 cup reduced-fat hard cheese, such as cheddar, shredded
¼ cup wheat germ

1 tbsp. freshly chopped oregano
salt and freshly ground black pepper
fresh salad leaves and crusty bread, to serve

1 Preheat the oven to 350° F. Grease and line a 3 x 9 inch loaf pan. Cut the pumpkin into cubes, and place in a saucepan of boiling water.

2 Simmer for 20 minutes or until the pumpkin is very tender. Drain and allow to cool, then mash well to form a purée.

3 Heat the oil in a nonstick skillet, and cook the chopped onion and pepper for about 4 minutes until softened.

4 Mix together the puréed pumpkin, softened vegetables, eggs, and yogurt. Add the cheese, wheat germ, and oregano. Season with salt and pepper.

5 When the pumpkin mixture is well blended, spoon it into the prepared pan and stand in a

baking dish. Fill the tray with hot water to come halfway up the sides of the pan, and carefully place in the preheated oven.

6 Cook for about 1 hour or until firm, then leave to cool. Chill in the refrigerator for 30 minutes before turning out onto a serving plate. Serve with crusty bread and a fresh salad.

TASTY TIP

This pâté, after being mixed together in Step 4, could also be used to stuff fresh pasta. Serve the pasta tossed in a little extra-virgin olive oil and some coarsely torn, fresh sage leaves.

SPANISH BAKED TOMATOES

INGREDIENTS

Serves 4

¾ cup brown rice
2½ cups vegetable stock
2 tsp. corn oil
2 shallots, peeled and finely chopped
1 garlic clove, peeled and crushed
1 green bell pepper, seeded and diced
1 red chili, seeded and finely chopped
½ cup button mushrooms, finely chopped

1 tbsp. freshly chopped oregano
salt and freshly ground black pepper
4 large ripe tomatoes
1 large egg, beaten
1 tsp. sugar
basil leaves, to garnish
crusty bread, to serve

1 Preheat the oven to 350° F. Place the rice in a saucepan, pour in the vegetable stock, and bring to a boil. Simmer gently for 30 minutes or until the rice is tender. Drain and turn into a large bowl.

2 Add 1 teaspoon of corn oil to a small nonstick skillet and cook the shallots, garlic, bell pepper, chili, and mushrooms for 2 minutes. Add to the rice, along with the chopped oregano. Season with salt and pepper.

3 Slice the top off each tomato. Cut and scoop out the flesh, removing the hard core. Pass the tomato flesh through a strainer. Add 1 tablespoon of the juice to the rice mixture. Stir in the beaten egg, and mix. Sprinkle sugar in the base of each tomato. Pile the rice mixture into the shells.

4 Place the tomatoes in a baking dish and pour a little cold water around them. Replace their lids and drizzle a few drops of corn oil over the tops.

5 Cook in the preheated oven for about 25 minutes. Garnish with the basil leaves and season with black pepper. Serve immediately with crusty bread.

TASTY TIP

This dish is also delicious when made with meat. Add ¼ lb. of lean ground beef in Step 2. Heat the skillet and fry the meat on a high heat until cooked through and brown, before adding the rest of the ingredients.

STUFFED ONIONS WITH PINE NUTS

INGREDIENTS

Serves 4

4 medium onions, peeled
2 garlic cloves, peeled and crushed
2 tbsp. fresh whole-wheat bread crumbs
2 tbsp. fresh white bread crumbs
2 tbsp. golden raisins
4 tbsp. pine nuts

½ cup reduced-fat hard cheese, such as cheddar, shredded, plus extra for sprinkling
2 tbsp. freshly chopped parsley
1 medium egg, beaten
salt and freshly ground black pepper
lettuce leaves, to serve

1 Preheat the oven to 400° F. Bring a saucepan of water to a boil, then add the onions and cook gently for about 15 minutes.

2 Drain well. Let the onions cool, then slice each one in half horizontally.

3 Scoop out most of the onion flesh, but leave a reasonably firm shell.

4 Chop up 4 tablespoons of the onion flesh and place in a bowl with the garlic, bread crumbs, golden raisins, pine nuts, shredded cheese, and parsley.

5 Mix the bread-crumb mixture together thoroughly. Bind together with as much of the beaten egg as necessary to make a firm filling. Season to taste with salt and pepper.

6 Pile the mixture back into the onion shells, and sprinkle with some shredded cheese. Place on a greased baking sheet and cook in the preheated oven for 20–30 minutes or until golden brown. Serve immediately with the lettuce leaves.

FOOD FACT

While this dish is delicious on its own, it also complements barbecued meat and fish. The onion takes on a mellow, nutty flavor when cooked.

WARM LEEK & TOMATO SALAD

INGREDIENTS
Serves 4

1 lb. baby leeks, trimmed
2 medium ripe tomatoes
2 shallots, peeled and cut into
  thin wedges

FOR THE DRESSING:
2 tbsp. honey
2 tsp. grated lime rind
4 tbsp. lime juice

1 tbsp. light olive oil
1 tsp. mustard
salt and freshly ground
  black pepper

TO GARNISH:
freshly chopped tarragon
freshly chopped basil

1 Trim the leeks so that they are all the same length. Place in a steamer over a saucepan of boiling water, and steam for 8 minutes or until just tender.

2 Drain the leeks thoroughly and arrange in a shallow serving dish.

3 Make a cross in the top of the tomatoes, place in a bowl, and cover them with boiling water until their skins start to peel away. Remove from the bowl and carefully remove the skins.

4 Quarter the tomatoes, remove the seeds, then dice. Spoon over the top of the leeks, along with the shallots.

5 In a small bowl, make the dressing by whisking the honey, lime rind, lime juice, olive oil, mustard, salt, and pepper. Pour 3 tablespoons of the dressing over the leeks and tomatoes, and garnish with the tarragon and

basil. Serve while the leeks are still warm, with the remaining dressing served separately.

HELPFUL HINT

An easy way to measure honey is to plunge a metal measuring spoon into boiling water. Drain the spoon, then dip into the honey.

HELPFUL HINT

Really flavorful tomatoes can make all the difference to tomato dishes. Use plum or vittoria tomatoes, as they have been left on the vine longer to ripen, and therefore have a better flavor.

WINTER COLESLAW

INGREDIENTS

Serves 6

½ lb. white cabbage
1 medium red onion, peeled
½ lb. carrots, peeled
1 head celeriac, peeled
2 celery stalks, trimmed
½ cup golden raisins

FOR THE DRESSING:
⅔ cup low-fat plain yogurt
1 garlic clove, peeled and
   crushed
1 tbsp. lemon juice
1 tsp. honey
1 tbsp. freshly cut chives

1 Remove the hard core from the cabbage with a small knife and shred finely.

2 Slice the onion finely and coarsely grate the carrot.

3 Place the raw vegetables in a large bowl and mix together.

4 Cut the celeriac into thin strips and simmer in boiling water for about 2 minutes.

5 Drain the celeriac and rinse thoroughly with cold water.

6 Chop the celery, add to the bowl with the celeriac and golden raisins, and mix well.

7 Make the yogurt and herb dressing by briskly beating the yogurt, garlic, lemon juice, honey, and chives together.

8 Pour the dressing over the top of the salad. Stir the vegetables thoroughly to coat evenly, and serve.

TASTY TIP

To make cheese coleslaw, simply replace the golden raisins with 3 oz. of reduced-fat cheese. Whether the winter or cheese variety, coleslaw is particularly good with baked potatoes and a little low-fat spread.

HELPFUL HINT

This dish is delicious all year round, and can be served as an accompaniment to many dishes, including salads, baked potatoes, roulades, and fish.

MEDITERRANEAN FEAST

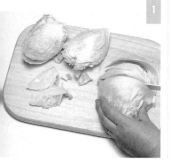

INGREDIENTS   Serves 4

1 small head of lettuce
1½ cups fine green beans
8 oz. baby new potatoes, scrubbed
4 medium eggs
1 green bell pepper
1 medium onion, peeled
7-oz. can tuna in water, drained and flaked into small pieces
½ cup reduced-fat hard cheese, such as cheddar, cut into small cubes
8 ripe but firm cherry tomatoes, quartered

5 tbsp. pitted ripe olives, halved
freshly chopped basil, to garnish

FOR THE LIME VINAIGRETTE:

3 tbsp. light olive oil
2 tbsp. white wine vinegar
4 tbsp. lime juice
2 tsp. grated lime rind
1 tsp. mustard
1-2 tsp. sugar
salt and freshly ground black pepper

1 Quarter the lettuce and remove the hard core. Tear into bite-size pieces and arrange on a large serving platter or four individual plates.

2 Cook the green beans in boiling, salted water for 8 minutes, and the potatoes for 10 minutes or until tender. Drain and rinse in cold water until cool, then cut both the beans and potatoes in half with a sharp knife.

3 Boil the eggs for 10 minutes, then rinse thoroughly under cold running water until cool. Remove the shells under the water, then cut each egg into 4.

4 Remove the seeds from the bell pepper and cut into thin strips. Finely chop the onion.

5 Arrange the beans, potatoes, eggs, bell peppers, and onion on top of the lettuce. Add the tuna, cheese, and tomatoes. Sprinkle with the olives and garnish with the basil.

6 To make the vinaigrette, place all the ingredients in a screw-top jar, and shake vigorously until everything is mixed thoroughly. Spoon 4 tablespoons over the top of the prepared salad, and serve the remainder separately.

FOOD FACT

Cans of tuna now include varieties such as albacore and yellowfin. Always choose tuna steaks over chunks.

BEET & POTATO MEDLEY

INGREDIENTS

Serves 4

¾ lb. raw baby beets
½ tsp. corn oil
8 oz. new potatoes
½ cucumber, peeled
3 tbsp. white wine vinegar
⅔ cup low-fat plain yogurt
salt and freshly ground
  black pepper

fresh lettuce leaves
1 tbsp. freshly cut chives,
  to garnish

1 Preheat the oven to 350° F. Scrub the beets thoroughly and place on a large baking sheet.

2 Brush the beets with a little oil and cook for 1½ hours or until a toothpick is easily inserted. Allow to cool slightly, then remove the skins from the beets.

3 Cook the potatoes in boiling water for about 10 minutes. Rinse in cold water and drain. Set the potatoes aside until cool. Dice evenly.

4 Cut the cucumber into cubes and place in a mixing bowl. Chop the beets into small cubes, and add to the bowl with the potatoes. Gently mix the vegetables together.

5 Mix together the vinegar and yogurt, and season to taste with a little salt and pepper. Pour over the vegetables and combine gently.

6 Arrange on a bed of lettuce leaves garnished with the cut chives, and serve.

HELPFUL HINT

Beets can also be cooked in the microwave. Place in a microwavable bowl. Add sufficient water to come halfway up the sides of the bowl. Cover and cook for 10–15 minutes on high. Leave for 5 minutes before removing the paper. Cool before peeling.

FOOD FACT

Like other fruits and vegetables that are red in color, beets have particularly high levels of antioxidants, which are essential to the body for fighting diseases.

LIGHT RATATOUILLE

INGREDIENTS

Serves 4

1 red bell pepper
2 zucchini, trimmed
1 small eggplant, trimmed
1 onion, peeled
2 ripe tomatoes
1½ cups button mushrooms,
  wiped and halved or
  quartered

¾ cup tomato juice
1 tbsp. freshly chopped basil
salt and freshly ground
  black pepper

1 Seed the peppers, remove the membrane with a small sharp knife, and dice. Thickly slice the zucchini and dice the eggplant. Slice the onion into rings.

2 Place the tomatoes in boiling water until their skins begin to peel away.

3 Remove the skins from the tomatoes, cut into quarters, and remove the seeds.

4 Place all the vegetables in a saucepan with the tomato juice and basil. Season to taste with salt and pepper.

5 Bring to a boil, cover, and simmer for 15 minutes or until the vegetables are tender.

6 Remove the vegetables with a slotted spoon and arrange in a serving dish.

7 Bring the liquid in the saucepan to a boil and boil for 20 seconds or until it is slightly thickened. Season the sauce to taste with salt and pepper.

8 Pass the sauce through a strainer to remove some of the seeds, and pour over the vegetables. Serve the ratatouille hot or cold.

TASTY TIP

This dish would be perfect, served as an accompaniment to any of the fish dishes in this book. It is also delicious in an omelette or as a baked-potato filling.

SICILIAN BAKED EGGPLANT

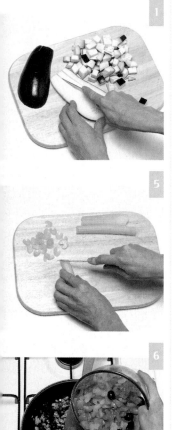

INGREDIENTS

Serves 4

1 large eggplant, trimmed
2 celery stalks, trimmed
4 large ripe tomatoes
1 tsp. corn oil
2 shallots, peeled and finely chopped
1½ tsp. tomato paste
2 tbsp. pitted green olives

2 tbsp. pitted ripe olives
salt and freshly ground black pepper
1 tbsp. white wine vinegar
2 tsp. sugar
1 tbsp. freshly chopped basil, to garnish
mixed lettuce leaves, to serve

1 Preheat the oven to 400° F. Cut the eggplant into small cubes and place on a greased baking sheet.

2 Cover the baking sheet with foil and cook in the preheated oven for about 15–20 minutes or until soft. Set aside to let the eggplant cool.

3 Place the celery and tomatoes in a large bowl, and cover with boiling water.

4 Remove the tomatoes from the bowl when their skins begin to peel away. Remove the skins, then seed and chop the flesh into small pieces.

5 Remove the celery from the bowl of water, finely chop, and set aside.

6 Pour the vegetable oil into a nonstick saucepan, add the chopped shallots, and cook gently for 2–3 minutes until soft. Add the celery, tomatoes, tomato

paste, and olives. Season to taste with salt and pepper.

7 Simmer gently for 3–4 minutes. Add the vinegar, sugar, and cooled eggplant to the saucepan and heat gently for 2–3 minutes until all the ingredients are well blended. Set aside to let the eggplant mixture cool. When cool, garnish with the chopped basil and serve with lettuce leaves.

FOOD FACT

It has been suggested that foods that are purple in color, such as eggplants, have particularly powerful antioxidants, which help the body protect itself from disease and strengthen the organs.

CARROT, CELERIAC, & SESAME SEED SALAD

INGREDIENTS

Serves 6

1 head celeriac
2 medium carrots, peeled
5 tbsp. seedless raisins
2 tbsp. sesame seeds
freshly chopped parsley,
   to garnish

FOR THE DRESSING:
1 tbsp. grated lemon rind
4 tbsp. lemon juice
2 tbsp. corn oil
2 tbsp. honey
1 red bird's eye chili, seeded
   and finely chopped
salt and freshly ground
   black pepper

1 Slice the celeriac into thin matchsticks. Place in a small saucepan of boiling, salted water, and boil for 2 minutes.

2 Drain and rinse the celeriac in cold water, and place in a mixing bowl.

3 Finely grate the carrot. Add the carrot and the raisins to the celeriac in the bowl.

4 Place the sesame seeds under a hot broiler or fry in a skillet for 1–2 minutes or until golden brown, then allow to cool.

5 Make the dressing by beating together the lemon rind, lemon juice, oil, honey, chili, and seasoning, or by shaking thoroughly in a screw-top jar.

6 Pour 2 tablespoons of the dressing over the salad and toss well. Turn into a serving dish, and sprinkle over the toasted sesame seeds and chopped parsley. Serve the remaining dressing separately.

FOOD FACT

Celeriac is a root vegetable that is similar in taste to fennel, but with a texture closer to parsnips. This versatile vegetable has a creamy taste and is also delicious in soups and gratins.

CRISPY BAKED POTATOES WITH PROSCIUTTO

INGREDIENTS

Serves 4

4 large baking potatoes
4 tsp. reduced-fat sour cream
salt and freshly ground
   black pepper
2 slices lean serrano ham or
   prosciutto, with fat removed
1 cup cooked baby fava beans
¼ cup cooked carrots, diced

1 cup cooked peas
½ cup reduced-fat hard cheese
   such as cheddar, shredded
fresh green salad, to serve

1 Preheat the oven to 400° F. Scrub the potatoes dry. Prick with a fork and place on a baking sheet. Cook for 1–1½ hours or until tender when squeezed. Use oven mitts to pick up the potatoes, as they will be very hot.

2 Cut the potatoes in half horizontally and scoop out all the flesh into a bowl.

3 Spoon the sour cream into the bowl and mix thoroughly with the potatoes. Season to taste with a little salt and pepper.

4 Cut the ham or prosciutto into fine strips, and carefully stir into the potato mixture with the fava beans, carrots, and peas.

5 Pile the mixture back into the 8 potato shells and sprinkle a little shredded cheese over the top.

6 Place under a hot broiler and cook until golden and heated through. Serve immediately with a fresh green salad.

FOOD FACT

Produced in Spain, serrano ham has a succulent, sweet taste and is traditionally carved along the grain. The nearest substitute is prosciutto. Serrano ham has a chewy texture and is often served in thin slices on bread.

LEEK & POTATO TART

INGREDIENTS

Serves 6

2 cups all-purpose flour
pinch of salt
⅔ cup butter, cubed
½ cup very finely chopped
  walnuts
1 large egg yolk

FOR THE FILLING:
1 lb. leeks, trimmed and thinly
  sliced
3 tbsp. butter

1 lb. large new potatoes,
  scrubbed
1¼ cups sour cream
3 medium eggs, lightly beaten
1½ cups shredded Gruyère
  cheese
freshly grated nutmeg
salt and freshly ground black
  pepper
fresh chives, to garnish

1 Preheat the oven to 400° F. Sift the flour and salt into a bowl. Rub in the butter until the mixture resembles bread crumbs. Stir in the nuts. Mix together the egg yolk and 3 tablespoons of cold water. Sprinkle over the dry ingredients. Mix to form a dough.

2 Knead on a lightly floured surface for a few seconds, then wrap in plastic wrap and chill in the refrigerator for 20 minutes. Roll out and use to line an 8-in. springform pan or very deep tart pan. Chill for an additional 30 minutes.

3 Cook the leeks in the butter over a high heat for 2–3 minutes, stirring constantly. Lower the heat, cover, and cook for 25 minutes until soft, stirring occasionally. Remove the leeks from the heat.

4 Cook the potatoes in boiling salted water for 15 minutes or until almost tender. Drain and slice thickly. Add to the leeks. Stir the sour cream into the leeks and potatoes, followed by the eggs, cheese, nutmeg, and salt and pepper. Pour into the pastry shell, and bake on the middle shelf in the preheated oven for 20 minutes.

5 Reduce the oven temperature to 375° F, and cook for an additional 30–35 minutes or until the filling is set. Garnish with chives and serve immediately.

TASTY TIP

Flavor the pastry with different nuts, such as hazelnuts or almonds, or replace the nuts with 3 tablespoons of freshly chopped mixed herbs.

POTATO GNOCCHI WITH PESTO SAUCE

INGREDIENTS

Serves 6

2 lbs. floury potatoes
3 tbsp. butter
1 medium egg, beaten
2 cups all-purpose flour
1 tsp. salt
freshly ground black pepper
⅓ cup shaved Parmesan cheese
arugula salad, to serve

FOR THE PESTO SAUCE:
packed 2 cups fresh basil leaves
1 large garlic clove, peeled
2 tbsp. pine nuts
½ cup olive oil
⅓ cup grated Parmesan cheese

1 Cook the potatoes in their skins in boiling water for 20 minutes or until tender. Drain and peel. While still warm, push the potatoes through a fine sieve into a bowl. Stir in the butter, egg, 1½ cups of the flour, and the salt and pepper.

2 Sift the remaining flour onto a board or work surface, and add the potato mixture. Gently knead in enough flour to form a soft, slightly sticky dough.

3 With floured hands, break off portions of the dough and roll into 1-in.-thick ropes. Cut into ¾-in. lengths. Lightly press each piece against the inner prongs of a fork. Put on a baking sheet covered with a floured dishtowel, and chill in the refrigerator for about 30 minutes.

4 To make the pesto sauce, put the basil, garlic, pine nuts,

and oil in a processor, and blend until smooth and creamy. Turn into a bowl and stir in the Parmesan cheese. Season to taste.

5 Cooking in several batches, drop the gnocchi into a saucepan of barely simmering salted water. Cook for 3–4 minutes or until they float to the surface. Remove with a slotted spoon and keep warm in a covered, greased baking dish in a low oven.

6 Add the gnocchi to the pesto sauce and toss gently to coat. Serve immediately, sprinkled with the Parmesan cheese and accompanied by an arugula salad.

HELPFUL HINT

Use a vegetable peeler to pare the Parmesan cheese into thin, decorative curls.

VEGETARIAN CASSOULET

INGREDIENTS

Serves 4

1⅛ cups dried kidney beans,
  soaked overnight
2 medium onions
1 bay leaf
6¼ cups cold water
2¾ cups peeled and thickly
  sliced potatoes
salt and freshly ground black
  pepper
5 tsp. olive oil
1 large garlic clove, peeled and
  crushed
2 leeks, trimmed and sliced
7-oz. can chopped tomatoes

1 tsp. dark brown sugar
1 tbsp. freshly chopped thyme
2 tbsp. freshly chopped
  parsley
3 zucchini, trimmed and sliced

FOR THE TOPPING:
1 cup fresh white bread
  crumbs
¼ cup finely shredded cheddar
  cheese

1 Preheat the oven to 350° F.
Drain the beans, rinse under
cold running water, and put in a
saucepan. Peel one of the onions
and add to the beans with the bay
leaf. Pour in the water.

2 Bring to a rapid boil and
cook for 10 minutes, then
turn down the heat, cover, and
simmer for 50 minutes or until
the beans are almost tender.
Drain the beans, setting aside the
liquid, but discarding the onion
and bay leaf.

3 Cook the potatoes in a
saucepan of lightly salted
boiling water for 6–7 minutes,
until almost tender when tested
with the point of a knife. Drain
and set aside.

4 Peel and chop the remaining
onion. Heat the oil in a skillet
and cook the onion with the
garlic and leeks for 10 minutes
until softened. Stir in the
tomatoes, sugar, thyme, and
parsley. Stir in the beans with 1¼
cups of the liquid and season to
taste. Simmer uncovered for 5
minutes.

5 Layer the potato slices,
zucchini, and ladlefuls of
the bean mixture in a large
flameproof casserole dish. To
make the topping, mix together
the bread crumbs and cheese, and
sprinkle over the top.

6 Bake in the preheated oven
for 40 minutes or until the
vegetables are cooked through,
and the topping is golden brown
and crisp. Serve immediately.

SWEET POTATO PATTIES WITH MANGO & TOMATO SALSA

INGREDIENTS

Serves 4

4 cups peeled and coarsely diced sweet potatoes
salt and freshly ground black pepper
2 tbsp. butter
1 onion, peeled and chopped
1 garlic clove, peeled and crushed
pinch of freshly grated nutmeg
1 medium egg, beaten
⅓ cup quick-cook polenta
2 tbsp. sunflower oil

FOR THE SALSA:

1 ripe mango, peeled, pitted, and diced
6 cherry tomatoes, cut in wedges
4 scallions, trimmed and thinly sliced
1 red chili, deseeded and finely chopped
finely grated zest and juice of ½ lime
2 tbsp. freshly chopped mint
1 tsp. honey
lettuce, to serve

1 Steam or cook the sweet potatoes in lightly salted, boiling water for 15–20 minutes until tender. Drain well, then mash until smooth.

2 Melt the butter in a saucepan. Add the onion and garlic, and cook gently for 10 minutes until soft. Add to the mashed sweet potatoes, and season with the nutmeg, salt, and pepper. Stir together until mixed thoroughly. Leave to cool.

3 Shape the mixture into 4 oval potato patties, about 1 in. thick. Dip first in the beaten egg, allowing the excess to fall back into the bowl, then coat in the polenta. Refrigerate for at least 30 minutes.

4 Meanwhile, mix together all the ingredients for the salsa. Spoon into a serving bowl, cover with plastic wrap, and leave at room temperature to allow the flavors to develop.

5 Heat the oil in a skillet and cook the potato patties for 4–5 minutes on each side. Serve with the salsa and salad leaves.

FOOD FACT

Polenta is finely ground, golden cornmeal from Italy. It is often made into a soft, savory mixture of the same name, but also makes an excellent coating for foods, such as these potato cakes.

CHEESE & ONION OAT PIE

INGREDIENTS

Serves 4

4 tsp. sunflower oil
2 tbsp. butter
2 medium onions, peeled and
  sliced
1 garlic clove, peeled and
  crushed
1¾ cups rolled oats
1 cup shredded sharp cheddar
  cheese

2 medium eggs, lightly beaten
2 tbsp. freshly chopped
  parsley
salt and freshly ground black
  pepper
1 baking potato, weighing
  about 10 oz., peeled

1 Preheat the oven to 350° F. Heat the oil and half the butter in a saucepan until melted. Add the onions and garlic, and gently cook for 10 minutes or until soft. Remove from the heat and transfer to a large bowl.

2 Spread the oats out on a baking sheet and toast in the hot oven for 12 minutes. Let cool, then add to the onions with the cheese, eggs, and parsley. Season to taste with salt and pepper, and mix well.

3 Line the base of an 8-in. round cake pan with waxed paper and grease well. Thinly slice the potato and arrange the slices on the base, overlapping them slightly.

4 Spoon the cheese and oat mixture on top of the potato, spreading evenly with the back of a spoon. Cover with foil and bake for 30 minutes.

5 Invert the pie onto a baking sheet so that the potato slices are on top. Carefully remove the pan and lining paper.

6 Set the oven to broil. Melt the remaining butter, and carefully brush over the potato topping. Cook under the broiler for 5–6 minutes, until the potatoes are lightly browned. Cut into wedges and serve.

TASTY TIP

To add extra flavor to this dish, cook the onions very slowly until soft and just beginning to brown and caramelize—either white or red onions can be used. For a crunchier texture, add ½ cup chopped hazelnuts instead of ⅓ cup of the oats, adding them to the baking sheet for the last 5 minutes of cooking time, in step 2.

VEGETABLE & GOAT CHEESE PIZZA

INGREDIENTS

Serves 4

4 oz. baking potato
1 tbsp. olive oil
2 cups white bread flour
½ tsp. salt
1 tsp. active dried yeast

FOR THE TOPPING:

1 medium eggplant, thinly sliced
2 small zucchini, trimmed and sliced lengthwise
1 yellow bell pepper, quartered and deseeded

1 red onion, peeled and sliced into very thin wedges
5 tbsp. olive oil
1½ cups halved, cooked new potatoes
14-oz. can chopped tomatoes, drained
2 tsp. freshly chopped oregano
⅓ cup diced mozzarella cheese
⅓ cup diced or crumbled goat cheese

1 Preheat the oven to 425° F. Put a cookie sheet in the oven to heat up. Cook the potato in lightly salted, boiling water until tender. Peel and mash with the olive oil until smooth.

2 Sift the flour and salt into a bowl. Stir in the yeast. Add the mashed potato and ⅔ cup warm water, and mix to a soft dough. Knead for 5–6 minutes, until smooth. Put the dough in a bowl, cover with plastic wrap, and leave to rise in a warm place for 30 minutes.

3 To make the topping, arrange the eggplant, zucchini, pepper, and onion, skin-side up, on a rack and brush with 4 tablespoons of the oil. Broil for 4–5 minutes. Turn the vegetables and brush with the remaining oil. Broil for 3–4 minutes. Cool, skin, and slice the pepper. Put all of the vegetables in a bowl, add the halved new potatoes, and toss gently together. Set aside.

4 Briefly reknead the dough then roll out to a 12–14 in. round, according to preferred thickness. Mix the tomatoes and oregano together, and spread over the pizza base. Sprinkle with the mozzarella cheese. Put the pizza on the preheated baking sheet and bake for 8 minutes.

5 Arrange the vegetables and goat cheese on top and bake for 8–10 minutes. Serve.

CHUNKY VEGETABLE & FENNEL GOULASH WITH DUMPLINGS

INGREDIENTS

Serves 4

2 fennel bulbs, weighing about 1 lb.
2 tbsp. sunflower oil
1 large onion, peeled and sliced
1½ tbsp. paprika
1 tbsp. all-purpose flour
1¼ cups vegetable stock
14-oz. can chopped tomatoes
2⅔ cups diced, peeled potatoes
¼ lb. small button mushrooms
salt and freshly ground black pepper

FOR THE DUMPLINGS:
1 tbsp. sunflower oil
1 small onion, peeled and finely chopped
1 medium egg
3 tbsp. milk
3 tbsp. freshly chopped parsley
2 cups fresh white bread crumbs

1 Cut the fennel bulbs in half widthwise. Thickly slice the stalks and cut the bulbs into 8 wedges. Heat the oil in a large saucepan or flameproof casserole. Add the onion and fennel, and cook gently for 10 minutes until soft. Stir in the paprika and flour.

2 Remove from the heat and gradually stir in the stock. Add the chopped tomatoes, potatoes, and mushrooms. Season to taste with salt and pepper. Bring to a boil, reduce the heat, and simmer for 20 minutes.

3 Meanwhile, make the dumplings. Heat the oil in a skillet and gently cook the onion for 10 minutes until soft. Leave to cool for a few minutes.

4 In a bowl, beat the egg and milk together, then add the onion, parsley, and bread crumbs, and season to taste. With damp hands, form the mixture into 12 round dumplings, each about the size of a walnut.

5 Arrange the dumplings on top of the goulash. Cover and cook for an additional 15 minutes until the dumplings are cooked and the vegetables are tender. Serve immediately.

TASTY TIP

Sour cream or crème fraîche is delicious spooned on top of the goulash.

CREAMY VEGETABLE KORMA

INGREDIENTS

Serves 4–6

2 tbsp. ghee or vegetable oil
1 large onion, peeled and
  chopped
2 garlic cloves, peeled and
  crushed
1-in. piece of ginger, peeled
  and grated
4 green cardamom pods
2 tsp. ground coriander
1 tsp. ground cumin
1 tsp. ground turmeric
finely grated zest and juice of ½
  lemon

½ cup ground almonds
1¾ cups vegetable stock
2⅔ cups peeled and diced
  potatoes
1 lb. mixed vegetables, such
  as cauliflower, carrots, and
  turnips, cut into chunks
⅔ cup heavy cream
3 tbsp. freshly chopped
  cilantro
salt and freshly ground black
  pepper
naan bread, to serve

1 Heat the ghee or oil in a large saucepan. Add the onion and cook for 5 minutes. Stir in the garlic and ginger, and cook for an additional 5 minutes or until soft and just beginning to brown.

2 Stir in the cardamom, coriander, cumin, and turmeric. Continue cooking over a low heat for 1 minute, while stirring.

3 Stir in the lemon zest and juice, and almonds. Blend in the vegetable stock. Slowly bring to a boil, stirring occasionally.

4 Add the potatoes and vegetables. Bring back to a boil, then reduce the heat, cover, and simmer for 35–40 minutes, or until the vegetables are just tender. Check after 25 minutes and add more stock if needed.

5 Slowly stir in the cream and chopped cilantro. Season to taste with salt and pepper. Cook very gently until heated through, but do not boil. Serve immediately with naan bread.

FOOD FACT

Ghee is butter, clarified by gently heating until all the water has evaporated and the milk solids separate from the pure fat, which can be used to cook at high temperatures without burning. You can buy butter-based ghee as well as a vegetable oil version in specialty shops and Indian groceries.

CABBAGE TIMBALE

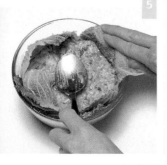

INGREDIENTS

Serves 4–6

1 small savoy cabbage,
  weighing about ¾ lb.
salt and freshly ground black
  pepper
2 tbsp. olive oil
1 leek, trimmed and chopped
1 garlic clove, peeled and
  crushed
½ cup long-grain rice
7-oz. can chopped tomatoes

1¼ cups vegetable stock
14-oz. can kidney beans,
  drained and rinsed
¾ cup shredded cheddar cheese
1 tbsp. freshly chopped
  oregano

TO GARNISH
plain yogurt with paprika
tomato wedges

1 Preheat the oven to 350° F. Remove 6 of the outer leaves of the cabbage. Cut off the thickest part of the stalk and blanch the leaves in lightly salted, boiling water for 2 minutes. Lift out with a slotted spoon, briefly rinse under cold water, and set aside.

2 Remove the stalks from the rest of the cabbage leaves. Shred the leaves and blanch in the boiling water for 1 minute. Drain, rinse under cold water, and pat dry on paper towels.

3 Heat the oil in a skillet and cook the leek and garlic for 5 minutes. Stir in the rice, chopped tomatoes with their juice, and stock. Bring to a boil, cover, and simmer for 15 minutes.

4 Remove the lid and simmer for an additional 4–5 minutes, stirring frequently, until the liquid is absorbed and the rice is tender. Stir in the kidney beans, cheese, and oregano. Season to taste with salt and pepper.

5 Line a greased, deep bowl with some of the large cabbage leaves, overlapping them slightly. Fill with alternate layers of rice mixture and shredded leaves, pressing down well.

6 Cover the top with the remaining leaves. Cover with greased foil and bake in the preheated oven for 30 minutes. Let stand for 10 minutes. Turn out, cut into wedges, and serve with yogurt, sprinkled with paprika and tomato wedges.

HANDY HINT

Avoid red or white cabbage for this recipe, as their leaves are not flexible enough.

INDONESIAN SALAD WITH PEANUT DRESSING

INGREDIENTS

Serves 4

½ lb. new potatoes, scrubbed
1 large carrot, peeled and
thinly sliced
¾ cup trimmed green beans
½ lb. tiny cauliflower florets
¾ cup cucumber, thinly sliced
1½ cups fresh bean sprouts
3 medium eggs, hard-boiled
and quartered

FOR THE PEANUT DRESSING:
2 tbsp. sesame oil
1 garlic clove, peeled and
crushed
1 red chili, deseeded and finely
chopped
⅔ cup crunchy peanut butter
6 tbsp. hot vegetable stock
2 tsp. light brown sugar
2 tsp. dark soy sauce
1 tbsp. lime juice

1 Cook the potatoes in a saucepan of salted, boiling water for 15–20 minutes until tender. Remove with a slotted spoon and slice thickly into a large bowl. Keep the saucepan of water boiling.

2 Add the carrot, green beans, and cauliflower to the water, return to a boil, and cook for 2 minutes or until just tender. Drain and rinse under cold running water, then drain well. Add to the potatoes with the cucumber and bean sprouts.

3 To make the dressing, gently heat the sesame oil in a small saucepan. Add the garlic and chili and cook for a few seconds, then remove from the heat. Stir in the peanut butter.

4 Stir in the stock, a little at a time. Add the remaining ingredients and mix together to make a thick, creamy dressing.

5 Divide the vegetables between 4 plates and arrange the eggs on top. Drizzle the dressing over the salad and serve immediately.

HELPFUL HINT

For perfect hard-boiled eggs with no green rings around the yolks, put the eggs in a saucepan and bring to a boil. Cover and remove from the heat. Allow eggs to sit for 15 minutes. Plunge in cold water, then refrigerate.

LAYERED CHEESE & HERB POTATO CAKE

INGREDIENTS

Serves 4

- 2 lbs. waxy potatoes
- 3 tbsp. freshly cut chives
- 2 tbsp. freshly chopped parsley
- 2 cups shredded mature cheddar cheese
- 2 large egg yolks
- 1 tsp. paprika
- 2 cups fresh white bread crumbs
- ½ cup toasted and roughly chopped almonds
- ¼ cup butter, melted
- salt and freshly ground black pepper
- mixed salad or steamed vegetables, to serve

1 Preheat the oven to 350° F. Lightly grease and line the base of an 8-in. round cake pan with lightly greased waxed paper. Peel and thinly slice the potatoes and set aside. Stir the chives, parsley, cheese, and egg yolks together in a small bowl and set aside. Mix the paprika into the bread crumbs.

2 Sprinkle the almonds over the base of the lined pan. Cover with half the potatoes, arranging them in layers, then sprinkle with the paprika and bread-crumb mixture, and season to taste with salt and pepper.

3 Spoon the cheese and herb mixture over the bread crumbs, sprinkle with a little more seasoning, then arrange the remaining potatoes on top. Drizzle the melted butter over and press the surface down firmly.

4 Bake in the preheated oven for 1¼ hours or until golden and cooked through. Let the potato cake stand for 10 minutes before carefully turning out and serving in thick wedges. Serve immediately with salad or freshly cooked vegetables.

HANDY HINT

Check that the potatoes are tender all the way through by pushing a thin skewer through the center. If the potatoes are still a little hard, and the top is already brown enough, loosely cover with aluminum foil and continue cooking until done.

ROAST BABY POTATO SALAD

INGREDIENTS

Serves 4

¾ lb. small shallots
sea salt and freshly ground
   black pepper
2 lbs. small, even-sized new
   potatoes
2 tbsp. olive oil
2 medium zucchini

2 sprigs of fresh rosemary
½ lb. cherry tomatoes
⅔ cup sour cream
2 tbsp. freshly cut chives
¼ tsp. paprika

1 Preheat the oven to 400° F. Trim the shallots, but leave the skins on. Put in a saucepan of lightly salted, boiling water with the potatoes, and cook for 5 minutes; drain. Separate the shallots and plunge them into cold water for 1 minute.

2 Put the oil on a baking sheet lined with aluminum foil or a roasting pan, and heat for a few minutes. Peel the skins off the shallots—they should now come away easily. Add to the baking sheet or roasting pan with the potatoes, and toss in the oil to coat. Sprinkle with a little sea salt. Roast in the preheated oven for 10 minutes.

3 Meanwhile, trim the zucchini, halve them lengthwise, and cut them into 2-in. chunks. Add to the baking sheet or roasting pan, toss to mix, and cook for 5 minutes.

4 Pierce the tomato skins with a sharp knife. Add to the sheet or pan with the rosemary, and cook for an additional 5 minutes or until all the vegetables are tender. Remove the rosemary and discard. Grind a little black pepper over the vegetables.

5 Spoon into a wide serving bowl. Mix together the sour cream and chives, and drizzle over the vegetables just before serving.

TASTY TIP

For a more substantial salad, or to serve six people rather than four, add ½ lb. eggplant, cut it in half lengthwise, and cook with the potatoes and shallots, along with an extra 1 tablespoon olive oil. If desired, crème fraîche or plain yogurt may be used instead of the sour cream.

RICE NUGGETS IN HERBED TOMATO SAUCE

INGREDIENTS

Serves 4

2½ cups vegetable stock
1 bay leaf
1 cup Arborio rice
½ cup shredded cheddar
  cheese
1 medium egg yolk
1 tbsp. all-purpose flour
2 tbsp. freshly chopped parsley
salt and freshly ground black
  pepper
grated Parmesan cheese, to
  serve

**FOR THE HERBED TOMATO
  SAUCE:**
1 tbsp. olive oil
1 onion, peeled and thinly
  sliced
1 garlic clove, peeled and
  crushed
1 small yellow bell pepper,
  deseeded and diced
14-oz. can chopped tomatoes
1 tbsp. freshly chopped basil

1 Pour the stock into a large saucepan. Add the bay leaf. Bring to a boil, add the rice, stir, then cover and simmer for 15 minutes.

2 Uncover, reduce the heat to low, and cook for an additional 5 minutes until the rice is tender and all the stock is absorbed, stirring often. Cool.

3 Stir the cheese, egg yolk, flour, and parsley into the rice. Season to taste, then shape into 20 walnut-sized balls. Cover and refrigerate.

4 To make the sauce, heat the oil in a large skillet and cook the onion for 5 minutes. Add the garlic and bell pepper, and cook for an additional 5 minutes until soft.

5 Stir in the chopped tomatoes and simmer gently for 3 minutes. Stir in the chopped basil and season to taste.

6 Add the rice nuggets to the sauce and simmer for an additional 10 minutes or until the rice nuggets are cooked through and the sauce has reduced a little. Spoon onto serving plates and serve hot, sprinkled with Parmesan cheese.

HELPFUL HINT

It is important that the stock is absorbed completely by the rice if these nuggets are to hold their shape. Stir constantly for the last minute of cooking to prevent the rice from sticking or burning.

MIXED GRAIN PILAF

INGREDIENTS

Serves 4

2 tbsp. olive oil
1 garlic clove, peeled and crushed
½ tsp. ground turmeric
⅔ cup mixed long-grain and wild rice
heaping ⅓ cup red lentils
1¼ cups vegetable stock
7-oz. can chopped tomatoes
2-in. piece cinnamon stick

salt and freshly ground black pepper
14-oz. can mixed beans, drained and rinsed
1 tbsp. butter
1 bunch scallions, trimmed and finely sliced
3 medium eggs
4 tbsp. freshly chopped herbs, such as parsley and chervil
sprigs of fresh dill, to garnish

1 Heat 1 tablespoon of the oil in a saucepan. Add the garlic and turmeric, and cook for a few seconds. Stir in the rice and lentils.

2 Add the stock, tomatoes, and cinnamon. Season to taste with salt and pepper. Stir once and bring to a boil. Lower the heat, cover, and simmer for 20 minutes until most of the stock is absorbed and the rice and lentils are tender.

3 Stir in the beans, replace the lid, and let stand for 2–3 minutes to allow the beans to heat through.

4 While the rice is cooking, heat the remaining oil and butter in a skillet. Add the scallions and cook for 4–5 minutes until soft. Lightly beat the eggs with 2 tablespoons of the herbs, then season with salt and pepper.

5 Pour the egg mixture over the scallions. Stir gently with a spatula over a low heat, drawing the mixture from the sides to the center as the omelette sets. When almost set, stop stirring, and cook for about 30 seconds, until golden underneath.

6 Remove the omelette from the pan, roll up, and slice into thin strips. Fluff up the rice with a fork and remove the cinnamon stick. Spoon onto serving plates, and top with strips of omelette and the remaining chopped herbs. Garnish with dill and serve.

HELPFUL HINT

Long-grain rice and wild rice have different cooking times, but in ready-mixed packages, the rice has been treated to even out the cooking times, making preparation easier.

CALYPSO RICE WITH CURRIED BANANAS

INGREDIENTS   Serves 4

2 tbsp. sunflower oil
1 medium onion, peeled and
   finely chopped
1 garlic clove, peeled and
   crushed
1 red chili, deseeded and finely
   chopped
1 red bell pepper, deseeded
   and chopped
1½ cups basmati rice
juice of 1 lime
1½ cups vegetable stock

7-oz. can black-eyed peas,
   drained and rinsed
2 tbsp. freshly chopped parsley
salt and freshly ground black
   pepper
sprigs of cilantro, to garnish

FOR THE CURRIED BANANAS:
4 green bananas
2 tbsp. sunflower oil
2 tsp. mild curry paste
¾ cup coconut milk

1 Heat the oil in a large skillet and gently cook the onion for 10 minutes until soft. Add the garlic, chili, and red pepper, and cook for 2–3 minutes.

2 Rinse the rice under cold running water, then add to the pan and stir. Pour in the lime juice and stock, bring to a boil, cover, and simmer for 12–15 minutes or until the rice is tender and the stock is absorbed.

3 Stir in the black-eyed peas and chopped parsley, and season to taste with salt and pepper. Let stand covered for 5 minutes before serving to allow the beans to warm through.

4 While the rice is cooking, make the curried green bananas. Remove the skins from

the bananas—you may have to cut them off with a sharp knife. Slice the flesh thickly. Heat the oil in a skillet and cook the bananas, in 2 batches, for 2–3 minutes or until lightly browned.

5 Pour the coconut milk into the pan, and stir in the curry paste.

6 Add the banana slices to the coconut milk and simmer uncovered over a low heat for 8–10 minutes or until the bananas are very soft and the coconut milk slightly reduced.

7 Spoon the rice onto warmed serving plates, garnish with sprigs of cilantro, and serve immediately with the curried bananas.

RED LENTIL KEDGEREE WITH AVOCADO & TOMATOES

INGREDIENTS

Serves 4

heaping ¾ cup basmati rice
¾ cup red lentils
½ tbsp. butter
1 tbsp. sunflower oil
1 medium onion, peeled and
  chopped
1 tsp. ground cumin
4 green cardamom pods,
  bruised
1 bay leaf
2 cups vegetable or chicken
  stock

1 ripe avocado, peeled, pitted,
  and diced
1 tbsp. lemon juice
4 plum tomatoes, peeled and
  diced
2 tbsp. freshly chopped
  cilantro
salt and freshly ground black
  pepper
lemon or lime slices, to
  garnish

1 Put the rice and lentils in a sieve and rinse under cold running water. Tip into a bowl, then pour over enough cold water to cover, and let soak for 10 minutes.

2 Heat the butter and oil in a saucepan. Add the sliced onion and cook gently, stirring occasionally for 10 minutes until softened. Stir in the cumin, cardamom pods, and bay leaf, and cook for an additional minute, stirring all the time.

3 Drain the rice and lentils, rinse again, and add to the onions in the saucepan. Stir in the vegetable stock and bring to a boil. Reduce the heat, cover the saucepan, and simmer for 15 minutes or until the rice and lentils are tender.

4 Place the diced avocado in a bowl and toss with the lemon juice. Stir in the tomatoes and chopped cilantro. Season to taste with salt and pepper.

5 Fluff up the rice with a fork, spoon into a warmed serving dish, and spoon the avocado mixture on top. Garnish with lemon or lime slices and serve.

TASTY TIP

Although basmati rice and red lentils do not usually need to be presoaked, it improves the results in this recipe: the rice will have very light, fluffy, separate grains, and the lentils will just begin to break down, giving the dish a creamier texture.

ADZUKI BEAN & RICE PATTIES

INGREDIENTS

Serves 4

2½ tbsp. sunflower oil
1 medium onion, peeled and very finely chopped
1 garlic clove, peeled and crushed
1 tsp. curry paste
1⅓ cups basmati rice
14-oz. can adzuki beans, drained and rinsed (kidney beans may also be used)
1 cup vegetable stock
¼ lb. firm tofu, crumbled
1 tsp. garam masala
2 tbsp. freshly chopped
cilantro
salt and freshly ground black pepper

FOR THE CARROT RAITA:
2 large carrots, peeled and shredded
½ cucumber, diced
⅔ cup plain yogurt

TO SERVE:
whole-wheat hamburger buns
tomato slices
lettuce leaves

1 Heat 1 tablespoon of the oil in a saucepan and gently cook the onion for 10 minutes until soft. Add the garlic and curry paste, and cook for a few more seconds. Stir in the rice and beans.

2 Pour in the stock, bring to a boil, and simmer for 12 minutes or until all the stock has been absorbed—do not lift the lid for the first 10 minutes of cooking. Set aside.

3 Lightly mash the tofu. Add to the rice mixture with the garam masala, cilantro, salt, and pepper. Mix.

4 Shape the mixture in 8 patties. Chill in the refrigerator for 30 minutes.

5 Meanwhile, make the raita. Mix together the carrots, cucumber, and plain yogurt. Spoon into a small bowl and chill in the refrigerator until ready to serve.

6 Heat the remaining oil in a large skillet. Fry the patties, in batches if necessary, for 4–5 minutes on each side or until lightly browned. Serve in the buns with tomato slices and lettuce. Accompany with the raita.

FOOD FACT

Firm tofu is sold in blocks. It is made in a similar way to soft cheese, and is the pressed curds of soy milk.

WILD RICE DOLMADES

INGREDIENTS

Serves 4–6

6 tbsp. olive oil
2½ tbsp. pine nuts
1½ cups wiped and finely
   chopped mushrooms
4 scallions, trimmed and finely
   chopped
1 garlic clove, peeled and
   crushed
1 cup cooked wild rice
2 tsp. freshly chopped dill
2 tsp. freshly chopped mint

salt and freshly ground black
   pepper
16–24 prepared medium grape
   leaves
about 1¼ cups vegetable stock

TO GARNISH:
lemon wedges
sprigs of fresh dill

1 Heat 1 tbsp. of the oil in a skillet and gently cook the pine nuts for 2–3 minutes, stirring frequently, until golden. Remove from the pan and set aside.

2 Add 1½ tablespoons of oil to the pan and gently cook the mushrooms, scallions, and garlic for 7–8 minutes until very soft. Stir in the rice, herbs, salt, and pepper.

3 Put a heaping teaspoon of stuffing in the center of each leaf (if the leaves are small, put 2 together, overlapping slightly). Fold over the stalk end, then the sides, and roll up to make a neat pocket. Continue until all the stuffing is used.

4 Arrange the stuffed grape leaves close together, seam-side down, in a large saucepan, drizzling each with a little of the

remaining oil—there will be several layers. Pour over just enough stock to cover.

5 Put an inverted plate over the dolmades to keep them from unrolling during cooking. Bring to a boil, then simmer very gently for 3 minutes. Cool in the saucepan.

6 Transfer the dolmades to a serving dish. Cover and chill. Sprinkle with pine nuts, and garnish with lemon and dill.

HELPFUL HINT

Fresh grape leaves should be blanched for 2–3 minutes in boiling water. Grape leaves preserved in brine can be found in supermarkets—soak in warm water for 20 minutes before using.

FAVA BEAN & ARTICHOKE RISOTTO

INGREDIENTS

Serves 4

2½ cups frozen fava beans
14-oz. can artichoke hearts, drained
1 tbsp. sunflower oil
⅔ cup dry white wine
3¾ cups vegetable stock
2 tbsp. butter
1 onion, peeled and finely chopped
heaping 1 cup Arborio rice
zest and juice of 1 lemon

½ cup grated Parmesan cheese
salt and freshly ground black pepper
freshly grated Parmesan cheese, to serve

1 Cook the beans in a saucepan of lightly salted, boiling water for 4–5 minutes or until just tender. Drain and plunge into cold water. Peel off the tough outer skins, if desired. Pat the artichokes dry on paper towels and cut each in half lengthwise through the stem end. Cut each half into 3 wedges.

2 Heat the oil in a large saucepan and cook the artichokes for 4–5 minutes, turning occasionally, until they are lightly browned. Remove and set aside. Bring the wine and s tock to a boil in a separate pan. Keep them barely simmering.

3 Melt the butter in a large skillet, add the onion, and cook for 5 minutes until beginning to soften. Add the rice and cook for 1 minute, stirring.

Pour in a ladleful of the hot wine and stock, simmer gently, stirring frequently, until the stock is absorbed. Continue to add the stock in this way for 20–25 minutes until the rice is just tender; the risotto should look creamy and soft.

4 Add the fava beans, artichokes, and lemon zest and juice. Gently mix in, cover, and leave to warm through for 1–2 minutes. Stir in the Parmesan cheese, and season to taste with salt and pepper. Serve sprinkled with extra Parmesan cheese.

HELPFUL HINT

If using fresh fava beans, buy about 1½ lb. in their pods. Young fresh beans do not need to be skinned.

MEDITERRANEAN RICE SALAD

INGREDIENTS

Serves 4

1½ cups Camargue red rice
2 sun-dried tomatoes, finely chopped
2 garlic cloves, peeled and finely chopped
4 tbsp. oil from a jar of sun-dried tomatoes
2 tsp. balsamic vinegar
2 tsp. red wine vinegar
salt and freshly ground black pepper
1 red onion, peeled and thinly sliced

1 yellow bell pepper, quartered and deseeded
1 red bell pepper, quartered and deseeded
½ cucumber, peeled and diced
6 ripe plum tomatoes, cut into wedges
1 fennel bulb, halved and thinly sliced
fresh basil leaves, to garnish

1 Cook the rice in a saucepan of lightly salted, boiling water for 35–40 minutes or until tender. Drain well and set aside.

2 Whisk the sun-dried tomatoes, garlic, oil, and vinegars together in a small bowl or pitcher. Season to taste with salt and pepper. Put the red onion in a large bowl, pour over the dressing, and leave to allow the flavors to develop.

3 Put the peppers skin-side up on a rack, and cook under a broiler for 5–6 minutes or until charred. Remove and place in a plastic bag. When cool enough to handle, peel off the skins and slice the peppers.

4 Add the peppers, cucumber, tomatoes, fennel, and rice to the onions. Mix gently together

to coat in the dressing. Cover and chill in the refrigerator for 30 minutes to allow the flavors to mingle.

5 Remove the salad from the refrigerator and let stand at room temperature for 20 minutes. Garnish with fresh basil leaves and serve.

FOOD FACT

Camargue red rice from the south of France is a reddish-brown color and gives salad a stunning appearance. It has a texture and cooking time similar to that of brown rice, which may be substituted in this recipe if Camargue red rice is unavailable.

CHEF'S RICE SALAD

INGREDIENTS

Serves 4

1⅓ cups wild rice
½ cucumber
½ lb. cherry tomatoes
6 scallions, trimmed
5 tbsp. extra-virgin olive oil
2 tbsp. balsamic vinegar
1 tsp. Dijon mustard
1 tsp. superfine sugar
salt and freshly ground black
  pepper
1 cup arugula

¼ lb. bacon
½ cup finely diced, cooked
  chicken meat
1 cup shredded Emmentaler
  cheese
¾ cup large cooked shrimp,
  peeled
1 avocado, pitted, peeled, and
  sliced, to garnish
warm, crusty bread, to serve

1 Put the rice in a saucepan of water and bring to a boil, stirring once or twice. Reduce the heat, cover, and simmer gently for 30–50 minutes, depending on the texture desired. Drain well and set aside.

2 Thinly peel the cucumber, cut in half, then remove the seeds with a spoon. Cut the cucumber into thin slices. Cut the tomatoes in quarters. Cut the scallions into diagonal slices.

3 Whisk the olive oil with the vinegar, then whisk in the Dijon mustard and sugar. Season the dressing with salt and pepper.

4 In a large bowl, gently toss together the cooled rice with the tomatoes, cucumber, scallions, and arugula. Pour over the dressing and toss lightly together.

5 Grill the bacon on both sides for 4–6 minutes or until crisp. Remove and chop. Arrange the prepared arugula salad on a platter, then arrange the bacon, chicken, cheese, and shrimp on top. Garnish with avocado slices, and serve with plenty of warm, crusty bread.

TASTY TIP

You can use any combination of your favorite cold meats in this salad; smoked duck or chicken work particularly well. Emmentaler cheese, famous for its large, round holes, has a mellow and sweet flavor that is good in this salad, or you can use your favorite hard cheese, such as cheddar or edam.

RICE WITH SMOKED SALMON & GINGER

INGREDIENTS

Serves 4

1⅓ cups basmati rice
2½ cups fish stock
1 bunch scallions, trimmed
   and diagonally sliced
3 tbsp. freshly chopped
   cilantro
1 tsp. freshly grated root
   ginger

½ lb. sliced smoked salmon
2 tbsp. soy sauce
1 tsp. sesame oil
2 tsp. lemon juice
4–6 slices pickled ginger
2 tsp. sesame seeds
arugula leaves, to serve

1 Place the rice in a sieve and rinse under cold water until the water runs clear. Drain, then place in a large saucepan with the stock and bring gently to a boil. Reduce to a simmer and cover with an airtight lid. Cook for 10 minutes, then remove from the heat and let sit, covered, for an additional 10 minutes.

2 Stir the scallions, cilantro, and fresh ginger into the cooked rice and mix well.

3 Spoon the rice into 4 tart pans, each measuring 4 in., and press down firmly with the back of a spoon to form patties. Invert a pan onto an individual serving plate, then tap the base firmly, and remove the pan. Repeat with the rest of the pans.

4 Top the rice with the salmon, folding if necessary, so the sides of the rice can still be seen in places. Mix together the soy sauce, sesame oil, and lemon juice to make a dressing, then drizzle over the salmon. Top with the pickled ginger and a sprinkling of sesame seeds. Scatter the arugula leaves around the edge of the plates, and serve immediately.

FOOD FACT

Good smoked salmon should look moist and firm, and have a peachy pink color. If you buy it from a delicatessan counter, ask for it to be freshly sliced, as any that has already been sliced may be dried out. Vacuum-packed salmon will keep for about 2 weeks in the refrigerator (check the use-by date), but once opened should be used within 3 days.

SWEET & SOUR RICE WITH CHICKEN

INGREDIENTS

Serves 4

4 scallions
2 tsp. sesame oil
1 tsp. Chinese five-spice powder
1 lb. chicken breast, cut into cubes
1 tbsp. oil
1 garlic clove, peeled and crushed
1 medium onion, peeled and sliced into thin wedges

1⅓ cups long-grain white rice
2½ cups water
4 tbsp. ketchup
1 tbsp. tomato paste
2 tbsp. honey
1 tbsp. vinegar
1 tbsp. dark soy sauce
1 carrot, peeled and thinly sliced

1 Trim the scallions, then cut lengthwise into fine strips. Drop into a large bowl of ice water and set aside.

2 Mix together the sesame oil and Chinese five-spice powder, and use to rub into the cubed chicken. Heat the wok, then add the oil, and when hot, cook the garlic and onion for 2–3 minutes or until transparent and softened.

3 Add the chicken and stir-fry over a medium-high heat until the chicken is golden and cooked through. Using a slotted spoon, remove from the wok and keep warm.

4 Stir the rice into the wok and add the water, ketchup, tomato paste, honey, vinegar, and soy sauce. Stir well to mix. Bring

to a boil, then simmer until almost all of the liquid is absorbed. Stir in the carrots and chicken, and continue to cook for 3–4 minutes.

5 Drain the scallions, which will have become curly. Garnish with the scallion curls, and serve immediately with the rice and chicken.

FOOD FACT

Five-spice powder is a popular Chinese seasoning available in most supermarkets. It is a mixture of finely ground star anise, fennel, cinnamon, cloves, and Szechuan pepper, and adds a unique sweet and spicy aniseed flavor to food.

SALMON & PHYLLO POCKETS

INGREDIENTS   Serves 4

1 tbsp. sunflower or vegetable oil

1 bunch of scallions, trimmed and finely chopped

1 tsp. paprika

1 cup long-grain white rice

1¼ cups fish stock

salt and freshly ground black pepper

1 lb. salmon fillet, cubed

1 tbsp. freshly chopped parsley

zest and juice of 1 lemon

1¼ cups arugula

generous ¼ lb. spinach

12 sheets phyllo pastry

¼ cup butter, melted

1 Preheat the oven to 400° F. Heat the oil in a small frying pan and gently cook the scallions for 2 minutes. Stir in the paprika and continue to cook for 1 minute, then remove from the heat and set aside.

2 Put the rice in a sieve and rinse under cold running water until the water runs clear; drain. Put the rice and stock in a saucepan, bring to a boil, then cover and simmer for 10 minutes or until the liquid is absorbed and the rice is tender. Add the scallion mixture and fork through. Season to taste with salt and pepper, then let cool.

3 In a nonmetallic bowl, mix together the salmon, parsley, lemon zest and juice, and salt and pepper. Set aside.

4 Blanch the arugula and spinach in a large saucepan of boiling water for 30 seconds or until just wilted. Drain well in a

colander, and rinse in plenty of cold water, then squeeze out as much moisture as possible.

5 Brush 3 sheets of phyllo pastry with melted butter and lay them on top of one another. Take a quarter of the rice mixture, and arrange it in an oblong shape in the center of the pastry. On top of this place a quarter of the salmon, followed by a quarter of the arugula and spinach.

6 Draw up the pastry around the filling and twist at the top to create a pocket. Repeat with the remaining pastry and filling to make 4 pockets. Brush with the remaining butter.

7 Place the pockets on a lightly greased baking sheet, and cook in the preheated oven for 20 minutes or until golden brown. Serve immediately.

WILD MUSHROOM RISOTTO

INGREDIENTS

Serves 4

½ oz. dried porcini
5 cups vegetable or chicken
  stock
⅓ cup butter
1 tbsp. olive oil
1 onion, peeled and chopped
2–4 garlic cloves, peeled and
  chopped
1–2 red chilies, deseeded and
  chopped
½ lb. wild mushrooms, halved
  if large

¼ lb. button mushrooms,
  wiped and sliced
2 cups Arborio rice
1 cup large cooked shrimp,
  peeled
⅔ cup white wine
salt and freshly ground black
  pepper
1 tbsp. lemon zest
1 tbsp. freshly cut chives
2 tbsp. freshly chopped parsley

1 Soak the porcini in 1¼ cups of very hot, but not boiling water for 30 minutes. Drain, setting aside the mushrooms and soaking liquid. Pour the stock into a saucepan, and bring to a boil, then reduce the heat to keep it simmering.

2 Melt the butter and oil in a large, deep skillet, add the onion, garlic, and chilies, and cook gently for 5 minutes. Add the mushrooms, along with the drained porcini, and continue to cook for 4–5 minutes, stirring frequently.

3 Stir in the rice and cook for 1 minute. Strain the soaking liquid and stir into the rice with a little of the hot stock. Cook gently, stirring frequently, until the liquid is absorbed. Continue to add most of the stock, a ladleful at a time, cooking after

each addition, until the rice is tender and the risotto looks creamy.

4 Add the shrimp and wine along with the last additions of stock. When the shrimp are hot and all the liquid is absorbed, season with salt and pepper. Remove from the heat and stir in the lemon zest, chives, and parsley, setting aside some for the garnish. Garnish and serve.

FOOD FACT

Porcini are wild mushrooms, also known by their French name *cèpes*. They have a meaty texture and an almost woody taste. Dried porcini are expensive, but you only need the tiniest amount to add an incredibly intense mushroom flavor to this risotto.

SPECIAL FRIED RICE

INGREDIENTS

Serves 4

1 large egg
1 tsp. sesame oil
1½ cups long-grain white rice
1 tbsp. peanut oil
1 lb. boneless, skinless chicken breast, diced
8 scallions, trimmed and sliced
2 large carrots, trimmed and thinly sliced
¾ cup snow peas
¾ cup raw tiger shrimp, peeled

2 tsp. Chinese five-spice powder
1 tbsp. soy sauce
1 tbsp. Thai fish sauce
1 tbsp. rice wine vinegar

1 Beat the egg in a bowl with ½ teaspoon of the sesame oil and 2 teaspoons of water. Heat a skillet over a medium-high heat, and swirl in 2 tablespoons of the egg mixture to form a paper-thin omelette. Remove and set aside. Repeat this process until all the egg has been used.

2 Cook the rice in lightly salted, boiling water for 12 minutes or until tender. Drain and set aside.

3 Heat a wok, then add the remaining sesame oil with the peanut oil, and stir-fry the chicken for 5 minutes until cooked through. Using a slotted spoon, remove from the wok and keep warm.

4 Add the scallions, carrot, and snow peas to the wok, and stir-fry for 2–3 minutes. Add the shrimp and stir-fry for 2–3

minutes, or until pink. Return the chicken to the wok with the Chinese five-spice powder, and stir-fry for 1 minute. Stir in the drained rice.

5 Mix together the soy sauce, fish sauce, and vinegar. Pour into the wok and continue to stir-fry for 2–3 minutes. Roll the papery omelettes into tight rolls and slice to form thin strips. Stir into the rice and serve immediately.

FOOD FACT

A classic Chinese ingredient, sesame oil is richly colored and strongly flavored. It has a low smoking temperature, so should not be heated to an extremely high temperature, otherwise the delicious sesame flavor will be lost.

LEG OF LAMB WITH MINTED RICE

INGREDIENTS

Serves 4

1 tbsp. olive oil
1 medium onion, peeled and finely chopped
1 garlic clove, peeled and crushed
1 celery stalk, trimmed and chopped
1 large mild red chili, deseeded and chopped

½ cup long-grain rice
⅔ cup lamb or chicken stock
2 tbsp. freshly chopped mint
salt and freshly ground black pepper
3 lb. boned leg of lamb
freshly cooked vegetables, to serve

1 Preheat the oven to 375° F. Heat the oil in a skillet and gently cook the onion for 5 minutes. Stir in the garlic, celery, and chili, and continue to cook for 3–4 minutes.

2 Place the rice and the stock in a large saucepan, and cook covered for 10–12 minutes or until the rice is tender and all the liquid is absorbed. Stir in the onion and celery mixture, then leave to cool. Once the rice mixture is cold, stir in the chopped mint, and season to taste with salt and pepper.

3 Place the boned lamb skin-side down and spoon the rice mixture along the center of the meat. Roll up the meat to enclose the stuffing and tie securely with string. Place in a roasting pan and roast in the preheated oven for 80 minutes. Remove from the oven and let rest in a warm place for

20 minutes before carving. Serve with a selection of cooked vegetables.

HELPFUL HINT

Weigh the lamb after stuffing and allow it to come to room temperature before roasting. For medium-cooked lamb, allow 25 minutes per pound, plus 25 minutes; for well-done, allow 30 minutes per pound, plus 30 minutes. Use a meat thermometer to check the joint, if cooked, or push a fine skewer into the thickest part: for medium meat they will be pink, for well-done, the juices will run clear.

LEMON CHICKEN RICE

INGREDIENTS

Serves 4

2 tbsp. sunflower or
   vegetable oil
4 chicken leg portions
1 medium onion, peeled and
   chopped
1–2 garlic cloves, peeled and
   crushed
1 tbsp. curry powder
2 tbsp. butter
1⅓ cups long-grain white rice

1 lemon, preferably unwaxed,
   sliced
2½ cups chicken stock
salt and freshly ground black
   pepper
2 tbsp. flaked, toasted almonds
sprigs of fresh cilantro, to
   garnish

1 Preheat the oven to 350° F. Heat the oil in a large skillet, add the chicken legs, and cook, turning, until sealed and golden all over. Using a slotted spoon, remove from the pan and set aside.

2 Add the onion and garlic to the oil remaining in the frying pan, and cook for 5–7 minutes, or until just beginning to brown. Sprinkle in the curry powder and cook, stirring, for an additional 1 minute. Return the chicken to the pan and stir well, then remove from the heat.

3 Melt the butter in a large heavy-based saucepan. Add the rice and cook, stirring, to ensure that all the grains are coated in the melted butter, then remove from the heat.

4 Stir the lemon slices into the chicken mixture, then spoon the mixture onto the rice, and

pour over the stock. Season to taste with salt and pepper.

5 Cover with an airtight lid and cook in the preheated oven for 45 minutes or until the rice is tender and the chicken is cooked thoroughly. Serve sprinkled with the toasted flaked almonds, and sprigs of cilantro.

TASTY TIP

Choose a strength of curry powder according to personal taste. There is a huge range of brands and mixtures available, from mild korma to medium Madras or hot vindaloo. Unless you use spices frequently, buy them in small quantities, as they quickly become stale and lose their flavor. Store in glass jars in a cool, dark place.

SCALLOP & POTATO GRATIN

INGREDIENTS

Serves 4

8 fresh scallops
scallop shells, for presentation
4 tbsp. white wine
salt and freshly ground black
  pepper
¼ cup butter
3 tbsp. all-purpose flour

2 tbsp. light cream
½ cup shredded cheddar
  cheese
2⅔ cups peeled and coarsely
  diced potatoes
1 tbsp. milk

1 Preheat the oven to 425° F. Clean 4 scallop shells to use as serving dishes and set aside. Place the scallops in a small saucepan with the wine, ⅔ cup water, and salt and pepper. Cover, and simmer very gently for 5 minutes or until just tender. Remove with a slotted spoon and cut each scallop into 3 pieces. Set aside the cooking juices.

2 Melt half the butter in a saucepan, stir in the flour, and cook for 1 minute, stirring, then gradually whisk in the cooking juices. Simmer, stirring, for 3–4 minutes until the sauce has thickened. Season to taste with salt and pepper. Remove from the heat and stir in the cream and half of the cheese. Fold in the scallops.

3 Boil the potatoes in lightly salted water until tender, then mash with the remaining butter and milk. Spoon or pipe the mashed potatoes around the edges of the cleaned scallop shells.

4 Divide the scallop mixture among the 4 shells, placing the mixture neatly in the center. Sprinkle with the remaining cheese, and bake in the preheated oven for about 10–15 minutes until golden brown and bubbling. Serve immediately.

FOOD FACT

Because scallops perish quickly out of water, they are usually sold shucked. Scallop shells are sold at many fish counters and gourmet stores for serving purposes.

WARM POTATO, PEAR, & PECAN SALAD

INGREDIENTS

Serves 4

2 lbs. new potatoes, preferably red-skinned, unpeeled
salt and freshly ground black pepper
1 tsp. Dijon mustard
2 tsp. white wine vinegar
3 tbsp. peanut oil

1 tbsp. hazelnut or walnut oil
2 tsp. poppy seeds
2 firm ripe dessert pears
2 tsp. lemon juice
scant ½ lb. baby spinach leaves
¾ cup toasted pecans

1 Scrub the potatoes, then cook in a saucepan of lightly salted, boiling water for 15 minutes or until tender. Drain, cut into halves, or quarters if large, and place in a serving bowl.

2 In a small bowl or pitcher, whisk together the mustard and vinegar. Gradually add the oils until the mixture begins to thicken. Stir in the poppy seeds, and season to taste.

3 Pour about two thirds of the dressing over the hot potatoes and toss gently to coat. Leave until the potatoes have soaked up the dressing and are just warm.

4 Meanwhile, quarter and core the pears. Cut into thin slices, then sprinkle with the lemon juice to prevent them from turning brown. Add to the potatoes with the spinach leaves and toasted pecans. Gently mix together.

5 Drizzle the remaining dressing over the salad. Serve immediately before the spinach starts to wilt.

FOOD FACT

To toast the pecans, place on a cookie sheet in a single layer and cook in a preheated oven at 350° F for 5 minutes, or under a broiler for 3–4 minutes, turning frequently. Watch them carefully—they burn easily. If you cannot get red-skinned new potatoes for this dish, add color by using red-skinned pears instead. Look for Red Bartlett, Red Williams, and Napolian.

HERBED HASSELBACK POTATOES WITH ROAST CHICKEN

INGREDIENTS

Serves 4

8 medium, evenly-sized
  potatoes, peeled
3 large sprigs of fresh rosemary
1 tbsp. oil
salt and freshly ground black
  pepper
¾ lb. baby parsnips, peeled
¾ lb. baby carrots, peeled

¾ lb. baby leeks, trimmed
⅓ cup butter
finely grated zest of 1 lemon,
  preferably unwaxed
3½ lbs. chicken

1 Preheat the oven to 400° F. Place a chopstick on either side of a potato, and with a sharp knife, cut down through the potato until you reach the chopsticks; take care not to cut right through the potato. Repeat these cuts every ¼ in. along the length of the potato. Carefully ease 2–4 of the slices apart and slip in a few rosemary sprigs. Repeat with remaining potatoes. Brush with the oil, and season well with salt and pepper.

2 Place the seasoned potatoes in a large roasting pan. Add the parsnips, carrots, and leeks to the potatoes, and cover with a wire rack or trivet.

3 Beat the butter and lemon zest together and season to taste. Smear the chicken with the lemon butter and place on the rack over the vegetables.

4 Roast in the preheated oven for 1 hour, 40 minutes, basting the chicken and vegetables occasionally until cooked thoroughly. The juices should run clear when the thigh is pierced with a skewer. Place the cooked chicken on a warmed serving platter, arrange the roast vegetables around it, and serve immediately.

FOOD FACT

Hasselback potatoes were named after the Stockholm restaurant of the same name. Using chopsticks is a great way of ensuring that you slice just far enough through the potatoes so that they fan out during cooking. The potatoes can be given an attractive golden finish by mixing ¼ tsp. ground turmeric or paprika with the oil.

SPICED INDIAN ROAST POTATOES WITH CHICKEN

INGREDIENTS

Serves 4

1½ lbs. waxy potatoes, peeled and cut into large chunks
salt and freshly ground black pepper
4 tbsp. sunflower oil
8 chicken drumsticks
1 large Spanish onion, peeled and roughly chopped
3 shallots, peeled and roughly chopped

2 large garlic cloves, peeled and crushed
1 red chili
2 tsp. finely grated ginger
2 tsp. ground cumin
2 tsp. ground coriander
pinch of cayenne pepper
4 green cardamom pods, crushed
sprigs of fresh cilantro, to garnish

1 Preheat the oven to 375° F. Parboil the potatoes for 5 minutes in lightly salted, boiling water, then drain thoroughly and set aside. Heat the oil in a large skillet, add the chicken drumsticks, and cook until sealed on all sides. Set aside.

2 Add the onions and shallots to the pan, and fry for 4–5 minutes. Stir in the garlic, chili, and ginger, and cook for 1 minute, stirring constantly. Stir in the ground cumin, coriander, cayenne pepper, and cardamom, and continue to cook, stirring, for an additional minute.

3 Add the potatoes and chicken to the pan. Season to taste with salt and pepper. Stir gently until the potatoes and chicken pieces are coated in the onion and spice mixture.

4 Spoon into a large roasting pan and roast in the preheated oven for 35 minutes, or until the chicken and potatoes are cooked thoroughly. Garnish with fresh cilantro and serve immediately.

HANDY HINT

Spanish onions are the largest white onions and they have a far milder flavor than many smaller varieties. When frying onions, as in this recipe, do not be tempted to chop them in a food processor, as this will make them too wet, and, as a result, the onions will steam rather than fry.

SPECIAL RÖSTI

INGREDIENTS

Serves 4

1½ lbs. potatoes, scrubbed but not peeled
salt and freshly ground black pepper
⅓ cup butter
1 large onion, peeled and finely chopped
1 garlic clove, peeled and crushed

2 tbsp. freshly chopped parsley
1 tbsp. olive oil
scant ¼ lb. prosciutto, thinly sliced
½ cup sun-dried tomatoes, chopped
1½ cups shredded Emmentaler cheese
mixed green salad, to serve

1 Cook the potatoes in a large saucepan of salted, boiling water for about 10 minutes until just tender. Drain in a colander, then rinse in cold water. Drain again. Leave until cool enough to handle, then peel off the skins.

2 Melt the butter in a large skillet and gently fry the onion and garlic for about 3 minutes until softened and beginning to color. Remove from the heat.

3 Shred the potatoes into a large bowl, then stir in the onion and garlic mixture. Sprinkle over the parsley and stir well to mix. Season to taste with salt and pepper.

4 Heat the oil in the frying pan and cover the bottom of the pan with half the potato mixture. Lay the slices of prosciutto on top. Sprinkle with the chopped sun-dried tomatoes first, then with the Emmentaler cheese.

5 Finally, top with the remaining potato mixture. Cook over a low heat, pressing down with a palette knife from time to time, for 10–15 minutes or until the bottom is golden brown. Carefully invert the rösti onto a large plate, then carefully slide it back into the pan and cook the other side until golden. Serve cut into wedges, with a mixed green salad.

HELPFUL HINT

To make sure the rösti is the right thickness, you will need a heavy-based, nonstick skillet with a diameter of about 9 in.

MEDITERRANEAN POTATO SALAD

INGREDIENTS

Serves 4

1½ lbs. small, waxy potatoes

2 red onions, peeled and roughly chopped

1 yellow bell pepper, deseeded and roughly chopped

1 green bell pepper, deseeded and roughly chopped

6 tbsp. extra-virgin olive oil

⅓ cup chopped ripe tomatoes

½ cup sliced, pitted black olives

¼ lb. feta cheese

3 tbsp. freshly chopped parsley

2 tbsp. white wine vinegar

1 tsp. Dijon mustard

1 tsp. honey

salt and freshly ground black pepper

sprigs of fresh parsley, to garnish

1 Preheat the oven to 400° F. Place the potatoes in a large saucepan of salted water, bring to a boil, and simmer until just tender. Do not overcook. Drain and plunge into cold water to keep them from cooking further.

2 Place the onions in a bowl with the yellow and green peppers, then pour 2 tablespoons of the olive oil over. Stir and spoon onto a large baking sheet. Cook in the preheated oven for 25–30 minutes or until the vegetables are tender and lightly charred in places, stirring occasionally. Remove from the oven and transfer to a large bowl.

3 Cut the potatoes into bite-sized pieces and mix with the roasted onions and peppers. Add the tomatoes and olives. Crumble over the feta cheese and sprinkle with the chopped parsley.

4 Whisk together the remaining olive oil, vinegar, mustard, and honey, then season to taste with salt and pepper. Pour the dressing over the potatoes and toss gently together. Garnish with parsley sprigs and serve immediately.

FOOD FACT

Tomatoes are such an integral part of many cuisines that it is hard to believe they were only introduced to Europe from the Americas a few hundred years ago. There are lots of new varieties now available to try. Those sold still attached to the vine tend to have a particularly good flavor.

POTATO & GOAT CHEESE TART

INGREDIENTS

Serves 6

10 oz. prepared basic pie
   dough, thawed if frozen
1¼ lbs. small, waxy potatoes
salt and freshly ground black
   pepper
beaten egg, for brushing
2 tbsp. sun-dried tomato paste
¼ tsp. chili powder, or to taste
1 large egg

⅔ cup sour cream
⅔ cup milk
2 tbsp. freshly cut chives
¾ lb. goat cheese, sliced
salad and warm, crusty bread,
   to serve

1 Preheat the oven to 375° F. Roll the pastry out on a lightly floured surface and use to line a 9-in. fluted quiche pan. Chill in the refrigerator for 30 minutes.

2 Scrub the potatoes, place in a large saucepan of lightly salted water, and bring to a boil. Simmer for 10–15 minutes or until the potatoes are tender. Drain and set aside until cool enough to handle.

3 Line the pie shell with waxed paper and baking beans and bake blind in the preheated oven for 15 minutes. Remove from the oven and discard the paper and beans. Brush the dough with a little beaten egg, then return to the oven and cook for an additional 5 minutes. Remove from the oven.

4 Cut the potatoes into ½-in.-thick slices; set aside. Spread the sun-dried tomato paste over

the base of pie shell, sprinkle with the chili powder, then arrange the potato slices on top in a decorative pattern.

5 Beat together the egg, sour cream, milk, and chives, then season to taste with salt and pepper. Pour over the potatoes. Arrange the goat cheese on top of the potatoes. Bake in the preheated oven for 30 minutes until golden brown. Serve immediately with salad and warm bread.

HELPFUL HINT

Using store-bought pie dough is a good way to save time, but always remove it from the refrigerator 10–15 minutes before rolling it out, otherwise it may be difficult to handle. Brushing the base with egg helps seal the dough, and keeps it crisp when filled.

POTATO PANCAKES WITH SMOKED SALMON

INGREDIENTS

Serves 4

2⅔ cups floury potatoes, diced
salt and freshly ground black
　pepper
1 large egg
1 large egg yolk
2 tbsp. butter
¼ cup all-purpose flour
⅔ cup heavy cream
2 tbsp. freshly chopped parsley
5 tbsp. crème fraîche

1 tbsp. horseradish sauce
½ lb. smoked salmon, sliced
lettuce leaves, to serve

TO GARNISH:
lemon slices
cut chives

1 Cook the potatoes in a saucepan of lightly salted, boiling water for 15–20 minutes or until tender. Drain thoroughly, then mash until free of lumps. Beat in the whole egg and egg yolk, along with the butter. Beat until smooth and creamy. Slowly beat in the flour and cream, then season to taste with salt and pepper. Stir in the chopped parsley.

2 Beat the crème fraîche and horseradish sauce together in a small bowl, cover with plastic wrap, and set aside until needed.

3 Heat a lightly greased, heavy-based skillet over a medium-high heat. Place a few spoonfuls of the potato mixture in the hot pan, and cook for 4–5 minutes or until cooked and golden, turning halfway through cooking time. Remove from the pan, drain on paper towels, and keep warm.

Repeat with the remaining mixture.

4 Arrange the pancakes on individual serving plates. Place the smoked salmon on the pancakes, and spoon over a little of the horseradish sauce. Serve with salad and the remaining horseradish sauce, and garnish with lemon slices and chives.

TASTY TIP

Horseradish is a pungent root, usually finely grated and mixed with oil and vinegar or cream to make horseradish sauce. Commercially-made sauces vary, so it is best to add a little at a time to the cream and taste after each addition until you have the desired flavor.

SALMON WITH HERBED POTATOES

INGREDIENTS

Serves 4

1 lb. baby new potatoes
salt and freshly ground black
  pepper
4 salmon steaks, each about
  6 oz.
1 carrot, peeled and cut into
  fine strips
12 asparagus spears, trimmed
1 cup snow peas, trimmed

finely grated zest and juice 1
  lemon
2 tbsp. butter
4 large sprigs of fresh parsley

1 Preheat the oven to 375° F. Parboil the potatoes in lightly salted, boiling water for 5–8 minutes until they are barely tender. Drain and set aside.

2 Cut out 4 pieces of baking parchment, measuring 8 in. square, and place on the work surface. Arrange the parboiled potatoes on top. Wipe the salmon steaks and place on top of the potatoes.

3 Place the carrot strips in a bowl with the asparagus spears, snow peas, and grated lemon zest and juice. Season to taste with salt and pepper. Toss lightly together.

4 Divide the vegetables evenly between the salmon. Dot the top of each pocket with butter and add a sprig of parsley.

5 To wrap a pocket, lift up 2 opposite sides of the paper and fold the edges together. Twist the paper at the other 2 ends to seal the pocket well. Repeat with the remaining pockets.

6 Place the pockets on a baking sheet and bake for 15 minutes. Place an unopened pocket on each plate, and open before eating.

HELPFUL HINT

Cooking fish *en papillote* is an excellent way of keeping in all the juices, flavor, and aroma of the fish and vegetables. Your guests will also enjoy the anticipation of opening these surprise packages. Let the pockets stand for a few minutes before serving, as the steam can be burning hot when opened.

LAMB & POTATO MOUSSAKA

INGREDIENTS

Serves 4

1½ lbs. cooked roast lamb
1½ lbs. potatoes, peeled
½ cup butter
1 large onion, peeled and chopped
2–4 garlic cloves, peeled and crushed
3 tbsp. tomato paste
1 tbsp. freshly chopped parsley
salt and freshly ground black pepper
3–4 tbsp. olive oil
2 medium eggplants, trimmed and sliced
4 medium tomatoes, sliced
2 medium eggs
1¼ cups plain yogurt
2–3 tbsp. grated Parmesan cheese

1 Preheat the oven to 400° F. Trim the lamb, discarding any fat, then dice and set aside. Thinly slice the potatoes and rinse thoroughly in cold water, then pat dry with a clean dishtowel.

2 Melt half the butter in a skillet and fry the potatoes in batches until crisp and golden. Using a slotted spoon, remove from the pan and set aside. Use a third of the potatoes to line the base of an ovenproof dish.

3 Add the onion and garlic to the butter remaining in the pan and cook for 5 minutes. Add the lamb and fry for 1 minute. Blend the tomato paste with 3 tablespoons of water and stir into the pan with the parsley and salt and pepper. Spoon over the layer of potatoes, then top with the remaining potato slices.

4 Heat the oil and the remaining butter in the pan, and brown the eggplant slices for 5–6 minutes. Arrange the tomatoes on top of the potatoes, then the eggplants on top of the tomatoes. Beat the eggs with the yogurt and Parmesan cheese, and pour over the eggplants and tomatoes. Bake in the preheated oven for 25 minutes or until golden and piping hot. Serve.

HANDY HINT

It is worth salting the eggplants to ensure that any bitterness is removed. Layer the slices in a colander, sprinkling a little salt between the layers. Leave for 20 minutes, then rinse under cold running water, and pat dry on paper towels. Salting helps the eggplants to absorb less oil when frying.

CROWN ROAST OF LAMB

INGREDIENTS

Serves 6

1 lamb crown roast
salt and freshly ground black pepper
1 tbsp. sunflower oil
1 small onion, peeled and finely chopped
2–3 garlic cloves, peeled and crushed
2 celery stalks, trimmed and finely chopped
½ cup cooked mixed basmati and wild rice

½ cup chopped dried apricots
⅓ cup pine nuts, toasted
1 tbsp. finely grated orange zest
2 tbsp. freshly chopped cilantro
1 small egg, beaten
freshly roasted potatoes and green vegetables, to serve

1 Preheat the oven to 350° F. Wipe the crown roast, and season the cavity with salt and pepper. Place in a roasting pan, and cover the ends of the bones with small pieces of aluminum foil.

2 Heat the oil in a small saucepan, and cook the onion, garlic, and celery for 5 minutes, then remove the saucepan from the heat. Add the cooked rice with the apricots, pine nuts, orange zest, and cilantro. Season with salt and pepper, then stir in the egg and mix well.

3 Carefully spoon the prepared stuffing into the cavity of the lamb, then roast in the preheated oven for 1–1½ hours. Remove the lamb from the oven, and remove and discard the aluminum foil from the bones. Return to the

oven and continue to cook for an additional 15 minutes.

4 Remove from the oven and let rest for 10 minutes before serving with the roast potatoes and freshly cooked vegetables.

FOOD FACT

The crown roast is made by joining 2 rib joints together, making a perfect central cavity to fill with stuffing. For a special occasion, when ready to serve, the trimmed bones may be topped with white paper frills, like tiny chefs' hats.

TERIYAKI BEEF

INGREDIENTS

Serves 4

1¼ lb. steak
1 medium onion, peeled and
 finely sliced
2-in. piece of ginger, peeled
 and coarsely chopped
1 bird's eye chili, deseeded
 and finely chopped
6 tbsp. light soy sauce
2 tbsp. sake or sweet sherry
1 tbsp. lemon juice

1 tsp. honey
1½ cups glutinous rice
sunflower oil, for spraying

TO GARNISH:
carrots, finely sliced
daikon, finely sliced
sprigs of fresh cilantro

1 Trim the steak, discarding any fat or gristle, and place in a shallow, nonmetallic dish. Spread the sliced onion over the steak. Mix the ginger with the chili, and sprinkle over the steak and onion.

2 Blend the soy sauce with the sake or sherry, the lemon juice, and honey. Stir well, then pour over the steak and onion. Cover and marinate in the refrigerator for at least 1 hour, longer if time permits. Turn the steak over or occasionally spoon the marinade over the meat during this time.

3 Place the rice in a saucepan with 2 cups of water and cook for 15 minutes or until tender. Drain if necessary, then pack into four warmed, greased, individual molds. Quickly invert onto four individual warm plates and keep warm.

4 Spray or brush a griddle with oil, then heat until really hot. Drain the steak and cook on the griddle for 2–3 minutes on each side, or until cooked as desired. Remove from the pan and slice thinly. Arrange on the warm serving plates, garnish with the carrots, daikon, and cilantro sprigs, then serve.

FOOD FACT

There are more than 200 different types of chilies. The heat comes from capsaicin, a compound found in the membranes and seeds, and, to a lesser extent, in the flesh. Chilies range in potency from very mild to blisteringly hot. Bird's eye chilies, whether red or green, are one of the smallest and the hottest.

ORANGE FREEZE

INGREDIENTS   Serves 4

4 large oranges
1¼ cups vanilla ice cream
2 cups raspberries

1½ cups confectioners' sugar,
    plus extra for dusting
red currant sprigs, to decorate

1 Using a sharp knife, carefully cut the top off each orange.

2 Scoop out the flesh from the orange, discarding any seeds and thick pith.

3 Place the peels and tops in the freezer, and chop any remaining orange flesh.

4 Beat together the orange juice, orange flesh, and vanilla ice cream until well blended.

5 Cover and freeze for about 2 hours, occasionally breaking up the ice crystals with a fork. Stir the mixture from around the edge of the container into the center, then level and return to the freezer. Do this 2–3 times, then leave until it is almost frozen solid.

6 Place a large scoop of the ice-cream mixture into the frozen peels. Add another scoop on top, so that there is plenty outside of the orange shell, and return to the freezer for 1 hour.

7 Arrange the lids on top and freeze for an additional 2 hours until the filled orange peel is completely frozen solid.

8 Meanwhile, using a nylon strainer, press the raspberries into a bowl using the back of a wooden spoon, and mix together with the confectioners' sugar. Spoon the raspberry coulis onto four serving plates and place an orange at the center of each. Dust with confectioners' sugar and serve decorated with the red currants.

TASTY TIP

The fresh citrus in this dish works to clear the palate. The acidity combines well with the creaminess of the ice cream. Oranges are very good with mangoes, so why not experiment by adding the flesh of a small, ripe mango in step 4 for a more fragrant dessert? Lemons would also work well in this recipe.

CHOCOLATE MOUSSE

INGREDIENTS

Serves 6

6 squares milk or
   unsweetened chocolate
1 lb. can reduced-fat,
   crème anglaise
2 cups reduced-fat cream

12 physallis or cherries,
   to decorate
reduced-fat cookies, to serve

1 Break the chocolate into segments and place in a bowl set over a saucepan of simmering water. Leave until melted, stirring occasionally. Remove the bowl in the saucepan from the heat, and allow the melted chocolate to cool slightly.

2 Place the custard in a bowl, and using a metal spoon or rubber spatula, fold the melted chocolate into it. Stir well until completely combined.

3 Pour the cream into a small bowl and beat until the cream forms soft peaks.

4 Using a metal spoon or rubber spatula, fold in most of the whipped cream into the chocolate mixture.

5 Spoon into 6 tall glasses and carefully top with the remaining cream.

6 Leave the desserts to chill in the refrigerator for at least 1 hour or preferably overnight.

7 Decorate the chocolate desserts with a few cherries and serve with some reduced-fat cookies.

FOOD FACT

Cape gooseberries are also known as "physallis" and can be found in gourmet supermarkets. They have a sweet flavor with a slight acidity. They are similar in taste to passion fruit.

HELPFUL HINT

Have fun with the presentation of this dish. Why not serve in large cappuccino cups and lightly dust with some cocoa or confectioners' sugar. Serve plenty of cherries on the side, for guests to dip into the chocolate mousse.

CREAMY PUDDINGS WITH MIXED BERRY COMPOTE

INGREDIENTS

Serves 6

1 cup reduced-fat cream
9 oz. ricotta cheese
¼ cup sugar
4 squares white chocolate,
   broken into pieces

2 cups mixed summer fruits
   such as strawberries,
   blueberries, and raspberries
2 tbsp. Cointreau

1 Beat the cream until soft peaks form. Fold in the ricotta cheese and half the sugar.

2 Place the chocolate in a bowl set over a saucepan of simmering water. Stir until melted.

3 Remove from the heat and allow to cool, stirring occasionally. Stir into the cheese mixture until well blended.

4 Spoon the mixture into 6 individual pudding molds and level the surface of each pudding with the back of a spoon. Place in the freezer and freeze for 4 hours.

5 Place the fruits and remaining sugar in a saucepan and heat, stirring occasionally, until the sugar has dissolved and the juices are beginning to run. Stir in the Cointreau to taste.

6 Dip the pudding molds in hot water for 30 seconds and invert onto six serving plates. Spoon the fruit compote over the desserts and serve immediately.

TASTY TIP

Don't just save this recipe for the summer. Why not try mulled fruit compote with this recipe? Poach 4–6 dark plums, quartered, and 4 dessert pears, sliced into thick wedges, in ⅔ cup of red wine. Add 1 mulled wine sachet, 1–2 tablespoons of sugar, and 2 cinnamon sticks. Simmer until reduced by half and the plums and pears are softened. Remove from the heat and discard the mulled wine sachet. Allow to cool a little before spooning over the dessert. Decorate with fine strips of orange rind.

RICE PUDDING

INGREDIENTS

Serves 4

¾ cup pudding rice
¼ cup granulated sugar
14-oz. can light evaporated
 milk
1¼ cups low-fat milk

pinch of freshly grated nutmeg
¼ stick reduced-fat butter
reduced-sugar jelly,
 to decorate

1 Preheat the oven to 300° F. Lightly grease a large ovenproof dish.

2 Sprinkle the rice and sugar into the dish, and mix together.

3 Bring the evaporated milk and milk to a boil in a small saucepan, stirring occasionally.

4 Stir the milks into the rice and mix well until the rice is coated thoroughly.

5 Sprinkle with the nutmeg, cover with foil, and cook in the preheated oven for 30 minutes.

6 Remove the pudding from the oven and stir well, breaking up any lumps.

7 Cover with the same foil and cook for an additional 30 minutes. Remove from the oven and stir well again.

8 Dot the pudding with butter and cook for an additional 45–60 minutes until the rice is tender and the skin is browned.

9 Divide the pudding among 4 individual serving bowls. Top with a large spoonful of the jelly and serve immediately.

TASTY TIP

Traditionally, rice pudding was cooked alongside the Sunday roast which, after many hours in the oven, came out rich and creamy. The main trick to achieving traditional creamy rice pudding is not using cream and whole milk, but instead long, slow cooking on a low temperature. Try adding a few golden raisins and lemon peel, or a few coarsely crushed cardamom pods for an alternative flavor. It is also delicious dusted with a little ground cinnamon.

LEMON SURPRISE

INGREDIENTS   Serves 4

½ stick reduced-fat butter
¾ cup sugar
3 medium eggs, separated
¾ cup self-rising flour
2 cups low-fat milk
4 tbsp. lemon juice

3 tbsp. orange juice
2 tsp. confectioners' sugar
lemon twists, to decorate
sliced strawberries, to serve

1 Preheat the oven to 375° F. Lightly grease a deep ovenproof dish.

2 Beat together the butter and sugar until pale and fluffy.

3 Add the egg yolks, one at a time, with 1 tablespoon of the flour, and beat well after each addition. Once added, stir in the remaining flour.

4 Stir in the milk, the lemon juice, and the orange juice.

5 Beat the egg whites until stiff, and fold into the dessert mixture with a metal spoon or rubber spatula until well combined. Pour into the prepared dish.

6 Stand the dish in a roasting pan and pour in just enough boiling water to come halfway up the sides of the dish.

7 Cook in the preheated oven for 45 minutes until well risen and spongy to the touch.

8 Remove the dessert from the oven and sprinkle with the confectioners' sugar. Decorate with the lemon twists and serve immediately with the strawberries.

FOOD FACT

This recipe uses a bain-marie, (when the dish is placed in a pan as in Step 6), which enables the pudding to cook slower. This is necessary, as reduced-fat butter does not respond well when cooked at higher temperatures.

ORANGE CURD & PLUM PUDDINGS

INGREDIENTS

Serves 4

1½ lbs. plums, pitted and
 quartered
2 tbsp. light brown sugar
1 tbsp. grated lemon rind
¼ stick butter, melted
1 tbsp. olive oil
6 sheets phyllo pastry
7 oz. orange (or lemon) curd

5 tbsp. golden raisins
confectioners' sugar,
 to decorate
low-fat plain yogurt, to serve

1 Preheat the oven to 400° F. Lightly grease an 8-inch round cake pan. Cook the plums with 2 tablespoons of the light brown sugar for 8–10 minutes to soften them, then remove from the heat and set aside.

2 Mix together the lemon rind, butter, and oil. Lay a sheet of phyllo pastry in the prepared cake pan and brush with the lemon rind mixture.

3 Cut the sheets of phyllo pastry in half and then place one half-sheet in the cake pan, and brush again.

4 Top with the remaining half-sheets of phyllo pastry, brushing each time with the lemon rind mixture. Fold each sheet in half lengthwise, to line the sides of the pan to make a phyllo shell.

5 Mix together the plums, orange curd, and golden raisins, and spoon into the phyllo pastry shell.

6 Draw the phyllo pastry edges up over the filling to enclose. Brush the remaining sheets of phyllo pastry with the lemon rind mixture and cut into thick strips.

7 Scrunch each strip of phyllo pastry and arrange on top of the pie. Cook in the preheated oven for 25 minutes until golden. Sprinkle with confectioners' sugar and serve with the plain yogurt.

HELPFUL HINT

Phyllo pastry dries out very quickly. Keep it wrapped when not using.

COFFEE & PEACH CREAMS

INGREDIENTS

Serves 4

4 peaches
¼ cup sugar
2 tbsp. coffee extract
7 oz. carton low-fat plain
   yogurt
11-oz. can reduced-fat, ready-
   made crème anglaise

TO DECORATE:
peach slices
sprigs of mint
reduced-fat sour cream

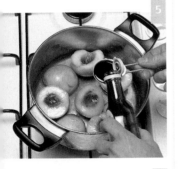

1 Cut the peaches in half and remove the pits. Place the peaches in a large bowl, cover with boiling water, and leave for 2–3 minutes.

2 Drain the peaches, then carefully remove the skin. Using a sharp knife, halve the peaches.

3 Place the sugar in a saucepan and add ¼ cup of water.

4 Bring the sugar mixture to a boil, stirring occasionally until the sugar has dissolved. Boil rapidly for about 2 minutes.

5 Add the peaches and coffee extract to the saucepan. Remove from the heat and let the peach mixture cool.

6 Meanwhile, mix together the plain yogurt and crème anglaise until well combined.

7 Divide the peach halves evenly among 4 individual glass dishes.

8 Spoon over the custard mixture, then top with the remaining peach mixture.

9 Chill in the refrigerator for 30 minutes and then serve decorated with peach slices, mint sprigs, and some sour cream.

FOOD FACT

It is generally believed that peaches originated from China. There are over 2000 varieties grown throughout the world.

SWEET-STEWED DRIED FRUITS

INGREDIENTS

Serves 4

1 lb. package mixed dried
  fruits
2 cups apple juice
2 tbsp. honey
2 tbsp. brandy
1 lemon
1 orange

TO DECORATE:
reduced-fat sour cream
fine strips of pared
  orange rind

1 Place the fruits, apple juice, honey, and brandy in a small saucepan.

2 Using a small, sharp knife or a zester, carefully remove the zest from the lemon and orange and place in the saucepan.

3 Squeeze the juice from the lemon and oranges and add to the saucepan.

4 Bring the fruit mixture to a boil, and simmer for about 1 minute. Remove the saucepan from the heat and let the mixture cool completely.

5 Transfer the mixture to a large bowl, cover with plastic wrap, and chill in the refrigerator overnight to allow the flavors to blend.

6 Spoon the stewed fruit in four shallow dessert dishes. Decorate with a large spoonful of reduced-fat sour cream and a few strips of the pared orange rind, and serve.

TASTY TIP

As a dessert, this dish is particularly good when served with cold rice pudding. However, these stewed fruits can also be very nice for breakfast. Simply pour some unsweetened granola into the bottom of a bowl, top with the stewed fruits and perhaps some low-fat plain yogurt, and serve.

TASTY TIP

Why not try for a Moroccan feel with this dish by choosing dried fruits with a selection of figs, apricots, and prunes? Add 1 teaspoon of whole cloves, a generous grating of fresh nutmeg and ginger, and 2 cinnamon sticks to the fruits in Step 1. Serve with the reduced-fat sour cream and sprinkle with a few chopped walnuts.

CHOCOLATE BRANDY DREAM

INGREDIENTS

Serves 4

6 squares low-fat chocolate,
 broken into pieces
1 cup whipping cream
2 tbsp. brandy
1 tbsp. coffee extract
1 medium egg white

TO DECORATE:
raspberries
blueberries
mint leaves
cocoa

1 Place the pieces of chocolate into a heatproof bowl placed over a saucepan of gently simmering water, and leave to slowly melt, stirring occasionally.

2 Carefully remove the saucepan and the bowl from the heat and set aside to allow the chocolate to cool.

3 Pour the cream into a small bowl, whip until soft peaks form, then set aside.

4 Gently stir the brandy and coffee extract into the chocolate. Mix together gently until blended, then fold in the whipped cream with a metal spoon or rubber spatula.

5 Briskly beat the egg white in a small bowl until stiff, then fold into the chocolate mixture with a metal spoon or rubber spatula.

6 Stir the chocolate mixture gently, taking care not to remove the air already beaten into the egg white.

7 Spoon into four tall glasses and chill in the refrigerator for at least 2 hours. Decorate with raspberries, blueberries, and mint leaves. Dust with cocoa and serve.

FOOD FACT

Careful blending is the key to recipe success in this dish, as it relies on the air beaten into both the cream and the egg whites to support the fairly heavy chocolate mixture. Take particular care when folding in the egg whites—you may find that folding just a tablespoon of the egg whites into the cream mixture may loosen the mixture, making it easier to fold in the rest of the egg whites.

FALL FRUIT LAYER

INGREDIENTS

Serves 4

1 lb. apples
2 cups blackberries
¼ cup soft brown sugar
3 tbsp. lemon juice
¼ cup low-fat spread
1¾ cups bread crumbs
2 cups nuts, chopped

red currants and mint leaves,
   to decorate
reduced-fat whipped cream or
   reduced fat ice cream,
   to serve

1 Peel, core, and slice the apples and place in a saucepan with the blackberries, sugar, and lemon juice.

2 Cover the fruit mixture and simmer, stirring occasionally, for about 15 minutes or until the apples and blackberries have formed a thick purée.

3 Remove the saucepan from the heat and allow to cool.

4 Melt the low-fat spread in a skillet and cook the bread crumbs for 5–10 minutes, stirring occasionally, until golden and crisp.

5 Remove the skillet from the heat and stir in the nuts. Allow to cool.

6 Alternately layer the fruit purée and bread crumbs into four tall glasses.

7 Store the desserts in the refrigerator to chill, and remove when ready to serve.

8 Decorate with red currants and mint leaves, and serve with reduced-fat whipped cream or reduced fat vanilla or raspberry ice cream.

TASTY TIP

Any fall fruit can be used in this recipe. Add pears to this recipe to make an apple and pear fruit layer, or use some plums if preferred. For a more textured dessert, reduce the amount of bread crumbs used to 1 cup and add ⅔ cup of rolled oats in Step 5.

FRUIT & OAT PUDDINGS

INGREDIENTS

Serves 4

1¼ cups rolled oats
¼ cup low-fat spread, melted
2 tbsp. chopped almonds
1 tbsp. honey
pinch of ground cinnamon
2 pears, peeled, cored, and
   finely chopped
1 tbsp. marmalade

orange zest, to decorate
low-fat custard or fruit-
   flavored low-fat yogurt,
   to serve

1 Preheat the oven to 400° F. Lightly grease and line the bases of 4 individual ovenproof bowls or muffin pans with a small circle of waxed paper.

2 Mix together the oats, low-fat spread, nuts, honey, and cinnamon in a small bowl.

3 Using a spoon, spread two thirds of the mixture over the base and around the sides of the ovenproof bowls or muffin pans.

4 Toss together the pears and marmalade, and spoon into the oat shells.

5 Sprinkle with the remaining oat mixture to cover the pears and marmalade.

6 Cook in the preheated oven for 15–20 minutes until cooked and the tops of the desserts are golden and crisp.

7 Leave for 5 minutes before removing the ovenproof bowls or the muffin pans. Decorate with orange zest and serve hot with low-fat custard or yogurt.

TASTY TIP

Liqueured crème anglaise is great with steamed desserts. Add 2–3 tablespoons of a liqueur of your choice to the crème anglaise, along with 1 teaspoon of vanilla extract. Taste, and add more liquer if desired.

FRUIT SALAD

INGREDIENTS

Serves 4

½ cup sugar
3 oranges
2 14-oz. cans lychees
1 small mango
1 small pineapple
1 papaya
4 pieces stem ginger, in syrup
4 tbsp. stem ginger syrup
¾ cup cherries

1 cup strawberries, hulled
½ tsp. almond extract

TO DECORATE:
mint leaves
lime zest

1 Place the sugar and 1¼ cups of water in a small saucepan and heat, gently stirring until the sugar has dissolved. Bring to a boil and simmer for 2 minutes. Once a syrup has formed, remove from the heat and allow to cool.

2 Using a sharp knife, cut away the skin from the oranges, then slice thickly. Cut each slice in half and place in a serving dish with the syrup and lychees.

3 Peel the mango, then cut into thick slices around each side of the pit. Discard the pit and cut the slices into bite-size pieces and add to the syrup.

4 Using a sharp knife again, carefully cut away the skin from the pineapple.

5 Remove the central core using the knife or an apple corer, then cut the pineapple into segments and add to the syrup.

6 Peel the papaya, then cut in half and remove the seeds. Cut the flesh into chunks, slice the ginger into matchsticks, and add with the ginger syrup to the fruit in the syrup.

7 Halve the strawberries, add to the fruit with the cherries and almond extract, and chill in the refrigerator for 30 minutes. Sprinkle with mint leaves and lime zest to decorate, and serve.

FOOD FACT

Lychees are native to China. If they are unavailable, try using grapes as a substitute.

SUMMER PAVLOVA

INGREDIENTS   Serves 6–8

4 medium egg whites
1 cup sugar
1 tsp. vanilla extract
2 tsp. white wine vinegar
1½ tsp. cornstarch
1 cup low-fat plain yogurt
2 tbsp. honey

2 cups strawberries, hulled
1 cup raspberries
1 cup blueberries
4 kiwis, peeled and sliced
confectioners' sugar,
  to decorate

1 Preheat the oven to 300° F. Line a baking sheet with a sheet of waxed paper or baking parchment.

2 Place the egg whites in a clean, grease-free bowl and beat until very stiff.

3 Beat in half the sugar, the vanilla extract, vinegar, and cornstarch, and continue beating until stiff.

4 Gradually, beat in the remaining sugar, a teaspoonful at a time, until very stiff and glossy.

5 Using a large spoon, arrange spoonfuls of the meringue in a circle on the waxed paper or baking parchment.

6 Cook the meringue in the preheated oven for 1 hour or until crisp and dry. Turn the oven off and leave the meringue in the oven to allow it to cool completely.

7 Remove the meringue from the baking sheet and peel away the baking parchment. Mix together the yogurt and honey. Place the pavlova on a serving plate and spoon the yogurt into the center.

8 Sprinkle with the strawberries, raspberries, blueberries, and kiwis. Dust with the confectioners' sugar and serve.

HELPFUL HINT

Always remember to double-check that the bowl being used to beat egg whites is completely clean, as you will find that any grease will prevent the egg whites from rising into the stiff consistency necessary for this recipe.

POACHED PEARS

INGREDIENTS   Serves 4

2 small cinnamon sticks
½ cup sugar
1¼ cups red wine
⅔ cup water
1 tbsp. thinly pared orange
  rind
1 tbsp. orange juice

4 firm pears
orange slices, to decorate
frozen vanilla yogurt or
  low-fat ice cream, to serve

1 Place the cinnamon sticks on the clean work surface, and with a rolling pin, slowly roll down the side of the cinnamon stick to bruise. Place in a large, heavy saucepan.

2 Add the sugar, wine, water, pared orange rind, and juice to the saucepan, and bring slowly to a boil, stirring occasionally until the sugar has dissolved.

3 Meanwhile, peel the pears, leaving the stalks on.

4 Cut out the cores from the bottoms of the pears, and level them so that they stand upright.

5 Stand the pears in the syrup, cover the saucepan, and simmer for 20 minutes or until tender.

6 Remove the saucepan from the heat and let the pears cool in the syrup, turning them occasionally.

7 Arrange the pears on serving plates and spoon over the syrup. Decorate with the orange slices and serve with the yogurt or low-fat ice cream and any remaining juices.

TASTY TIP

Poached pears are delicious served with a little reduced-fat sour cream and sprinkled with toasted almonds. To toast almonds, simply warm the broiler and place whole, blanched almonds or slivered almonds onto a piece of foil. Place under the broiler and toast lightly on both sides for 1–2 minutes until golden. Remove and cool; chop if desired.

GRAPE & ALMOND LAYER

INGREDIENTS

Serves 4

1 cup reduced-fat sour cream
1 cup low-fat plain yogurt
3 tbsp. confectioners' sugar, sifted
2 tbsp. crème de cassis
1 lb. red grapes
2 cups Amaretto cookies

2 ripe passion fruit

TO DECORATE:
confectioners' sugar
extra grapes (optional)

1 Mix together the sour cream and yogurt in a bowl, and lightly fold in the sifted confectioners' sugar and the crème de cassis with a large metal spoon or rubber spatula until lightly blended.

2 Using a small knife, remove the seeds from the grapes, if necessary. Rinse lightly and pat dry on absorbent paper towels.

3 Place the seeded grapes in a bowl and stir in any juice from the grapes left over from seeding.

4 Place the Amaretto cookies in a plastic bag and crush coarsely with a rolling pin. Alternatively, use a food processor.

5 Cut the passion fruit in half, scoop out the seeds with a teaspoon, and set aside.

6 Divide the yogurt mixture among 4 tall glasses, then layer alternately with grapes, crushed cookies, and most of the passion fruit seeds. Top with the yogurt mixture and the remaining passion fruit seeds. Chill in the refrigerator for 1 hour and decorate with extra grapes. Lightly dust with confectioners' sugar and serve.

FOOD FACT

Passion fruit is native to Brazil. They are purple in color and are about the size of an egg. Look for fruits that are wrinkled, not smooth. When wrinkled, they are ripe and at their best.

SUMMER PUDDING

INGREDIENTS

Serves 4

4 cups red currants
½ cup sugar
3 cups strawberries, hulled
and halved
1 cup raspberries
2 tbsp. Grand Marnier
or Cointreau
8–10 medium slices white
bread, crusts removed
mint sprigs, to decorate

low-fat plain yogurt or
reduced-fat sour cream,
to serve

1 Place the red currants, sugar, and 1 tablespoon of water in a large saucepan. Heat gently until the sugar has just dissolved and the juices have just begun to run.

2 Remove the saucepan from the heat and stir in the strawberries, raspberries, and the Grand Marnier or Cointreau.

3 Line the base and sides of a 1-quart ovenproof bowl with two thirds of the bread, making sure that the slices overlap each other slightly.

4 Spoon the fruit with their juices into the bread-lined ovenproof bowl, then top with the remaining bread slices.

5 Place a small plate on top of the dessert inside the ovenproof bowl. Ensure the plate fits tightly, then weigh down with a clean can or some weights, and chill in the refrigerator overnight.

6 When ready to serve, remove the weights and plate. Carefully loosen around the sides of the basin with a round-bladed knife. Invert the dessert onto a serving plate, decorate with the mint sprigs, and serve with the yogurt or sour cream.

TASTY TIP

This really is a summer dessert, using plump, juicy berries that are bursting with flavor. Why not try a fall version using seasonal fruit such as blackberries, plums, and flavorful apples? Place in just a few tablespoons of water, along with ¼ cup of sugar, and heat gently as in Step 1.

CARAMELIZED ORANGES IN AN ICED BOWL

INGREDIENTS   Serves 4

FOR THE ICE BOWL:
about 36 ice cubes
fresh flowers and fruits
8 medium oranges

1 cup sugar
4 tbsp. Grand Marnier
  or Cointreau

1 Place a few ice cubes in the base of a 2-quart freezable glass bowl. Place a 1-quart glass bowl on top of the ice cubes. Arrange the flowerheads and fruits between the 2 bowls, wedging in position with the ice cubes.

2 Weigh down the smaller bowl with some heavy weights, then carefully pour cold water between the 2 bowls, making sure that the flowers and the fruit are covered. Freeze for at least 6 hours or until the ice is frozen solid.

3 When ready to use, remove the weights, and using a hot, damp cloth, rub the inside of the smaller bowl with the cloth until it loosens sufficiently for you to remove the bowl. Place the larger bowl in the sink, half-filled with hot water. Leave for 30 seconds or until the ice loosens. Take care not to leave the bowl in the water for too long, otherwise the ice will melt. Remove the bowl from the sink and leave in the refrigerator. Return the freezer to its normal setting.

4 Thinly pare the rind from 2 oranges and then julienne. Using a sharp knife, cut away the rind and pith from all the oranges, holding over a bowl to catch the juices. Slice the oranges, discarding any seeds, and re-form each orange back to its original shape. Secure with toothpicks, then place in a bowl.

5 Heat 1¼ cups water, the orange rind, and sugar together in a saucepan. Stir the sugar until dissolved. Bring to a boil. Boil for 15 minutes until it is a caramel color. Remove from the heat.

6 Stir in the liqueur, then add the oranges. Allow to cool. Chill for 3 hours, turning the oranges occasionally. Spoon into the ice bowl and serve.

HELPFUL HINT

This ice bowl can hold any dessert. Why not fill it with flavored ice creams?

RASPBERRY SORBET CRUSH

INGREDIENTS

Serves 4

2 cups raspberries
2 tsp. grated lime rind
1 tbsp. lime juice

1¼ cups orange juice
1 cup sugar
2 medium egg whites

1 Pick over the raspberries and lightly rinse under cold running water.

2 Place the raspberries in a dish and, using a masher, mash to a chunky purée.

3 Place the lime rind and juice, orange juice, and half the sugar in a large, heavy saucepan.

4 Heat gently, stirring frequently, until the sugar has dissolved. Bring to a boil, and boil rapidly for about 5 minutes.

5 Remove the saucepan from the heat and pour carefully into a freezable container.

6 Allow to cool, then place in the freezer and freeze for 2 hours, stirring occasionally to break up the ice crystals.

7 Fold the ice mixture into the raspberry purée and freeze for an additional 2 hours, stirring occasionally.

8 Beat the egg whites until stiff, then gradually beat in the remaining sugar, a tablespoon at a time, until the egg white mixture is stiff and glossy.

9 Fold into the raspberry sorbet with a metal spoon and freeze for 1 hour. Spoon into tall glasses and serve immediately.

FOOD FACT

This recipe contains raw egg, and should not be given to babies, young children, pregnant women, the sick, the elderly, and those with a compromised immune system.

RASPBERRY SOUFFLÉ

INGREDIENTS   Serves 4

1 cup red currants
¼ cup sugar
3 tsp. powdered gelatin
3 medium eggs, separated
1 cup low-fat plain yogurt
4 cups raspberries, defrosted if
   frozen

TO DECORATE:
mint sprigs
extra fruits

1 Wrap a band of double-thickness waxed paper around 4 ramekin dishes, making sure that 2 inches of the paper stay above the top of each dish. Secure the paper to the dish with an elastic band or adhesive tape.

2 Place the red currants and 1 tablespoon of the sugar in a saucepan. Cook for 5 minutes until softened. Remove from the heat, strain, and set aside.

3 Place 3 tablespoons of water in a small bowl and sprinkle over the gelatin. Let stand for 5 minutes until spongy. Place the bowl over a saucepan of simmering water and leave until dissolved. Remove and let cool.

4 Beat together the remaining sugar and egg yolks until pale, thick, and creamy, then fold in the plain yogurt with a large metal spoon or rubber spatula until well blended.

5 Strain the raspberries and fold into the yogurt mixture with the gelatin. Beat the egg whites until stiff, and fold into the yogurt mixture. Pour into the prepared dishes and chill in the refrigerator for 2 hours until firm.

6 Remove the paper from the dishes and spread the red currant purée over the top of the soufflés. Decorate with mint sprigs and extra fruits, and serve.

HELPFUL HINT

Soufflés rely on air, so it is important that the egg whites in this recipe are beaten until very stiff in order to support the other mixture.

FRUITY ROULADE

INGREDIENTS

Serves 4

FOR THE SPONGE:
3 medium eggs
½ cup sugar
¾ cup all-purpose flour, sifted
1–2 tbsp. sugar, for sprinkling

FOR THE FILLING:
½ cup quark
½ cup low-fat plain yogurt
2 tbsp. sugar

1 tbsp. orange liqueur
(optional)
1 tbsp. grated orange rind
1 cup strawberries, hulled and
cut into quarters

TO DECORATE:
strawberries
sifted confectioners' sugar

1 Preheat the oven to 425° F. Lightly grease and line a 9 x 13 inch jelly-roll pan with baking parchment.

2 Using an electric whisk, beat the eggs and sugar until the mixture has doubled in volume and leaves a trail across the top.

3 Fold in the flour with a metal spoon or rubber spatula. Pour into the prepared pan and cook in the preheated oven for 10–12 minutes until well risen and golden.

4 Place a whole sheet of baking parchment out on a clean, flat work surface and sprinkle evenly with the sugar.

5 Turn the cooked sponge out onto the paper, discard the paper, trim the sponge, and roll up, encasing the paper inside. Set aside until cool.

6 To make the filling, mix together the quark, yogurt, sugar, liqueur (if using), and orange rind. Unroll the roulade and spread over the mixture. Sprinkle with the strawberries and roll up.

7 Decorate the roulade with strawberries. Dust with the confectioners' sugar and serve.

FOOD FACT

Quark is a soft, unripened cheese with the flavor and texture of sour cream. It comes in two varieties, low-fat and nonfat. It can be used as a sour cream substitute to top baked potatoes or in dips and cheesecakes.

INDEX